Compendium of maritime labour instruments

Maritime Labour Convention, 2006
Seafarers' Identity Documents (Revised) Convention, 2003
Work in Fishing Convention and Recommendation, 2007

The International Labour Organization

The *International Labour Organization* was founded in 1919 to promote social justice and, thereby, to contribute to universal and lasting peace. Its tripartite structure is unique among agencies affiliated to the United Nations; the ILO's Governing Body includes representatives of governments, and of employers' and workers' organizations. These three constituencies are active participants in regional and other meetings sponsored by the ILO, as well as in the International Labour Conference – a world forum that meets annually to discuss social and labour questions.

Over the years the ILO has issued for adoption by member States a widely respected code of international labour Conventions and Recommendations on freedom of association, employment, social policy, conditions of work, social security, industrial relations and labour administration, and child labour, among others.

The ILO provides expert advice and technical assistance to member States through a network of offices and multidisciplinary teams in over 40 countries. This assistance takes the form of labour rights and industrial relations counselling, employment promotion, training in small business development, project management, advice on social security, workplace safety and working conditions, the compiling and dissemination of labour statistics, and workers' education.

ILO Publications

The *International Labour Office* is the Organization's secretariat, research body and publishing house. ILO Publications produces and distributes material on major social and economic trends. It publishes policy studies on issues affecting labour around the world, reference works, technical guides, research-based books and monographs, codes of practice on safety and health prepared by experts, and training and workers' education manuals. The magazine *World of Work* is published three times a year in printed form by the Department of Communication and Public Information and is also available online at www.ilo.org.

You may purchase ILO publications and other resources securely online at www.ilo.org/publns; or request a free catalogue by writing to ILO Publications, International Labour Office, CH-1211 Geneva 22, Switzerland; fax +41 (0) 22 799 6938; email: pubvente@ilo.org.

Compendium of maritime labour instruments

Maritime Labour Convention, 2006
Seafarers' Identity Document (Revised) Convention, 2003
Work in Fishing Convention and Recommendation, 2007

International Labour Office Geneva

ILO
Compendium of maritime labour instruments: Maritime Labour Convention, 2006, Seafarers' Identity Documents (Revised) Convention, 2003, Work in Fishing Convention and Recommendation, 2007
Geneva, International Labour Office, 2008

merchant marine / seafarer / identity card / fishery worker / working conditions / conditions of employment / workers' rights / ILO Convention / ILO Recommendation / ILO Declaration / ILO Resolution / text

10.05.3

ISBN 978-92-2-120612-5

Also published in French: *Compilation des instruments sur le travail maritime: convention du travail maritime, 2006, convention sur les pièces d'identité des gens de mer (révisée), 2003, convention et recommandation sur le travail dans la pêche, 2007* (ISBN 978-92-2-220612-4, Geneva, 2008); and in Spanish: *Compilación de los instrumentos sobre el trabajo marítimo: Convenio sobre el trabajo marítimo, 2006, Convenio sobre los documentos de identidad de la gente de mar (revisado), 2003, Convenio y Recomendación sobre el trabajo en la pesca, 2007* (ISBN 978-92-2-320612-3, Geneva, 2008).

ILO Cataloguing in Publication Data

ILO publications can be obtained through major booksellers or ILO local offices in many countries, or direct from ILO Publications, International Labour Office, CH-1211 Geneva 22, Switzerland. Catalogues or lists of new publications are available free of charge from the above address, or by email: pubvente@ilo.org.

Visit our web site: www.ilo.org/publns.

Printed by the International Labour Office, Geneva, Switzerland DTP

CONTENTS

Part B. Seafarers' identity documents

Part C. Fishing

Part D. The fundamental Conventions

Annexes

PREFACE

This book contains three Conventions relating to the maritime sector. The first is one of the International Labour Organization's newest and most innovative international labour Conventions, the Maritime Labour Convention, 2006, and two other key related Conventions, the Seafarers' Identity Documents Convention, (Revised) 2003, and the Work in Fishing Convention, 2007.

The Maritime Labour Convention, 2006, is often described as a charter for decent work or a "bill of rights" for the world's maritime workers and a framework for creating a level playing field for shipowners. Governments, seafarers and shipowners all saw the adoption of this Convention as a landmark development for the world's most globalized sector.

The Maritime Labour Convention, 2006, consolidates and updates the majority (68 out of 72) of the ILO's maritime Conventions and Recommendations adopted since 1920. This in itself is a major step forward in assisting countries to improve labour conditions on ships operating under their flags - ships, for which they have international responsibility. This Convention demonstrates that social dialogue and international cooperation can effectively address the challenges of living, working and conducting business at sea. But it goes even further by showing how dialogue and tripartism can also address the challenges of globalization.

The Convention takes forward the ILO's 21st century approach of actively seeking innovative ways to ensure the relevance and effectiveness of international labour standards in modern economic and social conditions.

The Maritime Labour Convention, 2006, is based on certification by flag States of maritime labour standards with an important focus on the development of national enforcement and compliance systems. It is addressed to flag States, port States and countries with labour supplying interests.

The Seafarers' Identity Documents Convention (Revised), 2003 (No. 185), also reflects important new maritime concerns. Seafarers typically work as part of a multinational crew, for a foreign shipowner on a ship flying the flag of still another country. Their ship's voyage may take them to several foreign ports, often with short notice. For their health and wellbeing and to carry out their work, they need temporary admission into the territories of the countries visited: shore leave after working at sea for perhaps several months at a time; and permission to transit through a country to join or change ship or for repatriation.

How can these needs be reconciled with the security measures being taken by countries to confront the modern day phenomena of terrorism and clandestine immigration? This is taken up in Convention No. 185, the second subject of this book.

This Convention responded to the needs and priorities of all parties. It addresses the concerns of shipowner and seafarer representatives by including an assurance that would allow seafarers the necessary facilities to go ashore in foreign countries upon presentation of the new identity document. The Convention aims to ensure that the issuance procedures for the document respect the dignity and rights of workers, especially with respect to fingerprint technology. The Convention also responds to government concerns by including a strong and comprehensive security system which assures that the holders of the document requesting admission to their territory are indeed genuine seafarers. It also provides assurances for their country's own seafarers and ships flying their flag.

Finally, the Work in Fishing Convention (No. 188) and Recommendation (No. 199), adopted in 2007, revises and consolidates five ILO standards concerned with working conditions of fishers. The world's fisheries are, of course, an essential aspect of human food security: we all rely and will continue to rely on their work. The new Convention tackles many of the key challenges in ensuring decent work for fishers: minimum age and medical fitness to work as fishers; fishers' work agreements; manning of vessels and hours of rest; accommodation and food on board fishing vessels; occupational safety and health and medical care at sea; and social security protection. The Recommendation provides guidance on the implementation of the Convention's requirements.

Together these instruments offer comprehensive protection of fishers in a variety of work arrangements, including those paid on the basis of a share of the catch and those considered self-employed. At the same time, it ensures that fishing vessel owners retain responsibility for providing the protection set out in the Convention.

Convention No. 188 is aimed at all fishers and fishing vessels in commercial fishing. However, it recognizes the great diversity in the sector. Some countries, for example, may not yet have in place the institutions and infrastructure to implement certain provisions. It therefore sets basic standards for all fishing vessels and higher ones for larger vessels (i.e. 24 metres in length and over) or those that remain at sea for extended periods. Certain provisions can be implemented progressively – if the State puts in place a plan for extending the full protection of the Convention to all fishers and periodically reports to the ILO on progress. The Convention also contains improved provisions on compliance and enforcement, including on inspection by States of foreign vessels visiting their ports.

Although these three Conventions address one sector, they cover a very large number of the world's workers. The Maritime Labour Convention, 2006, and the Seafarers' Identity Documents Convention seek to meet the decent work needs of the more than 1.2 million people working as seafarers and their employers on ships that carry 90 per cent of the world's trade. The Work in Fishing Convention, 2007, is designed to improve conditions for the nearly 30 million men and women working in the fishing sector worldwide.

All three Conventions provide clear evidence of the continued relevance of international labour standards, developed through tripartite social dialogue, as key to effectively responding to many of the challenges facing both workers and employers in today's globalized workplaces.

Juan Somavia
Director-General

PART A

MARITIME LABOUR CONVENTION, 2006

Contents

Page

MARITIME LABOUR CONVENTION, 2006

Adopted: 23 February 2006

PREAMBLE

The General Conference of the International Labour Organization,

Having been convened at Geneva by the Governing Body of the International Labour Office, and having met in its Ninety-fourth Session on 7 February 2006, and

Desiring to create a single, coherent instrument embodying as far as possible all up-to-date standards of existing international maritime labour Conventions and Recommendations, as well as the fundamental principles to be found in other international labour Conventions, in particular:

- the Forced Labour Convention, 1930 (No. 29);
- the Freedom of Association and Protection of the Right to Organise Convention, 1948 (No. 87);
- the Right to Organise and Collective Bargaining Convention, 1949 (No. 98);
- the Equal Remuneration Convention, 1951 (No. 100);
- the Abolition of Forced Labour Convention, 1957 (No. 105);
- the Discrimination (Employment and Occupation) Convention, 1958 (No. 111);
- the Minimum Age Convention, 1973 (No. 138);
- the Worst Forms of Child Labour Convention, 1999 (No. 182); and

Mindful of the core mandate of the Organization, which is to promote decent conditions of work, and

Recalling the ILO Declaration on Fundamental Principles and Rights at Work, 1998, and

Mindful also that seafarers are covered by the provisions of other ILO instruments and have other rights which are established as fundamental rights and freedoms applicable to all persons, and

Considering that, given the global nature of the shipping industry, seafarers need special protection, and

Mindful also of the international standards on ship safety, human security and quality ship management in the International Convention for the Safety of Life at Sea, 1974, as amended, the Convention on the International Regulations for Preventing Collisions at Sea, 1972, as amended, and the seafarer training and competency requirements in the International Convention on Standards of Training, Certification and Watchkeeping for Seafarers, 1978, as amended, and

Recalling that the United Nations Convention on the Law of the Sea, 1982, sets out a general legal framework within which all activities in the oceans and seas must be carried out and is of strategic importance as the basis for national, regional and global action and cooperation in the marine sector, and that its integrity needs to be maintained, and

Recalling that Article 94 of the United Nations Convention on the Law of the Sea, 1982, establishes the duties and obligations of a flag State with regard to, inter alia, labour conditions, crewing and social matters on ships that fly its flag, and

Recalling paragraph 8 of article 19 of the Constitution of the International Labour Organisation which provides that in no case shall the adoption of any Convention or Recommendation by the Conference or the ratification of any Convention by any Member be deemed to affect any law, award, custom or agreement which ensures more favourable conditions to the workers concerned than those provided for in the Convention or Recommendation, and

Determined that this new instrument should be designed to secure the widest possible acceptability among governments, shipowners and seafarers committed to the principles of decent work, that it should be readily updateable and that it should lend itself to effective implementation and enforcement, and

Having decided upon the adoption of certain proposals for the realization of such an instrument, which is the only item on the agenda of the session, and

Having determined that these proposals shall take the form of an international Convention;

adopts this twenty-third day of February of the year two thousand and six the following Convention, which may be cited as the Maritime Labour Convention, 2006.

General obligations

Article I

1. Each Member which ratifies this Convention undertakes to give complete effect to its provisions in the manner set out in Article VI in order to secure the right of all seafarers to decent employment.

2. Members shall cooperate with each other for the purpose of ensuring the effective implementation and enforcement of this Convention.

DEFINITIONS AND SCOPE OF APPLICATION

Article II

1. For the purpose of this Convention and unless provided otherwise in particular provisions, the term:

(a) *competent authority* means the minister, government department or other authority having power to issue and enforce regulations, orders or other instructions having the force of law in respect of the subject matter of the provision concerned;

(b) *declaration of maritime labour compliance* means the declaration referred to in Regulation 5.1.3;

(c) *gross tonnage* means the gross tonnage calculated in accordance with the tonnage measurement regulations contained in Annex I to the International Convention on Tonnage Measurement of Ships, 1969, or any successor Convention; for ships covered by the tonnage measurement interim scheme adopted by the International Maritime Organization, the gross tonnage is that which is included in the REMARKS column of the International Tonnage Certificate (1969);

(d) *maritime labour certificate* means the certificate referred to in Regulation 5.1.3;

(e) *requirements of this Convention* refers to the requirements in these Articles and in the Regulations and Part A of the Code of this Convention;

(f) *seafarer* means any person who is employed or engaged or works in any capacity on board a ship to which this Convention applies;

(g) *seafarers' employment agreement* includes both a contract of employment and articles of agreement;

(h) *seafarer recruitment and placement service* means any person, company, institution, agency or other organization, in the public or the private sector, which is engaged in recruiting seafarers on behalf of shipowners or placing seafarers with shipowners;

(i) *ship* means a ship other than one which navigates exclusively in inland waters or waters within, or closely adjacent to, sheltered waters or areas where port regulations apply;

(j) *shipowner* means the owner of the ship or another organization or person, such as the manager, agent or bareboat charterer, who has assumed the responsibility for the operation of the ship from the owner and who, on assuming such responsibility, has agreed to take over the duties and responsibilities imposed on shipowners in accordance with this Convention, regardless of whether any other organization or persons fulfil certain of the duties or responsibiities on behalf of the shipowner.

2. Except as expressly provided otherwise, this Convention applies to all seafarers.

3. In the event of doubt as to whether any categories of persons are to be regarded as seafarers for the purpose of this Convention, the question shall be determined by the competent authority in each Member after consultation with the shipowners' and seafarers' organizations concerned with this question.

4. Except as expressly provided otherwise, this Convention applies to all ships, whether publicly or privately owned, ordinarily engaged in commercial activities, other than ships engaged in fishing or in similar pursuits and ships of traditional build such as dhows and junks. This Convention does not apply to warships or naval auxiliaries.

5. In the event of doubt as to whether this Convention applies to a ship or particular category of ships, the question shall be determined by the competent authority in each Member after consultation with the shipowners' and seafarers' organizations concerned.

6. Where the competent authority determines that it would not be reasonable or practicable at the present time to apply certain details of the Code referred to in Article VI, paragraph 1, to a ship or particular categories of ships flying the flag of the Member, the relevant provisions of the Code shall not apply to the extent that the subject matter is dealt with differently by national laws or regulations or collective bargaining agreements or other measures. Such a determination may only be made in consultation with the shipowners' and seafarers' organizations concerned and may only be made with respect to ships of less than 200 gross tonnage not engaged in international voyages.

7. Any determinations made by a Member under paragraph 3 or 5 or 6 of this Article shall be communicated to the Director-General of the International Labour Office, who shall notify the Members of the Organization.

8. Unless expressly provided otherwise, a reference to this Convention constitutes at the same time a reference to the Regulations and the Code.

Fundamental rights and principles

Article III

Each Member shall satisfy itself that the provisions of its law and regulations respect, in the context of this Convention, the fundamental rights to:

(a) freedom of association and the effective recognition of the right to collective bargaining;

(b) the elimination of all forms of forced or compulsory labour;

(c) the effective abolition of child labour; and

(d) the elimination of discrimination in respect of employment and occupation.

Seafarers' employment and social rights

Article IV

1. Every seafarer has the right to a safe and secure workplace that complies with safety standards.

2. Every seafarer has a right to fair terms of employment.

3. Every seafarer has a right to decent working and living conditions on board ship.

4. Every seafarer has a right to health protection, medical care, welfare measures and other forms of social protection.

5. Each Member shall ensure, within the limits of its jurisdiction, that the seafarers' employment and social rights set out in the preceding paragraphs of this Article are fully implemented in accordance with the requirements of this Convention. Unless specified otherwise in the Convention, such implementation may be achieved through national laws or regulations, through applicable collective bargaining agreements or through other measures or in practice.

Implementation and enforcement responsibilities

Article V

1. Each Member shall implement and enforce laws or regulations or other measures that it has adopted to fulfil its commitments under this Convention with respect to ships and seafarers under its jurisdiction.

2. Each Member shall effectively exercise its jurisdiction and control over ships that fly its flag by establishing a system for ensuring compliance with the requirements of this Convention, including regular inspections, reporting, monitoring and legal proceedings under the applicable laws.

3. Each Member shall ensure that ships that fly its flag carry a maritime labour certificate and a declaration of maritime labour compliance as required by this Convention.

4. A ship to which this Convention applies may, in accordance with international law, be inspected by a Member other than the flag State, when the ship is in one of its ports, to determine whether the ship is in compliance with the requirements of this Convention.

5. Each Member shall effectively exercise its jurisdiction and control over seafarer recruitment and placement services, if these are established in its territory.

6. Each Member shall prohibit violations of the requirements of this Convention and shall, in accordance with international law, establish sanctions or require the adoption of corrective measures under its laws which are adequate to discourage such violations.

7. Each Member shall implement its responsibilities under this Convention in such a way as to ensure that the ships that fly the flag of any State that has not ratified this Convention do not receive more favourable treatment than the ships that fly the flag of any State that has ratified it.

Regulations and Parts A and B of the Code

Article VI

1. The Regulations and the provisions of Part A of the Code are mandatory. The provisions of Part B of the Code are not mandatory.

2. Each Member undertakes to respect the rights and principles set out in the Regulations and to implement each Regulation in the manner set out in the corresponding provisions of Part A of the Code. In addition, the Member shall give due consideration to implementing its responsibilities in the manner provided for in Part B of the Code.

3. A Member which is not in a position to implement the rights and principles in the manner set out in Part A of the Code may, unless expressly provided otherwise in this Convention, implement Part A through provisions in its laws and regulations or other measures which are substantially equivalent to the provisions of Part A.

4. For the sole purpose of paragraph 3 of this Article, any law, regulation, collective agreement or other implementing measure shall be considered to be substantially equivalent, in the context of this Convention, if the Member satisfies itself that:

(a) it is conducive to the full achievement of the general object and purpose of the provision or provisions of Part A of the Code concerned; and

(b) it gives effect to the provision or provisions of Part A of the Code concerned.

Consultation with shipowners' and seafarers' organizations

Article VII

Any derogation, exemption or other flexible application of this Convention for which the Convention requires consultation with shipowners' and seafarers' organizations may, in cases where representative organizations of shipowners or of seafarers do not exist within a Member, only be decided by that Member through consultation with the Committee referred to in Article XIII.

Entry into force

Article VIII

1. The formal ratifications of this Convention shall be communicated to the Director-General of the International Labour Office for registration.

2. This Convention shall be binding only upon those Members of the International Labour Organization whose ratifications have been registered by the Director-General.

3. This Convention shall come into force 12 months after the date on which there have been registered ratifications by at least 30 Members with a total share in the world gross tonnage of ships of at least 33 per cent.

4. Thereafter, this Convention shall come into force for any Member 12 months after the date on which its ratification has been registered.

Denunciation

Article IX

1. A Member which has ratified this Convention may denounce it after the expiration of ten years from the date on which the Convention first comes into force, by an act communicated to the Director-General of the International Labour Office for registration. Such denunciation shall not take effect until one year after the date on which it is registered.

2. Each Member which does not, within the year following the expiration of the period of ten years mentioned in paragraph 1 of this Article, exercise the right of denunciation provided for in this Article, shall be bound for another period of ten years and, thereafter, may denounce this Convention at the expiration of each new period of ten years under the terms provided for in this Article.

Effect of entry into force

Article X

This Convention revises the following Conventions:

Minimum Age (Sea) Convention, 1920 (No. 7)

Unemployment Indemnity (Shipwreck) Convention, 1920 (No. 8)

Placing of Seamen Convention, 1920 (No. 9)

Medical Examination of Young Persons (Sea) Convention, 1921 (No. 16)

Seamen's Articles of Agreement Convention, 1926 (No. 22)

Repatriation of Seamen Convention, 1926 (No. 23)

Officers' Competency Certificates Convention, 1936 (No. 53)

Holidays with Pay (Sea) Convention, 1936 (No. 54)

Shipowners' Liability (Sick and Injured Seamen) Convention, 1936 (No. 55)

Sickness Insurance (Sea) Convention, 1936 (No. 56)

Hours of Work and Manning (Sea) Convention, 1936 (No. 57)

Minimum Age (Sea) Convention (Revised), 1936 (No. 58)

Food and Catering (Ships' Crews) Convention, 1946 (No. 68)

Certification of Ships' Cooks Convention, 1946 (No. 69)

Social Security (Seafarers) Convention, 1946 (No. 70)

Paid Vacations (Seafarers) Convention, 1946 (No. 72)

Medical Examination (Seafarers) Convention, 1946 (No. 73)

Certification of Able Seamen Convention, 1946 (No. 74)

Accommodation of Crews Convention, 1946 (No. 75)

Wages, Hours of Work and Manning (Sea) Convention, 1946 (No. 76)

Paid Vacations (Seafarers) Convention (Revised), 1949 (No. 91)

Accommodation of Crews Convention (Revised), 1949 (No. 92)

Wages, Hours of Work and Manning (Sea) Convention (Revised), 1949 (No. 93)

Wages, Hours of Work and Manning (Sea) Convention (Revised), 1958 (No. 109)

Accommodation of Crews (Supplementary Provisions) Convention, 1970 (No. 133)

Prevention of Accidents (Seafarers) Convention, 1970 (No. 134)

Continuity of Employment (Seafarers) Convention, 1976 (No. 145)

Seafarers' Annual Leave with Pay Convention, 1976 (No. 146)

Merchant Shipping (Minimum Standards) Convention, 1976 (No. 147)

Protocol of 1996 to the Merchant Shipping (Minimum Standards) Convention, 1976 (No. 147)

Seafarers' Welfare Convention, 1987 (No. 163)

Health Protection and Medical Care (Seafarers) Convention, 1987 (No. 164)

Social Security (Seafarers) Convention (Revised), 1987 (No. 165)

Repatriation of Seafarers Convention (Revised), 1987 (No. 166)

Labour Inspection (Seafarers) Convention, 1996 (No. 178)

Recruitment and Placement of Seafarers Convention, 1996 (No. 179)

Seafarers' Hours of Work and the Manning of Ships Convention, 1996 (No. 180).

Depositary functions

Article XI

1. The Director-General of the International Labour Office shall notify all Members of the International Labour Organization of the registration of all ratifications, acceptances and denunciations under this Convention.

2. When the conditions provided for in paragraph 3 of Article VIII have been fulfilled, the Director-General shall draw the attention of the Members of the Organization to the date upon which the Convention will come into force.

Article XII

The Director-General of the International Labour Office shall communicate to the Secretary-General of the United Nations for registration in accordance with Article 102 of the Charter of the United Nations full particulars of all ratifications, acceptances and denunciations registered under this Convention.

Special Tripartite Committee

Article XIII

1. The Governing Body of the International Labour Office shall keep the working of this Convention under continuous review through a committee established by it with special competence in the area of maritime labour standards.

2. For matters dealt with in accordance with this Convention, the Committee shall consist of two representatives nominated by the Government of each Member which has ratified this Convention, and the representatives of Shipowners and Seafarers appointed by the Governing Body after consultation with the Joint Maritime Commission.

3. The Government representatives of Members which have not yet ratified this Convention may participate in the Committee but shall have no right to vote on any matter dealt with in accordance with this Convention. The Governing Body may invite other organizations or entities to be represented on the Committee by observers.

4. The votes of each Shipowner and Seafarer representative in the Committee shall be weighted so as to ensure that the Shipowners' group and the Seafarers' group each have half the voting power of the total number of governments which are represented at the meeting concerned and entitled to vote.

Amendment of this Convention

Article XIV

1. Amendments to any of the provisions of this Convention may be adopted by the General Conference of the International Labour Organization in the framework of article 19 of the Constitution of the International Labour Organisation and the rules and procedures of the Organization for the adoption of Conventions. Amendments to the Code may also be adopted following the procedures in Article XV.

2. In the case of Members whose ratifications of this Convention were registered before the adoption of the amendment, the text of the amendment shall be communicated to them for ratification.

3. In the case of other Members of the Organization, the text of the Convention as amended shall be communicated to them for ratification in accordance with art-icle 19 of the Constitution.

4. An amendment shall be deemed to have been accepted on the date when there have been registered ratifications, of the amendment or of the Convention as amended, as the case may be, by at least 30 Members with a total share in the world gross tonnage of ships of at least 33 per cent.

5. An amendment adopted in the framework of article 19 of the Constitution shall be binding only upon those Members of the Organization whose ratifications have been registered by the Director-General of the International Labour Office.

6. For any Member referred to in paragraph 2 of this Article, an amendment shall come into force 12 months after the date of acceptance referred to in paragraph 4 of this Article or 12 months after the date on which its ratification of the amendment has been registered, whichever date is later.

7. Subject to paragraph 9 of this Article, for Members referred to in paragraph 3 of this Article, the Convention as amended shall come into force 12 months after the date of acceptance referred to in paragraph 4 of this Article or 12 months after the date on which their ratifications of the Convention have been registered, whichever date is later.

8. For those Members whose ratification of this Convention was registered before the adoption of an amendment but which have not ratified the amendment, this Convention shall remain in force without the amendment concerned.

9. Any Member whose ratification of this Convention is registered after the adoption of the amendment but before the date referred to in paragraph 4 of this Article may, in a declaration accompanying the instrument of ratification, specify that its ratification relates to the Convention without the amendment concerned. In the case of a ratification with such a declaration, the Convention shall come into force for the Member concerned 12 months after the date on which the ratification was registered. Where an instrument of ratification is not accompanied by such a declaration, or where the ratification is registered on or after the date referred to in paragraph 4, the Convention shall come into force for the Member concerned 12 months after the date on which the ratification was registered and, upon its entry into force in accordance with paragraph 7 of this Article, the amendment shall be binding on the Member concerned unless the amendment provides otherwise.

Amendments to the Code

Article XV

1. The Code may be amended either by the procedure set out in Article XIV or, unless expressly provided otherwise, in accordance with the procedure set out in the present Article.

2. An amendment to the Code may be proposed to the Director-General of the International Labour Office by the government of any Member of the Organization or by the group of Shipowner representatives or the group of Seafarer representatives who have been appointed to the Committee referred to in Article XIII. An amendment proposed by a government must have been proposed by, or be supported by, at least five governments of Members that have ratified the Convention or by the group of Shipowner or Seafarer representatives referred to in this paragraph.

3. Having verified that the proposal for amendment meets the requirements of paragraph 2 of this Article, the Director-General shall promptly communicate the proposal, accompanied by any comments or suggestions deemed appropriate, to all Members of the Organization, with an invitation to them to transmit their observations or suggestions concerning the proposal within a period of six months or such other period (which shall not be less than three months nor more than nine months) prescribed by the Governing Body.

4. At the end of the period referred to in paragraph 3 of this Article, the proposal, accompanied by a summary of any observations or suggestions made under that paragraph, shall be transmitted to the Committee for consideration at a meeting. An amendment shall be considered adopted by the Committee if:

(a) at least half the governments of Members that have ratified this Convention are represented in the meeting at which the proposal is considered; and

(b) a majority of at least two-thirds of the Committee members vote in favour of the amendment; and

(c) this majority comprises the votes in favour of at least half the government voting power, half the Shipowner voting power and half the Seafarer voting power of the Committee members registered at the meeting when the proposal is put to the vote.

5. Amendments adopted in accordance with paragraph 4 of this Article shall be submitted to the next session of the Conference for approval. Such approval shall require a majority of two-thirds of the votes cast by the delegates present. If such majority is not obtained, the proposed amendment shall be referred back to the Committee for reconsideration should the Committee so wish.

6. Amendments approved by the Conference shall be notified by the Director-General to each of the Members whose ratifications of this Convention were registered before the date of such approval by the Conference. These Members are referred to below as "the ratifying Members". The notification shall contain a reference to the present Article and shall prescribe the period for the communication of any formal disagreement. This period shall be two years from the date of the notification unless, at the time of approval, the Conference has set a different period, which shall be a period of at least one year. A copy of the notification shall be communicated to the other Members of the Organization for their information.

7. An amendment approved by the Conference shall be deemed to have been accepted unless, by the end of the prescribed period, formal expressions of disagreement have been received by the Director-General from more than 40 per cent of the Members which have ratified the Convention and which represent not less than 40 per cent of the gross tonnage of the ships of the Members which have ratified the Convention.

8. An amendment deemed to have been accepted shall come into force six months after the end of the prescribed period for all the ratifying Members except those which had formally expressed their disagreement in accordance with paragraph 7 of this Article and have not withdrawn such disagreement in accordance with paragraph 11. However:

(a) before the end of the prescribed period, any ratifying Member may give notice to the Director-General that it shall be bound by the amendment only after a subsequent express notification of its acceptance; and

(b) before the date of entry into force of the amendment, any ratifying Member may give notice to the Director-General that it will not give effect to that amendment for a specified period.

9. An amendment which is the subject of a notice referred to in paragraph 8(a) of this Article shall enter into force for the Member giving such notice six months after the Member has notified the Director-General of its acceptance of the amendment or on the date on which the amendment first comes into force, whichever date is later.

10. The period referred to in paragraph 8(b) of this Article shall not go beyond one year from the date of entry into force of the amendment or beyond any longer period determined by the Conference at the time of approval of the amendment.

11. A Member that has formally expressed disagreement with an amendment may withdraw its disagreement at any time. If notice of such withdrawal is received by the Director-General after the amendment has entered into force, the amendment shall enter into force for the Member six months after the date on which the notice was registered.

12. After entry into force of an amendment, the Convention may only be ratified in its amended form.

13. To the extent that a maritime labour certificate relates to matters covered by an amendment to the Convention which has entered into force:

(a) a Member that has accepted that amendment shall not be obliged to extend the benefit of the Convention in respect of the maritime labour certificates issued to ships flying the flag of another Member which:

   (i) pursuant to paragraph 7 of this Article, has formally expressed disagreement to the amendment and has not withdrawn such disagreement; or

   (ii) pursuant to paragraph 8(a) of this Article, has given notice that its acceptance is subject to its subsequent express notification and has not accepted the amendment; and

(b) a Member that has accepted the amendment shall extend the benefit of the Convention in respect of the maritime labour certificates issued to ships flying the flag of another Member that has given notice, pursuant to paragraph 8(b) of this Article, that it will not give effect to that amendment for the period specified in accordance with paragraph 10 of this Article.

Authoritative languages

Article XVI

The English and French versions of the text of this Convention are equally authoritative.

Explanatory note to the Regulations and Code of the Maritime Labour Convention

1. This explanatory note, which does not form part of the Maritime Labour Convention, is intended as a general guide to the Convention.

2. The Convention comprises three different but related parts: the Articles, the Regulations and the Code.

3. The Articles and Regulations set out the core rights and principles and the basic obligations of Members ratifying the Convention. The Articles and Regulations can only be changed by the Conference in the framework of article 19 of the Constitution of the International Labour Organisation (see Article XIV of the Convention).

4. The Code contains the details for the implementation of the Regulations. It comprises Part A (mandatory Standards) and Part B (non-mandatory Guidelines). The Code can be amended through the simplified procedure set out in Article XV of the Convention. Since the Code relates to detailed implementation, amendments to it must remain within the general scope of the Articles and Regulations.

5. The Regulations and the Code are organized into general areas under five Titles:

Title 1: Minimum requirements for seafarers to work on a ship

Title 2: Conditions of employment

Title 3: Accommodation, recreational facilities, food and catering

Title 4: Health protection, medical care, welfare and social security protection

Title 5: Compliance and enforcement

6. Each Title contains groups of provisions relating to a particular right or principle (or enforcement measure in Title 5), with connected numbering. The first group in Title 1, for example, consists of Regulation 1.1, Standard A1.1 and Guideline B1.1, relating to minimum age.

7. The Convention has three underlying purposes:

(a) to lay down, in its Articles and Regulations, a firm set of rights and principles;

(b) to allow, through the Code, a considerable degree of flexibility in the way Members implement those rights and principles; and

(c) to ensure, through Title 5, that the rights and principles are properly complied with and enforced.

8. There are two main areas for flexibility in implementation: one is the possibility for a Member, where necessary (see Article VI, paragraph 3), to give effect to the detailed requirements of Part A of the Code through substantial equivalence (as defined in Article VI, paragraph 4).

9. The second area of flexibility in implementation is provided by formulating the mandatory requirements of many provisions in Part A in a more general way, thus leaving a wider scope for discretion as to the precise action to be provided for at the national level. In such cases, guidance on implementation is given in the non-mandatory Part B of the Code. In this way, Members which have ratified this Convention can ascertain the kind of action that might be expected of them under the corresponding general obligation in Part A, as well as action that would not necessarily be required. For example, Standard A4.1 requires all ships to provide prompt access to the necessary medicines for medical care on board ship (paragraph 1(b)) and to "carry a medicine chest" (paragraph 4(a)). The fulfilment in good faith of this latter obligation clearly means something more than simply having a medicine chest on board each ship. A more precise indication of what is involved is provided in the corresponding Guideline B4.1.1 (paragraph 4) so as to ensure that the contents of the chest are properly stored, used and maintained.

10. Members which have ratified this Convention are not bound by the guidance concerned and, as indicated in the provisions in Title 5 on port State control, inspections would deal only with the relevant requirements of this Convention (Articles, Regulations and the Standards in Part A). However, Members are required under paragraph 2 of Article VI to give due consideration to implementing their responsibilities under Part A of the Code in the manner provided for in Part B. If, having duly considered the relevant Guidelines, a Member decides to provide for different arrangements which ensure the proper storage, use and maintenance of the contents of the medicine chest, to take the example given above, as required by the Standard in Part A, then that is acceptable. On the other hand, by following the guidance provided in Part B, the Member concerned, as well as the ILO bodies responsible for reviewing implementation of international labour Conventions, can be sure without further consideration that the arrangements the Member has provided for are adequate to implement the responsibilities under Part A to which the Guideline relates.

THE REGULATIONS AND THE CODE

Title 1. Minimum requirements for seafarers to work on a ship

Regulation 1.1 – Minimum age

Purpose: To ensure that no under-age persons work on a ship

1. No person below the minimum age shall be employed or engaged or work on a ship.

2. The minimum age at the time of the initial entry into force of this Convention is 16 years.

3. A higher minimum age shall be required in the circumstances set out in the Code.

Standard A1.1 – Minimum age

1. The employment, engagement or work on board a ship of any person under the age of 16 shall be prohibited.

2. Night work of seafarers under the age of 18 shall be prohibited. For the purposes of this Standard, "night" shall be defined in accordance with national law and practice. It shall cover a period of at least nine hours starting no later than midnight and ending no earlier than 5 a.m.

3. An exception to strict compliance with the night work restriction may be made by the competent authority when:

(a) the effective training of the seafarers concerned, in accordance with established programmes and schedules, would be impaired; or

(b) the specific nature of the duty or a recognized training programme requires that the seafarers covered by the exception perform duties at night and the authority determines, after consultation with the shipowners' and seafarers' organizations concerned, that the work will not be detrimental to their health or well-being.

4. The employment, engagement or work of seafarers under the age of 18 shall be prohibited where the work is likely to jeopardize their health or safety. The types of such work shall be determined by national laws or regulations or by the competent authority, after consultation with the shipowners' and seafarers' organizations concerned, in accordance with relevant international standards.

Guideline B1.1 – Minimum age

1. When regulating working and living conditions, Members should give special attention to the needs of young persons under the age of 18.

Regulation 1.2 – Medical certificate

Purpose: To ensure that all seafarers are medically fit to perform their duties at sea

1. Seafarers shall not work on a ship unless they are certified as medically fit to perform their duties.

2. Exceptions can only be permitted as prescribed in the Code.

Standard A1.2 – Medical certificate

1. The competent authority shall require that, prior to beginning work on a ship, seafarers hold a valid medical certificate attesting that they are medically fit to perform the duties they are to carry out at sea.

2. In order to ensure that medical certificates genuinely reflect seafarers' state of health, in light of the duties they are to perform, the competent authority shall, after consultation with the shipowners' and seafarers' organizations concerned, and giving due consideration to applicable international guidelines referred to in Part B of this Code, prescribe the nature of the medical examination and certificate.

3. This Standard is without prejudice to the International Convention on Standards of Training, Certification and Watchkeeping for Seafarers, 1978, as amended ("STCW"). A medical certificate issued in accordance with the requirements of STCW shall be accepted by the competent authority, for the purpose of Regulation 1.2. A medical certificate meeting the substance of those requirements, in the case of seafarers not covered by STCW, shall similarly be accepted.

4. The medical certificate shall be issued by a duly qualified medical practitioner or, in the case of a certificate solely concerning eyesight, by a person recognized by the competent authority as qualified to issue such a certificate. Practitioners must enjoy full professional independence in exercising their medical judgement in undertaking medical examination procedures.

5. Seafarers that have been refused a certificate or have had a limitation imposed on their ability to work, in particular with respect to time, field of work or trading area, shall be given the opportunity to have a further examination by another independent medical practitioner or by an independent medical referee.

6. Each medical certificate shall state in particular that:

(a) the hearing and sight of the seafarer concerned, and the colour vision in the case of a seafarer to be employed in capacities where fitness for the work to be performed is liable to be affected by defective colour vision, are all satisfactory; and

(b) the seafarer concerned is not suffering from any medical condition likely to be aggravated by service at sea or to render the seafarer unfit for such service or to endanger the health of other persons on board.

7. Unless a shorter period is required by reason of the specific duties to be performed by the seafarer concerned or is required under STCW:

(a) a medical certificate shall be valid for a maximum period of two years unless the seafarer is under the age of 18, in which case the maximum period of validity shall be one year;

(b) a certification of colour vision shall be valid for a maximum period of six years.

8. In urgent cases the competent authority may permit a seafarer to work without a valid medical certificate until the next port of call where the seafarer can obtain a medical certificate from a qualified medical practitioner, provided that:

(a) the period of such permission does not exceed three months; and

(b) the seafarer concerned is in possession of an expired medical certificate of recent date.

9. If the period of validity of a certificate expires in the course of a voyage, the certificate shall continue in force until the next port of call where the seafarer can obtain a medical certificate from a qualified medical practitioner, provided that the period shall not exceed three months.

10. The medical certificates for seafarers working on ships ordinarily engaged on international voyages must as a minimum be provided in English.

Guideline B1.2 – Medical certificate

Guideline B1.2.1 – International guidelines

1. The competent authority, medical practitioners, examiners, shipowners, seafarers' representatives and all other persons concerned with the conduct of medical fitness examinations of seafarer candidates and serving seafarers should follow the ILO/WHO *Guidelines for Conducting Pre-sea and Periodic Medical Fitness Examinations for Seafarers*, including any subsequent versions, and any other applicable international guidelines published by the International Labour Organization, the International Maritime Organization or the World Health Organization.

Regulation 1.3 – Training and qualifications

Purpose: To ensure that seafarers are trained or qualified to carry out their duties on board ship

1. Seafarers shall not work on a ship unless they are trained or certified as competent or otherwise qualified to perform their duties.

2. Seafarers shall not be permitted to work on a ship unless they have successfully completed training for personal safety on board ship.

3. Training and certification in accordance with the mandatory instruments adopted by the International Maritime Organization shall be considered as meeting the requirements of paragraphs 1 and 2 of this Regulation.

4. Any Member which, at the time of its ratification of this Convention, was bound by the Certification of Able Seamen Convention, 1946 (No. 74), shall continue to carry out the obligations under that Convention unless and until mandatory

provisions covering its subject matter have been adopted by the International Maritime Organization and entered into force, or until five years have elapsed since the entry into force of this Convention in accordance with paragraph 3 of Article VIII, whichever date is earlier.

Regulation 1.4 – Recruitment and placement

Purpose: To ensure that seafarers have access to an efficient and well-regulated seafarer recruitment and placement system

1. All seafarers shall have access to an efficient, adequate and accountable system for finding employment on board ship without charge to the seafarer.

2. Seafarer recruitment and placement services operating in a Member's territory shall conform to the standards set out in the Code.

3. Each Member shall require, in respect of seafarers who work on ships that fly its flag, that shipowners who use seafarer recruitment and placement services that are based in countries or territories in which this Convention does not apply, ensure that those services conform to the requirements set out in the Code.

Standard A1.4 – Recruitment and placement

1. Each Member that operates a public seafarer recruitment and placement service shall ensure that the service is operated in an orderly manner that protects and promotes seafarers' employment rights as provided in this Convention.

2. Where a Member has private seafarer recruitment and placement services operating in its territory whose primary purpose is the recruitment and placement of seafarers or which recruit and place a significant number of seafarers, they shall be operated only in conformity with a standardized system of licensing or certification or other form of regulation. This system shall be established, modified or changed only after consultation with the shipowners' and seafarers' organizations concerned. In the event of doubt as to whether this Convention applies to a private recruitment and placement service, the question shall be determined by the competent authority in each Member after consultation with the shipowners' and seafarers' organizations concerned. Undue proliferation of private seafarer recruitment and placement services shall not be encouraged.

3. The provisions of paragraph 2 of this Standard shall also apply – to the extent that they are determined by the competent authority, in consultation with the shipowners' and seafarers' organizations concerned, to be appropriate – in the context of recruitment and placement services operated by a seafarers' organization in the territory of the Member for the supply of seafarers who are nationals of that Member to ships which fly its flag. The services covered by this paragraph are those fulfilling the following conditions:

(a) the recruitment and placement service is operated pursuant to a collective bargaining agreement between that organization and a shipowner;

(b) both the seafarers' organization and the shipowner are based in the territory of the Member;

(c) the Member has national laws or regulations or a procedure to authorize or register the collective bargaining agreement permitting the operation of the recruitment and placement service; and

(d) the recruitment and placement service is operated in an orderly manner and measures are in place to protect and promote seafarers' employment rights comparable to those provided in paragraph 5 of this Standard.

4. Nothing in this Standard or Regulation 1.4 shall be deemed to:

(a) prevent a Member from maintaining a free public seafarer recruitment and placement service for seafarers in the framework of a policy to meet the needs of seafarers and shipowners, whether the service forms part of or is coordinated with a public employment service for all workers and employers; or

(b) impose on a Member the obligation to establish a system for the operation of private seafarer recruitment or placement services in its territory.

5. A Member adopting a system referred to in paragraph 2 of this Standard shall, in its laws and regulations or other measures, at a minimum:

(a) prohibit seafarer recruitment and placement services from using means, mechanisms or lists intended to prevent or deter seafarers from gaining employment for which they are qualified;

(b) require that no fees or other charges for seafarer recruitment or placement or for providing employment to seafarers are borne directly or indirectly, in whole or in part, by the seafarer, other than the cost of the seafarer obtaining a national statutory medical certificate, the national seafarer's book and a passport or other similar personal travel documents, not including, however, the cost of visas, which shall be borne by the shipowner; and

(c) ensure that seafarer recruitment and placement services operating in its territory:

  (i) maintain an up-to-date register of all seafarers recruited or placed through them, to be available for inspection by the competent authority;

  (ii) make sure that seafarers are informed of their rights and duties under their employment agreements prior to or in the process of engagement and that proper arrangements are made for seafarers to examine their employment agreements before and after they are signed and for them to receive a copy of the agreements;

  (iii) verify that seafarers recruited or placed by them are qualified and hold the documents necessary for the job concerned, and that the seafarers' employment agreements are in accordance with applicable laws and regulations and any collective bargaining agreement that forms part of the employment agreement;

  (iv) make sure, as far as practicable, that the shipowner has the means to protect seafarers from being stranded in a foreign port;

  (v) examine and respond to any complaint concerning their activities and advise the competent authority of any unresolved complaint;

  (vi) establish a system of protection, by way of insurance or an equivalent appropriate measure, to compensate seafarers for monetary loss that they may incur as a result of the failure of a recruitment and placement service or the relevant shipowner under the seafarers' employment agreement to meet its obligations to them.

6. The competent authority shall closely supervise and control all seafarer recruitment and placement services operating in the territory of the Member concerned. Any licences or certificates or similar authorizations for the operation of private services in the territory are granted or renewed only after verification that the seafarer recruitment and placement service concerned meets the requirements of national laws and regulations.

7. The competent authority shall ensure that adequate machinery and procedures exist for the investigation, if necessary, of complaints concerning the activities of seafarer recruitment and placement services, involving, as appropriate, representatives of shipowners and seafarers.

8. Each Member which has ratified this Convention shall, in so far as practicable, advise its nationals on the possible problems of signing on a ship that flies the flag of a State which has not ratified the Convention, until it is satisfied that standards equivalent to those fixed by this Convention are being applied. Measures taken to this effect by the Member that has ratified this Convention shall not be in contradiction with the principle of free movement of workers stipulated by the treaties to which the two States concerned may be parties.

9. Each Member which has ratified this Convention shall require that shipowners of ships that fly its flag, who use seafarer recruitment and placement services based in countries or territories in which this Convention does not apply, ensure, as far as practicable, that those services meet the requirements of this Standard.

10. Nothing in this Standard shall be understood as diminishing the obligations and responsibilities of shipowners or of a Member with respect to ships that fly its flag.

Guideline B1.4 – Recruitment and placement

Guideline B1.4.1 – Organizational and operational guidelines

1. When fulfilling its obligations under Standard A1.4, paragraph 1, the competent authority should consider:

(a) taking the necessary measures to promote effective cooperation among seafarer recruitment and placement services, whether public or private;

(b) the needs of the maritime industry at both the national and international levels, when developing training programmes for seafarers that form the part of the ship's crew that is responsible for the ship's safe navigation and pollution prevention operations, with the participation of shipowners, seafarers and the relevant training institutions;

(c) making suitable arrangements for the cooperation of representative shipowners' and seafarers' organizations in the organization and operation of the public seafarer recruitment and placement services, where they exist;

(d) determining, with due regard to the right to privacy and the need to protect confidentiality, the conditions under which seafarers' personal data may be processed by seafarer recruitment and placement services, including the collection, storage, combination and communication of such data to third parties;

(e) maintaining an arrangement for the collection and analysis of all relevant information on the maritime labour market, including the current and prospective supply of seafarers that work as crew classified by age, sex, rank and qualifications, and the industry's requirements, the collection of data on age or sex being admissible only for statistical purposes or if used in the framework of a programme to prevent discrimination based on age or sex;

(f) ensuring that the staff responsible for the supervision of public and private seafarer recruitment and placement services for ship's crew with responsibility for the ship's safe navigation and pollution prevention operations have had adequate training, including approved sea-service experience, and have relevant knowledge of the maritime industry, including the relevant maritime international instruments on training, certification and labour standards;

(g) prescribing operational standards and adopting codes of conduct and ethical practices for seafarer recruitment and placement services; and

(h) exercising supervision of the licensing or certification system on the basis of a system of quality standards.

2. In establishing the system referred to in Standard A1.4, paragraph 2, each Member should consider requiring seafarer recruitment and placement services, established in its territory, to develop and maintain verifiable operational practices. These operational practices for private seafarer recruitment and placement services and, to the extent that they are applicable, for public seafarer recruitment and placement services should address the following matters:

(a) medical examinations, seafarers' identity documents and such other items as may be required for the seafarer to gain employment;

(b) maintaining, with due regard to the right to privacy and the need to protect confidentiality, full and complete records of the seafarers covered by their recruitment and placement system, which should include but not be limited to:

    (i) the seafarers' qualifications;

    (ii) record of employment;

    (iii) personal data relevant to employment; and

    (iv) medical data relevant to employment;

(c) maintaining up-to-date lists of the ships for which the seafarer recruitment and placement services provide seafarers and ensuring that there is a means by which the services can be contacted in an emergency at all hours;

(d) procedures to ensure that seafarers are not subject to exploitation by the seafarer recruitment and placement services or their personnel with regard to the offer of engagement on particular ships or by particular companies;

(e) procedures to prevent the opportunities for exploitation of seafarers arising from the issue of joining advances or any other financial transaction between the shipowner and the seafarers which are handled by the seafarer recruitment and placement services;

(f) clearly publicizing costs, if any, which the seafarer will be expected to bear in the recruitment process;

(g) ensuring that seafarers are advised of any particular conditions applicable to the job for which they are to be engaged and of the particular shipowner's policies relating to their employment;

(h) procedures which are in accordance with the principles of natural justice for dealing with cases of incompetence or indiscipline consistent with national laws and practice and, where applicable, with collective agreements;

(i) procedures to ensure, as far as practicable, that all mandatory certificates and documents submitted for employment are up to date and have not been fraudulently obtained and that employment references are verified;

(j) procedures to ensure that requests for information or advice by families of seafarers while the seafarers are at sea are dealt with promptly and sympathetically and at no cost; and

(k) verifying that labour conditions on ships where seafarers are placed are in conformity with applicable collective bargaining agreements concluded between a shipowner and a representative seafarers' organization and, as a matter of policy, supplying seafarers only to shipowners that offer terms and conditions of employment to seafarers which comply with applicable laws or regulations or collective agreements.

3. Consideration should be given to encouraging international cooperation between Members and relevant organizations, such as:

(a) the systematic exchange of information on the maritime industry and labour market on a bilateral, regional and multilateral basis;

(b) the exchange of information on maritime labour legislation;

(c) the harmonization of policies, working methods and legislation governing recruitment and placement of seafarers;

(d) the improvement of procedures and conditions for the international recruitment and placement of seafarers; and

(e) workforce planning, taking account of the supply of and demand for seafarers and the requirements of the maritime industry.

Title 2. Conditions of employment

Regulation 2.1 – Seafarers' employment agreements

Purpose: To ensure that seafarers have a fair employment agreement

1. The terms and conditions for employment of a seafarer shall be set out or referred to in a clear written legally enforceable agreement and shall be consistent with the standards set out in the Code.

2. Seafarers' employment agreements shall be agreed to by the seafarer under conditions which ensure that the seafarer has an opportunity to review and seek advice on the terms and conditions in the agreement and freely accepts them before signing.

3. To the extent compatible with the Member's national law and practice, seafarers' employment agreements shall be understood to incorporate any applicable collective bargaining agreements.

Standard A2.1 – Seafarers' employment agreements

1. Each Member shall adopt laws or regulations requiring that ships that fly its flag comply with the following requirements:

(a) seafarers working on ships that fly its flag shall have a seafarers' employment agreement signed by both the seafarer and the shipowner or a representative of the shipowner (or, where they are not employees, evidence of contractual or similar arrangements) providing them with decent working and living conditions on board the ship as required by this Convention;

(b) seafarers signing a seafarers' employment agreement shall be given an opportunity to examine and seek advice on the agreement before signing, as well as such other facilities as are necessary to ensure that they have freely entered into an agreement with a sufficient understanding of their rights and responsibilities;

(c) the shipowner and seafarer concerned shall each have a signed original of the seafarers' employment agreement;

(d) measures shall be taken to ensure that clear information as to the conditions of their employment can be easily obtained on board by seafarers, including the ship's master, and that such information, including a copy of the seafarers' employment agreement, is also accessible for review by officers of a competent authority, including those in ports to be visited; and

(e) seafarers shall be given a document containing a record of their employment on board the ship.

2. Where a collective bargaining agreement forms all or part of a seafarers' employment agreement, a copy of that agreement shall be available on board. Where the language of the seafarers' employment agreement and any applicable collective bargaining agreement is not English, the following shall also be available in English (except for ships engaged only in domestic voyages):

(a) a copy of a standard form of the agreement; and

(b) the portions of the collective bargaining agreement that are subject to a port State inspection under Regulation 5.2.

3. The document referred to in paragraph 1(e) of this Standard shall not contain any statement as to the quality of the seafarers' work or as to their wages. The form of the document, the particulars to be recorded and the manner in which such particulars are to be entered, shall be determined by national law.

4. Each Member shall adopt laws and regulations specifying the matters that are to be included in all seafarers' employment agreements governed by its national law. Seafarers' employment agreements shall in all cases contain the following particulars:

(a) the seafarer's full name, date of birth or age, and birthplace;

(b) the shipowner's name and address;

(c) the place where and date when the seafarers' employment agreement is entered into;

(d) the capacity in which the seafarer is to be employed;

(e) the amount of the seafarer's wages or, where applicable, the formula used for calculating them;

(f) the amount of paid annual leave or, where applicable, the formula used for calculating it;

(g) the termination of the agreement and the conditions thereof, including:

  (i) if the agreement has been made for an indefinite period, the conditions entitling either party to terminate it, as well as the required notice period, which shall not be less for the shipowner than for the seafarer;

  (ii) if the agreement has been made for a definite period, the date fixed for its expiry; and

  (iii) if the agreement has been made for a voyage, the port of destination and the time which has to expire after arrival before the seafarer should be discharged;

(h) the health and social security protection benefits to be provided to the seafarer by the shipowner;

(i) the seafarer's entitlement to repatriation;

(j) reference to the collective bargaining agreement, if applicable; and

(k) any other particulars which national law may require.

5. Each Member shall adopt laws or regulations establishing minimum notice periods to be given by the seafarers and shipowners for the early termination of a seafarers' employment agreement. The duration of these minimum periods shall be determined after consultation with the shipowners' and seafarers' organizations concerned, but shall not be shorter than seven days.

6. A notice period shorter than the minimum may be given in circumstances which are recognized under national law or regulations or applicable collective bargaining agreements as justifying termination of the employment agreement at shorter notice or without notice. In determining those circumstances, each Member shall ensure that the need of the seafarer to terminate, without penalty, the employment agreement on shorter notice or without notice for compassionate or other urgent reasons is taken into account.

Guideline B2.1 – Seafarers' employment agreements

Guideline B2.1.1 – Record of employment

1. In determining the particulars to be recorded in the record of employment referred to in Standard A2.1, paragraph 1(e), each Member should ensure that this document contains sufficient information, with a translation in English, to facilitate the acquisition of further work or to satisfy the sea-service requirements for upgrading or promotion. A seafarers' discharge book may satisfy the requirements of paragraph 1(e) of that Standard.

Regulation 2.2 – Wages

Purpose: To ensure that seafarers are paid for their services

1. All seafarers shall be paid for their work regularly and in full in accordance with their employment agreements.

Standard A2.2 – Wages

1. Each Member shall require that payments due to seafarers working on ships that fly its flag are made at no greater than monthly intervals and in accordance with any applicable collective agreement.

2. Seafarers shall be given a monthly account of the payments due and the amounts paid, including wages, additional payments and the rate of exchange used where payment has been made in a currency or at a rate different from the one agreed to.

3. Each Member shall require that shipowners take measures, such as those set out in paragraph 4 of this Standard, to provide seafarers with a means to transmit all or part of their earnings to their families or dependants or legal beneficiaries.

4. Measures to ensure that seafarers are able to transmit their earnings to their families include:

(a) a system for enabling seafarers, at the time of their entering employment or during it, to allot, if they so desire, a proportion of their wages for remittance at regular intervals to their families by bank transfers or similar means; and

(b) a requirement that allotments should be remitted in due time and directly to the person or persons nominated by the seafarers.

5. Any charge for the service under paragraphs 3 and 4 of this Standard shall be reasonable in amount, and the rate of currency exchange, unless otherwise provided, shall, in accordance with national laws or regulations, be at the prevailing market rate or the official published rate and not unfavourable to the seafarer.

6. Each Member that adopts national laws or regulations governing seafarers' wages shall give due consideration to the guidance provided in Part B of the Code.

Guideline B2.2 – Wages

Guideline B2.2.1 – Specific definitions

1. For the purpose of this Guideline, the term:

(a) *able seafarer* means any seafarer who is deemed competent to perform any duty which may be required of a rating serving in the deck department, other than the duties of a supervisory or specialist rating, or who is defined as such by national laws, regulations or practice, or by collective agreement;

(b) *basic pay or wages* means the pay, however composed, for normal hours of work; it does not include payments for overtime worked, bonuses, allowances, paid leave or any other additional remuneration;

(c) *consolidated wage* means a wage or salary which includes the basic pay and other pay-related benefits; a consolidated wage may include compensation for all overtime hours which are worked and all other pay-related benefits, or it may include only certain benefits in a partial consolidation;

(d) *hours of work* means time during which seafarers are required to do work on account of the ship;

(e) *overtime* means time worked in excess of the normal hours of work.

Guideline B2.2.2 – Calculation and payment

1. For seafarers whose remuneration includes separate compensation for overtime worked:

(a) for the purpose of calculating wages, the normal hours of work at sea and in port should not exceed eight hours per day;

(b) for the purpose of calculating overtime, the number of normal hours per week covered by the basic pay or wages should be prescribed by national laws or regulations, if not determined by collective agreements, but should not exceed 48 hours per week; collective agreements may provide for a different but not less favourable treatment;

(c) the rate or rates of compensation for overtime, which should be not less than one and one-quarter times the basic pay or wages per hour, should be prescribed by national laws or regulations or by collective agreements, if applicable; and

(d) records of all overtime worked should be maintained by the master, or a person assigned by the master, and endorsed by the seafarer at no greater than monthly intervals.

2. For seafarers whose wages are fully or partially consolidated:

(a) the seafarers' employment agreement should specify clearly, where appropriate, the number of hours of work expected of the seafarer in return for this remuneration, and any additional allowances which might be due in addition to the consolidated wage, and in which circumstances;

(b) where hourly overtime is payable for hours worked in excess of those covered by the consolidated wage, the hourly rate should be not less than one and one-quarter times the basic rate corresponding to the normal hours of work as defined in paragraph 1 of this Guideline; the same principle should be applied to the overtime hours included in the consolidated wage;

(c) remuneration for that portion of the fully or partially consolidated wage representing the normal hours of work as defined in paragraph 1(a) of this Guideline should be no less than the applicable minimum wage; and

(d) for seafarers whose wages are partially consolidated, records of all overtime worked should be maintained and endorsed as provided for in paragraph 1(d) of this Guideline.

3. National laws or regulations or collective agreements may provide for compensation for overtime or for work performed on the weekly day of rest and on public holidays by at least equivalent time off duty and off the ship or additional leave in lieu of remuneration or any other compensation so provided.

4. National laws and regulations adopted after consulting the representative shipowners' and seafarers' organizations or, as appropriate, collective agreements should take into account the following principles:

(a) equal remuneration for work of equal value should apply to all seafarers employed on the same ship without discrimination based upon race, colour, sex, religion, political opinion, national extraction or social origin;

(b) the seafarers' employment agreement specifying the applicable wages or wage rates should be carried on board the ship; information on the amount of wages or wage rates should be made available to each seafarer, either by providing at least one signed copy of the relevant information to the seafarer in a language which the seafarer understands, or by posting a copy of the agreement in a place accessible to seafarers or by some other appropriate means;

(c) wages should be paid in legal tender; where appropriate, they may be paid by bank transfer, bank cheque, postal cheque or money order;

(d) on termination of engagement all remuneration due should be paid without undue delay;

(e) adequate penalties or other appropriate remedies should be imposed by the competent authority where shipowners unduly delay, or fail to make, payment of all remuneration due;

(f) wages should be paid directly to seafarers' designated bank accounts unless they request otherwise in writing;

(g) subject to subparagraph (h) of this paragraph, the shipowner should impose no limit on seafarers' freedom to dispose of their remuneration;

(h) deduction from remuneration should be permitted only if:

(i) there is an express provision in national laws or regulations or in an applicable collective agreement and the seafarer has been informed, in the manner deemed most appropriate by the competent authority, of the conditions for such deductions; and

(ii) the deductions do not in total exceed the limit that may have been established by national laws or regulations or collective agreements or court decisions for making such deductions;

(i) no deductions should be made from a seafarer's remuneration in respect of obtaining or retaining employment;

(j) monetary fines against seafarers other than those authorized by national laws or regulations, collective agreements or other measures should be prohibited;

(k) the competent authority should have the power to inspect stores and services provided on board ship to ensure that fair and reasonable prices are applied for the benefit of the seafarers concerned; and

(l) to the extent that seafarers' claims for wages and other sums due in respect of their employment are not secured in accordance with the provisions of the International Convention on Maritime Liens and Mortgages, 1993, such claims should be protected in accordance with the Protection of Workers' Claims (Employer's Insolvency) Convention, 1992 (No. 173).

5. Each Member should, after consulting with representative shipowners' and seafarers' organizations, have procedures to investigate complaints relating to any matter contained in this Guideline.

Guideline B2.2.3 – Minimum wages

1. Without prejudice to the principle of free collective bargaining, each Member should, after consulting representative shipowners' and seafarers' organizations, establish procedures for determining minimum wages for seafarers. Representative shipowners' and seafarers' organizations should participate in the operation of such procedures.

2. When establishing such procedures and in fixing minimum wages, due regard should be given to international labour standards concerning minimum wage fixing, as well as the following principles:

(a) the level of minimum wages should take into account the nature of maritime employment, crewing levels of ships, and seafarers' normal hours of work; and

(b) the level of minimum wages should be adjusted to take into account changes in the cost of living and in the needs of seafarers.

3. The competent authority should ensure:

(a) by means of a system of supervision and sanctions, that wages are paid at not less than the rate or rates fixed; and

(b) that any seafarers who have been paid at a rate lower than the minimum wage are enabled to recover, by an inexpensive and expeditious judicial or other procedure, the amount by which they have been underpaid.

Guideline B2.2.4 – Minimum monthly basic pay or wage figure for able seafarers

1. The basic pay or wages for a calendar month of service for an able seafarer should be no less than the amount periodically set by the Joint Maritime Commission or another body authorized by the Governing Body of the International Labour Office. Upon a decision of the Governing Body, the Director-General shall notify any revised amount to the Members of the Organization.

2. Nothing in this Guideline should be deemed to prejudice arrangements agreed between shipowners or their organizations and seafarers' organizations with regard to the regulation of standard minimum terms and conditions of employment, provided such terms and conditions are recognized by the competent authority.

Regulation 2.3 – Hours of work and hours of rest

Purpose: To ensure that seafarers have regulated hours of work or hours of rest

1. Each Member shall ensure that the hours of work or hours of rest for seafarers are regulated.

2. Each Member shall establish maximum hours of work or minimum hours of rest over given periods that are consistent with the provisions in the Code.

Standard A2.3 – Hours of work and hours of rest

1. For the purpose of this Standard, the term:

(a) *hours of work* means time during which seafarers are required to do work on account of the ship;

(b) *hours of rest* means time outside hours of work; this term does not include short breaks.

2. Each Member shall within the limits set out in paragraphs 5 to 8 of this Standard fix either a maximum number of hours of work which shall not be exceeded in a given period of time, or a minimum number of hours of rest which shall be provided in a given period of time.

3. Each Member acknowledges that the normal working hours' standard for seafarers, like that for other workers, shall be based on an eight-hour day with one day of rest per week and rest on public holidays. However, this shall not prevent the Member from having procedures to authorize or register a collective agreement which determines seafarers' normal working hours on a basis no less favourable than this standard.

4. In determining the national standards, each Member shall take account of the danger posed by the fatigue of seafarers, especially those whose duties involve navigational safety and the safe and secure operation of the ship.

5. The limits on hours of work or rest shall be as follows:

(a) maximum hours of work shall not exceed:

(i) 14 hours in any 24-hour period; and

(ii) 72 hours in any seven-day period;

or

(b) minimum hours of rest shall not be less than:

(i) ten hours in any 24-hour period; and

(ii) 77 hours in any seven-day period.

6. Hours of rest may be divided into no more than two periods, one of which shall be at least six hours in length, and the interval between consecutive periods of rest shall not exceed 14 hours.

7. Musters, fire-fighting and lifeboat drills, and drills prescribed by national laws and regulations and by international instruments, shall be conducted in a manner that minimizes the disturbance of rest periods and does not induce fatigue.

8. When a seafarer is on call, such as when a machinery space is unattended, the seafarer shall have an adequate compensatory rest period if the normal period of rest is disturbed by call-outs to work.

9. If no collective agreement or arbitration award exists or if the competent authority determines that the provisions in the agreement or award in respect of paragraph 7 or 8 of this Standard are inadequate, the competent authority shall determine such provisions to ensure the seafarers concerned have sufficient rest.

10. Each Member shall require the posting, in an easily accessible place, of a table with the shipboard working arrangements, which shall contain for every position at least:

(a) the schedule of service at sea and service in port; and

(b) the maximum hours of work or the minimum hours of rest required by national laws or regulations or applicable collective agreements.

11. The table referred to in paragraph 10 of this Standard shall be established in a standardized format in the working language or languages of the ship and in English.

12. Each Member shall require that records of seafarers' daily hours of work or of their daily hours of rest be maintained to allow monitoring of compliance with paragraphs 5 to 11 inclusive of this Standard. The records shall be in a standardized format established by the competent authority taking into account any available guidelines of the International Labour Organization or shall be in any standard format prepared by the Organization. They shall be in the languages required by paragraph 11 of this Standard. The seafarers shall receive a copy of the records pertaining to them which shall be endorsed by the master, or a person authorized by the master, and by the seafarers.

13. Nothing in paragraphs 5 and 6 of this Standard shall prevent a Member from having national laws or regulations or a procedure for the competent authority to authorize or register collective agreements permitting exceptions to the limits set out. Such exceptions shall, as far as possible, follow the provisions of this Standard but may take account of more frequent or longer leave periods or the granting of compensatory leave for watchkeeping seafarers or seafarers working on board ships on short voyages.

14. Nothing in this Standard shall be deemed to impair the right of the master of a ship to require a seafarer to perform any hours of work necessary for the immediate safety of the ship, persons on board or cargo, or for the purpose of giving assistance to other ships or persons in distress at sea. Accordingly, the master may suspend the schedule of hours of work or hours of rest and require a seafarer to perform any hours of work necessary until the normal situation has been restored. As soon as practicable after the normal situation has been restored, the master shall ensure that any seafarers who have performed work in a scheduled rest period are provided with an adequate period of rest.

Guideline B2.3 – Hours of work and hours of rest

Guideline B2.3.1 – Young seafarers

1. At sea and in port the following provisions should apply to all young seafarers under the age of 18:

(a) working hours should not exceed eight hours per day and 40 hours per week and overtime should be worked only where unavoidable for safety reasons;

(b) sufficient time should be allowed for all meals, and a break of at least one hour for the main meal of the day should be assured; and

(c) a 15-minute rest period as soon as possible following each two hours of continuous work should be allowed.

2. Exceptionally, the provisions of paragraph 1 of this Guideline need not be applied if:

(a) they are impracticable for young seafarers in the deck, engine room and catering departments assigned to watchkeeping duties or working on a rostered shift-work system; or

(b) the effective training of young seafarers in accordance with established programmes and schedules would be impaired.

3. Such exceptional situations should be recorded, with reasons, and signed by the master.

4. Paragraph 1 of this Guideline does not exempt young seafarers from the general obligation on all seafarers to work during any emergency as provided for in Standard A2.3, paragraph 14.

Regulation 2.4 – Entitlement to leave

Purpose: To ensure that seafarers have adequate leave

1. Each Member shall require that seafarers employed on ships that fly its flag are given paid annual leave under appropriate conditions, in accordance with the provisions in the Code.

2. Seafarers shall be granted shore leave to benefit their health and well-being and consistent with the operational requirements of their positions.

Standard A2.4 – Entitlement to leave

1. Each Member shall adopt laws and regulations determining the minimum standards for annual leave for seafarers serving on ships that fly its flag, taking proper account of the special needs of seafarers with respect to such leave.

2. Subject to any collective agreement or laws or regulations providing for an appropriate method of calculation that takes account of the special needs of seafarers in this respect, the annual leave with pay entitlement shall be calculated on the basis of a minimum of 2.5 calendar days per month of employment. The manner in which the length of service is calculated shall be determined by the competent authority or through the appropriate machinery in each country. Justified absences from work shall not be considered as annual leave.

3. Any agreement to forgo the minimum annual leave with pay prescribed in this Standard, except in cases provided for by the competent authority, shall be prohibited.

Guideline B2.4 – Entitlement to leave

Guideline B2.4.1 – Calculation of entitlement

1. Under conditions as determined by the competent authority or through the appropriate machinery in each country, service off-articles should be counted as part of the period of service.

2. Under conditions as determined by the competent authority or in an applicable collective agreement, absence from work to attend an approved maritime vocational training course or for such reasons as illness or injury or for maternity should be counted as part of the period of service.

3. The level of pay during annual leave should be at the seafarer's normal level of remuneration provided for by national laws or regulations or in the applicable seafarers' employment agreement. For seafarers employed for periods shorter than one year or in the event of termination of the employment relationship, entitlement to leave should be calculated on a pro-rata basis.

4. The following should not be counted as part of annual leave with pay:

(a) public and customary holidays recognized as such in the flag State, whether or not they fall during the annual leave with pay;

(b) periods of incapacity for work resulting from illness or injury or from maternity, under conditions as determined by the competent authority or through the appropriate machinery in each country;

(c) temporary shore leave granted to a seafarer while under an employment agreement; and

(d) compensatory leave of any kind, under conditions as determined by the competent authority or through the appropriate machinery in each country.

Guideline B2.4.2 – Taking of annual leave

1. The time at which annual leave is to be taken should, unless it is fixed by regulation, collective agreement, arbitration award or other means consistent

with national practice, be determined by the shipowner after consultation and, as far as possible, in agreement with the seafarers concerned or their representatives.

2. Seafarers should in principle have the right to take annual leave in the place with which they have a substantial connection, which would normally be the same as the place to which they are entitled to be repatriated. Seafarers should not be required without their consent to take annual leave due to them in another place except under the provisions of a seafarers' employment agreement or of national laws or regulations.

3. If seafarers are required to take their annual leave from a place other than that permitted by paragraph 2 of this Guideline, they should be entitled to free transportation to the place where they were engaged or recruited, whichever is nearer their home; subsistence and other costs directly involved should be for the account of the shipowner; the travel time involved should not be deducted from the annual leave with pay due to the seafarer.

4. A seafarer taking annual leave should be recalled only in cases of extreme emergency and with the seafarer's consent.

Guideline B2.4.3 – Division and accumulation

1. The division of the annual leave with pay into parts, or the accumulation of such annual leave due in respect of one year together with a subsequent period of leave, may be authorized by the competent authority or through the appropriate machinery in each country.

2. Subject to paragraph 1 of this Guideline and unless otherwise provided in an agreement applicable to the shipowner and the seafarer concerned, the annual leave with pay recommended in this Guideline should consist of an uninterrupted period.

Guideline B2.4.4 – Young seafarers

1. Special measures should be considered with respect to young seafarers under the age of 18 who have served six months or any other shorter period of time under a collective agreement or seafarers' employment agreement without leave on a foreign-going ship which has not returned to their country of residence in that time, and will not return in the subsequent three months of the voyage. Such measures could consist of their repatriation at no expense to themselves to the place of original engagement in their country of residence for the purpose of taking any leave earned during the voyage.

Regulation 2.5 – Repatriation

Purpose: To ensure that seafarers are able to return home

1. Seafarers have a right to be repatriated at no cost to themselves in the circumstances and under the conditions specified in the Code.

2. Each Member shall require ships that fly its flag to provide financial security to ensure that seafarers are duly repatriated in accordance with the Code.

Standard A2.5 – Repatriation

1. Each Member shall ensure that seafarers on ships that fly its flag are entitled to repatriation in the following circumstances:

(a) if the seafarers' employment agreement expires while they are abroad;

(b) when the seafarers' employment agreement is terminated:

  (i) by the shipowner; or

  (ii) by the seafarer for justified reasons; and also

(c) when the seafarers are no longer able to carry out their duties under their employment agreement or cannot be expected to carry them out in the specific circumstances.

2. Each Member shall ensure that there are appropriate provisions in its laws and regulations or other measures or in collective bargaining agreements, prescribing:

(a) the circumstances in which seafarers are entitled to repatriation in accordance with paragraph 1(b) and (c) of this Standard;

(b) the maximum duration of service periods on board following which a seafarer is entitled to repatriation – such periods to be less than 12 months; and

(c) the precise entitlements to be accorded by shipowners for repatriation, including those relating to the destinations of repatriation, the mode of transport, the items of expense to be covered and other arrangements to be made by shipowners.

3. Each Member shall prohibit shipowners from requiring that seafarers make an advance payment towards the cost of repatriation at the beginning of their employment, and also from recovering the cost of repatriation from the seafarers' wages or other entitlements except where the seafarer has been found, in accordance with national laws or regulations or other measures or applicable collective bargaining agreements, to be in serious default of the seafarer's employment obligations.

4. National laws and regulations shall not prejudice any right of the shipowner to recover the cost of repatriation under third-party contractual arrangements.

5. If a shipowner fails to make arrangements for or to meet the cost of repatriation of seafarers who are entitled to be repatriated:

(a) the competent authority of the Member whose flag the ship flies shall arrange for repatriation of the seafarers concerned; if it fails to do so, the State from which the seafarers are to be repatriated or the State of which they are a national may arrange for their repatriation and recover the cost from the Member whose flag the ship flies;

(b) costs incurred in repatriating seafarers shall be recoverable from the shipowner by the Member whose flag the ship flies;

(c) the expenses of repatriation shall in no case be a charge upon the seafarers, except as provided for in paragraph 3 of this Standard.

6. Taking into account applicable international instruments, including the International Convention on Arrest of Ships, 1999, a Member which has paid the cost

of repatriation pursuant to this Code may detain, or request the detention of, the ships of the shipowner concerned until the reimbursement has been made in accordance with paragraph 5 of this Standard.

7. Each Member shall facilitate the repatriation of seafarers serving on ships which call at its ports or pass through its territorial or internal waters, as well as their replacement on board.

8. In particular, a Member shall not refuse the right of repatriation to any seafarer because of the financial circumstances of a shipowner or because of the shipowner's inability or unwillingness to replace a seafarer.

9. Each Member shall require that ships that fly its flag carry and make available to seafarers a copy of the applicable national provisions regarding repatriation written in an appropriate language.

Guideline B2.5 – Repatriation

Guideline B2.5.1 – Entitlement

1. Seafarers should be entitled to repatriation:

(a) in the case covered by Standard A2.5, paragraph 1(a), upon the expiry of the period of notice given in accordance with the provisions of the seafarers' employment agreement;

(b) in the cases covered by Standard A2.5, paragraph 1(b) and (c):

  (i) in the event of illness or injury or other medical condition which requires their repatriation when found medically fit to travel;

  (ii) in the event of shipwreck;

  (iii) in the event of the shipowner not being able to continue to fulfil their legal or contractual obligations as an employer of the seafarers by reason of insolvency, sale of ship, change of ship's registration or any other similar reason;

  (iv) in the event of a ship being bound for a war zone, as defined by national laws or regulations or seafarers' employment agreements, to which the seafarer does not consent to go; and

  (v) in the event of termination or interruption of employment in accordance with an industrial award or collective agreement, or termination of employment for any other similar reason.

2. In determining the maximum duration of service periods on board following which a seafarer is entitled to repatriation, in accordance with this Code, account should be taken of factors affecting the seafarers' working environment. Each Member should seek, wherever possible, to reduce these periods in the light of technological changes and developments and might be guided by any recommendations made on the matter by the Joint Maritime Commission.

3. The costs to be borne by the shipowner for repatriation under Standard A2.5 should include at least the following:

(a) passage to the destination selected for repatriation in accordance with paragraph 6 of this Guideline;

(b) accommodation and food from the moment the seafarers leave the ship until they reach the repatriation destination;
(c) pay and allowances from the moment the seafarers leave the ship until they reach the repatriation destination, if provided for by national laws or regulations or collective agreements;
(d) transportation of 30 kg of the seafarers' personal luggage to the repatriation destination; and
(e) medical treatment when necessary until the seafarers are medically fit to travel to the repatriation destination.

4. Time spent awaiting repatriation and repatriation travel time should not be deducted from paid leave accrued to the seafarers.

5. Shipowners should be required to continue to cover the costs of repatriation until the seafarers concerned are landed at a destination prescribed pursuant to this Code or are provided with suitable employment on board a ship proceeding to one of those destinations.

6. Each Member should require that shipowners take responsibility for repatriation arrangements by appropriate and expeditious means. The normal mode of transport should be by air. The Member should prescribe the destinations to which seafarers may be repatriated. The destinations should include the countries with which seafarers may be deemed to have a substantial connection including:
(a) the place at which the seafarer agreed to enter into the engagement;
(b) the place stipulated by collective agreement;
(c) the seafarer's country of residence; or
(d) such other place as may be mutually agreed at the time of engagement.

7. Seafarers should have the right to choose from among the prescribed destinations the place to which they are to be repatriated.

8. The entitlement to repatriation may lapse if the seafarers concerned do not claim it within a reasonable period of time to be defined by national laws or regulations or collective agreements.

Guideline B2.5.2 – Implementation by Members

1. Every possible practical assistance should be given to a seafarer stranded in a foreign port pending repatriation and in the event of delay in the repatriation of the seafarer, the competent authority in the foreign port should ensure that the consular or local representative of the flag State and the seafarer's State of nationality or State of residence, as appropriate, is informed immediately.

2. Each Member should have regard to whether proper provision is made:
(a) for the return of seafarers employed on a ship that flies the flag of a foreign country who are put ashore in a foreign port for reasons for which they are not responsible:
  (i) to the port at which the seafarer concerned was engaged; or
  (ii) to a port in the seafarer's State of nationality or State of residence, as appropriate; or

(iii) to another port agreed upon between the seafarer and the master or shipowner, with the approval of the competent authority or under other appropriate safeguards;

(b) for medical care and maintenance of seafarers employed on a ship that flies the flag of a foreign country who are put ashore in a foreign port in consequence of sickness or injury incurred in the service of the ship and not due to their own wilful misconduct.

3. If, after young seafarers under the age of 18 have served on a ship for at least four months during their first foreign-going voyage, it becomes apparent that they are unsuited to life at sea, they should be given the opportunity of being repatriated at no expense to themselves from the first suitable port of call in which there are consular services of the flag State, or the State of nationality or residence of the young seafarer. Notification of any such repatriation, with the reasons therefor, should be given to the authority which issued the papers enabling the young seafarers concerned to take up seagoing employment.

Regulation 2.6 – Seafarer compensation for the ship's loss or foundering

Purpose: To ensure that seafarers are compensated when a ship is lost or has foundered

1. Seafarers are entitled to adequate compensation in the case of injury, loss or unemployment arising from the ship's loss or foundering.

Standard A2.6 – Seafarer compensation for the ship's loss or foundering

1. Each Member shall make rules ensuring that, in every case of loss or foundering of any ship, the shipowner shall pay to each seafarer on board an indemnity against unemployment resulting from such loss or foundering.

2. The rules referred to in paragraph 1 of this Standard shall be without prejudice to any other rights a seafarer may have under the national law of the Member concerned for losses or injuries arising from a ship's loss or foundering.

Guideline B2.6 – Seafarer compensation for the ship's loss or foundering

Guideline B2.6.1 – Calculation of indemnity against unemployment

1. The indemnity against unemployment resulting from a ship's foundering or loss should be paid for the days during which the seafarer remains in fact unemployed at the same rate as the wages payable under the employment agreement, but the total indemnity payable to any one seafarer may be limited to two months' wages.

2. Each Member should ensure that seafarers have the same legal remedies for recovering such indemnities as they have for recovering arrears of wages earned during the service.

Regulation 2.7 – Manning levels

Purpose: To ensure that seafarers work on board ships with sufficient personnel for the safe, efficient and secure operation of the ship

1. Each Member shall require that all ships that fly its flag have a sufficient number of seafarers employed on board to ensure that ships are operated safely, efficiently and with due regard to security under all conditions, taking into account concerns about seafarer fatigue and the particular nature and conditions of the voyage.

Standard A2.7 – Manning levels

1. Each Member shall require that all ships that fly its flag have a sufficient number of seafarers on board to ensure that ships are operated safely, efficiently and with due regard to security. Every ship shall be manned by a crew that is adequate, in terms of size and qualifications, to ensure the safety and security of the ship and its personnel, under all operating conditions, in accordance with the minimum safe manning document or an equivalent issued by the competent authority, and to comply with the standards of this Convention.

2. When determining, approving or revising manning levels, the competent authority shall take into account the need to avoid or minimize excessive hours of work to ensure sufficient rest and to limit fatigue, as well as the principles in applicable international instruments, especially those of the International Maritime Organization, on manning levels.

3. When determining manning levels, the competent authority shall take into account all the requirements within Regulation 3.2 and Standard A3.2 concerning food and catering.

Guideline B2.7 – Manning levels

Guideline B2.7.1 – Dispute settlement

1. Each Member should maintain, or satisfy itself that there is maintained, efficient machinery for the investigation and settlement of complaints or disputes concerning the manning levels on a ship.

2. Representatives of shipowners' and seafarers' organizations should participate, with or without other persons or authorities, in the operation of such machinery.

Regulation 2.8 – Career and skill development and opportunities for seafarers' employment

Purpose: To promote career and skill development and employment opportunities for seafarers

1. Each Member shall have national policies to promote employment in the maritime sector and to encourage career and skill development and greater employment opportunities for seafarers domiciled in its territory.

Standard A2.8 – Career and skill development and employment opportunities for seafarers

1. Each Member shall have national policies that encourage career and skill development and employment opportunities for seafarers, in order to provide the maritime sector with a stable and competent workforce.

2. The aim of the policies referred to in paragraph 1 of this Standard shall be to help seafarers strengthen their competencies, qualifications and employment opportunities.

3. Each Member shall, after consulting the shipowners' and seafarers' organizations concerned, establish clear objectives for the vocational guidance, education and training of seafarers whose duties on board ship primarily relate to the safe operation and navigation of the ship, including ongoing training.

Guideline B2.8 – Career and skill development and employment opportunities for seafarers

Guideline B2.8.1 – Measures to promote career and skill development and employment opportunities for seafarers

1. Measures to achieve the objectives set out in Standard A2.8 might include:

(a) agreements providing for career development and skills training with a shipowner or an organization of shipowners; or

(b) arrangements for promoting employment through the establishment and maintenance of registers or lists, by categories, of qualified seafarers; or

(c) promotion of opportunities, both on board and ashore, for further training and education of seafarers to provide for skill development and portable competencies in order to secure and retain decent work, to improve individual employment prospects and to meet the changing technology and labour market conditions of the maritime industry.

Guideline B2.8.2 – Register of seafarers

1. Where registers or lists govern the employment of seafarers, these registers or lists should include all occupational categories of seafarers in a manner determined by national law or practice or by collective agreement.

2. Seafarers on such a register or list should have priority of engagement for seafaring.

3. Seafarers on such a register or list should be required to be available for work in a manner to be determined by national law or practice or by collective agreement.

4. To the extent that national laws or regulations permit, the number of seafarers on such registers or lists should be periodically reviewed so as to achieve levels adapted to the needs of the maritime industry.

5. When a reduction in the number of seafarers on such a register or list becomes necessary, all appropriate measures should be taken to prevent or minimize detrimental effects on seafarers, account being taken of the economic and social situation of the country concerned.

Title 3. Accommodation, recreational facilities, food and catering

Regulation 3.1 – Accommodation and recreational facilities

Purpose: To ensure that seafarers have decent accommodation and recreational facilities on board

1. Each Member shall ensure that ships that fly its flag provide and maintain decent accommodations and recreational facilities for seafarers working or living on board, or both, consistent with promoting the seafarers' health and well-being.

2. The requirements in the Code implementing this Regulation which relate to ship construction and equipment apply only to ships constructed on or after the date when this Convention comes into force for the Member concerned. For ships constructed before that date, the requirements relating to ship construction and equipment that are set out in the Accommodation of Crews Convention (Revised), 1949 (No. 92), and the Accommodation of Crews (Supplementary Provisions) Convention, 1970 (No. 133), shall continue to apply to the extent that they were applicable, prior to that date, under the law or practice of the Member concerned. A ship shall be deemed to have been constructed on the date when its keel is laid or when it is at a similar stage of construction.

3. Unless expressly provided otherwise, any requirement under an amendment to the Code relating to the provision of seafarer accommodation and recreational facilities shall apply only to ships constructed on or after the amendment takes effect for the Member concerned.

Standard A3.1 – Accommodation and recreational facilities

1. Each Member shall adopt laws and regulations requiring that ships that fly its flag:

(a) meet minimum standards to ensure that any accommodation for seafarers, working or living on board, or both, is safe, decent and in accordance with the relevant provisions of this Standard; and

(b) are inspected to ensure initial and ongoing compliance with those standards.

2. In developing and applying the laws and regulations to implement this Standard, the competent authority, after consulting the shipowners' and seafarers' organizations concerned, shall:

(a) take into account Regulation 4.3 and the associated Code provisions on health and safety protection and accident prevention, in light of the specific needs of seafarers that both live and work on board ship, and

(b) give due consideration to the guidance contained in Part B of this Code.

3. The inspections required under Regulation 5.1.4 shall be carried out when:

(a) a ship is registered or re-registered; or

(b) the seafarer accommodation on a ship has been substantially altered.

4. The competent authority shall pay particular attention to ensuring implementation of the requirements of this Convention relating to:

(a) the size of rooms and other accommodation spaces;

(b) heating and ventilation;

(c) noise and vibration and other ambient factors;

(d) sanitary facilities;

(e) lighting; and

(f) hospital accommodation.

5. The competent authority of each Member shall require that ships that fly its flag meet the minimum standards for on-board accommodation and recreational facilities that are set out in paragraphs 6 to 17 of this Standard.

6. With respect to general requirements for accommodation:

(a) there shall be adequate headroom in all seafarer accommodation; the minimum permitted headroom in all seafarer accommodation where full and free movement is necessary shall be not less than 203 centimetres; the competent authority may permit some limited reduction in headroom in any space, or part of any space, in such accommodation where it is satisfied that such reduction:
   (i) is reasonable; and
   (ii) will not result in discomfort to the seafarers;

(b) the accommodation shall be adequately insulated;

(c) in ships other than passenger ships, as defined in Regulation 2(e) and (f) of the International Convention for the Safety of Life at Sea, 1974, as amended (the "SOLAS Convention"), sleeping rooms shall be situated above the load line amidships or aft, except that in exceptional cases, where the size, type or intended service of the ship renders any other location impracticable, sleeping rooms may be located in the fore part of the ship, but in no case forward of the collision bulkhead;

(d) in passenger ships, and in special ships constructed in compliance with the IMO *Code of Safety for Special Purpose Ships*, 1983, and subsequent versions (hereinafter called "special purpose ships"), the competent authority may, on condition that satisfactory arrangements are made for lighting and ventilation, permit the location of sleeping rooms below the load line, but in no case shall they be located immediately beneath working alleyways;

(e) there shall be no direct openings into sleeping rooms from cargo and machinery spaces or from galleys, storerooms, drying rooms or communal sanitary areas; that part of a bulkhead separating such places from sleeping rooms and external bulkheads shall be efficiently constructed of steel or other approved substance and be watertight and gas-tight;

(f) the materials used to construct internal bulkheads, panelling and sheeting, floors and joinings shall be suitable for the purpose and conducive to ensuring a healthy environment;

(g) proper lighting and sufficient drainage shall be provided; and

(h) accommodation and recreational and catering facilities shall meet the requirements in Regulation 4.3, and the related provisions in the Code, on health and safety protection and accident prevention, with respect to preventing the risk of exposure to hazardous levels of noise and vibration and other ambient factors and chemicals on board ships, and to provide an acceptable occupational and on-board living environment for seafarers.

7. With respect to requirements for ventilation and heating:

(a) sleeping rooms and mess rooms shall be adequately ventilated;

(b) ships, except those regularly engaged in trade where temperate climatic conditions do not require this, shall be equipped with air conditioning for seafarer accommodation, for any separate radio room and for any centralized machinery control room;

(c) all sanitary spaces shall have ventilation to the open air, independently of any other part of the accommodation; and

(d) adequate heat through an appropriate heating system shall be provided, except in ships exclusively on voyages in tropical climates.

8. With respect to requirements for lighting, subject to such special arrangements as may be permitted in passenger ships, sleeping rooms and mess rooms shall be lit by natural light and provided with adequate artificial light.

9. When sleeping accommodation on board ships is required, the following requirements for sleeping rooms apply:

(a) in ships other than passenger ships, an individual sleeping room shall be provided for each seafarer; in the case of ships of less than 3,000 gross tonnage or special purpose ships, exemptions from this requirement may be granted by the competent authority after consultation with the shipowners' and seafarers' organizations concerned;

(b) separate sleeping rooms shall be provided for men and for women;

(c) sleeping rooms shall be of adequate size and properly equipped so as to ensure reasonable comfort and to facilitate tidiness;

(d) a separate berth for each seafarer shall in all circumstances be provided;

(e) the minimum inside dimensions of a berth shall be at least 198 centimetres by 80 centimetres;

(f) in single berth seafarers' sleeping rooms the floor area shall not be less than:

    (i) 4.5 square metres in ships of less than 3,000 gross tonnage;

    (ii) 5.5 square metres in ships of 3,000 gross tonnage or over but less than 10,000 gross tonnage;

    (iii) 7 square metres in ships of 10,000 gross tonnage or over;

(g) however, in order to provide single berth sleeping rooms on ships of less than 3,000 gross tonnage, passenger ships and special purpose ships, the competent authority may allow a reduced floor area;

(h) in ships of less than 3,000 gross tonnage other than passenger ships and special purpose ships, sleeping rooms may be occupied by a maximum of two seafarers; the floor area of such sleeping rooms shall not be less than 7 square metres;

(i) on passenger ships and special purpose ships the floor area of sleeping rooms for seafarers not performing the duties of ships' officers shall not be less than:

 (i) 7.5 square metres in rooms accommodating two persons;

 (ii) 11.5 square metres in rooms accommodating three persons;

 (iii) 14.5 square metres in rooms accommodating four persons;

(j) on special purpose ships sleeping rooms may accommodate more than four persons; the floor area of such sleeping rooms shall not be less than 3.6 square metres per person;

(k) on ships other than passenger ships and special purpose ships, sleeping rooms for seafarers who perform the duties of ships' officers, where no private sitting room or day room is provided, the floor area per person shall not be less than:

 (i) 7.5 square metres in ships of less than 3,000 gross tonnage;

 (ii) 8.5 square metres in ships of 3,000 gross tonnage or over but less than 10,000 gross tonnage;

 (iii) 10 square metres in ships of 10,000 gross tonnage or over;

(l) on passenger ships and special purpose ships the floor area for seafarers performing the duties of ships' officers where no private sitting room or day room is provided, the floor area per person for junior officers shall not be less than 7.5 square metres and for senior officers not less than 8.5 square metres; junior officers are understood to be at the operational level, and senior officers at the management level;

(m) the master, the chief engineer and the chief navigating officer shall have, in addition to their sleeping rooms, an adjoining sitting room, day room or equivalent additional space; ships of less than 3,000 gross tonnage may be exempted by the competent authority from this requirement after consultation with the shipowners' and seafarers' organizations concerned;

(n) for each occupant, the furniture shall include a clothes locker of ample space (minimum 475 litres) and a drawer or equivalent space of not less than 56 litres; if the drawer is incorporated in the clothes locker then the combined minimum volume of the clothes locker shall be 500 litres; it shall be fitted with a shelf and be able to be locked by the occupant so as to ensure privacy;

(o) each sleeping room shall be provided with a table or desk, which may be of the fixed, drop-leaf or slide-out type, and with comfortable seating accommodation as necessary.

10. With respect to requirements for mess rooms:

(a) mess rooms shall be located apart from the sleeping rooms and as close as practicable to the galley; ships of less than 3,000 gross tonnage may be exempted by the competent authority from this requirement after consultation with the shipowners' and seafarers' organizations concerned; and

(b) mess rooms shall be of adequate size and comfort and properly furnished and equipped (including ongoing facilities for refreshment), taking account of the number of seafarers likely to use them at any one time; provision shall be made for separate or common mess room facilities as appropriate.

11. With respect to requirements for sanitary facilities:

(a) all seafarers shall have convenient access on the ship to sanitary facilities meeting minimum standards of health and hygiene and reasonable standards of comfort, with separate sanitary facilities being provided for men and for women;

(b) there shall be sanitary facilities within easy access of the navigating bridge and the machinery space or near the engine room control centre; ships of less than 3,000 gross tonnage may be exempted by the competent authority from this requirement after consultation with the shipowners' and seafarers' organizations concerned;

(c) in all ships a minimum of one toilet, one wash basin and one tub or shower or both for every six persons or less who do not have personal facilities shall be provided at a convenient location;

(d) with the exception of passenger ships, each sleeping room shall be provided with a washbasin having hot and cold running fresh water, except where such a washbasin is situated in the private bathroom provided;

(e) in passenger ships normally engaged on voyages of not more than four hours' duration, consideration may be given by the competent authority to special arrangements or to a reduction in the number of facilities required; and

(f) hot and cold running fresh water shall be available in all wash places.

12. With respect to requirements for hospital accommodation, ships carrying 15 or more seafarers and engaged in a voyage of more than three days' duration shall provide separate hospital accommodation to be used exclusively for medical purposes; the competent authority may relax this requirement for ships engaged in coastal trade; in approving on-board hospital accommodation, the competent authority shall ensure that the accommodation will, in all weathers, be easy of access, provide comfortable housing for the occupants and be conducive to their receiving prompt and proper attention.

13. Appropriately situated and furnished laundry facilities shall be available.

14. All ships shall have a space or spaces on open deck to which the seafarers can have access when off duty, which are of adequate area having regard to the size of the ship and the number of seafarers on board.

15. All ships shall be provided with separate offices or a common ship's office for use by deck and engine departments; ships of less than 3,000 gross tonnage may be exempted by the competent authority from this requirement after consultation with the shipowners' and seafarers' organizations concerned.

16. Ships regularly trading to mosquito-infested ports shall be fitted with appropriate devices as required by the competent authority.

17. Appropriate seafarers' recreational facilities, amenities and services, as adapted to meet the special needs of seafarers who must live and work on ships, shall be provided on board for the benefit of all seafarers, taking into account Regulation 4.3 and the associated Code provisions on health and safety protection and accident prevention.

18. The competent authority shall require frequent inspections to be carried out on board ships, by or under the authority of the master, to ensure that sea-

farer accommodation is clean, decently habitable and maintained in a good state of repair. The results of each such inspection shall be recorded and be available for review.

19. In the case of ships where there is need to take account, without discrimination, of the interests of seafarers having differing and distinctive religious and social practices, the competent authority may, after consultation with the shipowners' and seafarers' organizations concerned, permit fairly applied variations in respect of this Standard on condition that such variations do not result in overall facilities less favourable than those which would result from the application of this Standard.

20. Each Member may, after consultation with the shipowners' and seafarers' organizations concerned, exempt ships of less than 200 gross tonnage where it is reasonable to do so, taking account of the size of the ship and the number of persons on board in relation to the requirements of the following provisions of this Standard:

(a) paragraphs 7(b), 11(d) and 13; and

(b) paragraph 9(f) and (h) to (l) inclusive, with respect to floor area only.

21. Any exemptions with respect to the requirements of this Standard may be made only where they are expressly permitted in this Standard and only for particular circumstances in which such exemptions can be clearly justified on strong grounds and subject to protecting the seafarers' health and safety.

Guideline B3.1 – Accommodation and recreational facilities

Guideline B3.1.1 – Design and construction

1. External bulkheads of sleeping rooms and mess rooms should be adequately insulated. All machinery casings and all boundary bulkheads of galleys and other spaces in which heat is produced should be adequately insulated where there is a possibility of resulting heat effects in adjoining accommodation or passageways. Measures should also be taken to provide protection from heat effects of steam or hot-water service pipes or both.

2. Sleeping rooms, mess rooms, recreation rooms and alleyways in the accommodation space should be adequately insulated to prevent condensation or overheating.

3. The bulkhead surfaces and deckheads should be of material with a surface easily kept clean. No form of construction likely to harbour vermin should be used.

4. The bulkhead surfaces and deckheads in sleeping rooms and mess rooms should be capable of being easily kept clean and light in colour with a durable, nontoxic finish.

5. The decks in all seafarer accommodation should be of approved material and construction and should provide a non-slip surface impervious to damp and easily kept clean.

6. Where the floorings are made of composite materials, the joints with the sides should be profiled to avoid crevices.

Guideline B3.1.2 – Ventilation

1. The system of ventilation for sleeping rooms and mess rooms should be controlled so as to maintain the air in a satisfactory condition and to ensure a sufficiency of air movement in all conditions of weather and climate.

2. Air-conditioning systems, whether of a centralized or individual unit type, should be designed to:

(a) maintain the air at a satisfactory temperature and relative humidity as compared to outside air conditions, ensure a sufficiency of air changes in all air-conditioned spaces, take account of the particular characteristics of operations at sea and not produce excessive noises or vibrations; and

(b) facilitate easy cleaning and disinfection to prevent or control the spread of disease.

3. Power for the operation of the air conditioning and other aids to ventilation required by the preceding paragraphs of this Guideline should be available at all times when seafarers are living or working on board and conditions so require. However, this power need not be provided from an emergency source.

Guideline B3.1.3 – Heating

1. The system of heating the seafarer accommodation should be in operation at all times when seafarers are living or working on board and conditions require its use.

2. In all ships in which a heating system is required, the heating should be by means of hot water, warm air, electricity, steam or equivalent. However, within the accommodation area, steam should not be used as a medium for heat transmission. The heating system should be capable of maintaining the temperature in seafarer accommodation at a satisfactory level under normal conditions of weather and climate likely to be met within the trade in which the ship is engaged. The competent authority should prescribe the standard to be provided.

3. Radiators and other heating apparatus should be placed and, where necessary, shielded so as to avoid risk of fire or danger or discomfort to the occupants.

Guideline B3.1.4 – Lighting

1. In all ships, electric light should be provided in the seafarer accommodation. If there are not two independent sources of electricity for lighting, additional lighting should be provided by properly constructed lamps or lighting apparatus for emergency use.

2. In sleeping rooms an electric reading lamp should be installed at the head of each berth.

3. Suitable standards of natural and artificial lighting should be fixed by the competent authority.

Guideline B3.1.5 – Sleeping rooms

1. There should be adequate berth arrangements on board, making it as comfortable as possible for the seafarer and any partner who may accompany the seafarer.

2. Where the size of the ship, the activity in which it is to be engaged and its layout make it reasonable and practicable, sleeping rooms should be planned and equipped with a private bathroom, including a toilet, so as to provide reasonable comfort for the occupants and to facilitate tidiness.

3. As far as practicable, sleeping rooms of seafarers should be so arranged that watches are separated and that no seafarers working during the day share a room with watchkeepers.

4. In the case of seafarers performing the duty of petty officers there should be no more than two persons per sleeping room.

5. Consideration should be given to extending the facility referred to in Standard A3.1, paragraph 9(m), to the second engineer officer when practicable.

6. Space occupied by berths and lockers, chests of drawers and seats should be included in the measurement of the floor area. Small or irregularly shaped spaces which do not add effectively to the space available for free movement and cannot be used for installing furniture should be excluded.

7. Berths should not be arranged in tiers of more than two; in the case of berths placed along the ship's side, there should be only a single tier where a sidelight is situated above a berth.

8. The lower berth in a double tier should be not less than 30 centimetres above the floor; the upper berth should be placed approximately midway between the bottom of the lower berth and the lower side of the deckhead beams.

9. The framework and the lee-board, if any, of a berth should be of approved material, hard, smooth, and not likely to corrode or to harbour vermin.

10. If tubular frames are used for the construction of berths, they should be completely sealed and without perforations which would give access to vermin.

11. Each berth should be fitted with a comfortable mattress with cushioning bottom or a combined cushioning mattress, including a spring bottom or a spring mattress. The mattress and cushioning material used should be made of approved material. Stuffing of material likely to harbour vermin should not be used.

12. When one berth is placed over another, a dust-proof bottom should be fitted beneath the bottom mattress or spring bottom of the upper berth.

13. The furniture should be of smooth, hard material not liable to warp or corrode.

14. Sleeping rooms should be fitted with curtains or equivalent for the sidelights.

15. Sleeping rooms should be fitted with a mirror, small cabinets for toilet requisites, a book rack and a sufficient number of coat hooks.

Guideline B3.1.6 – Mess rooms

1. Mess room facilities may be either common or separate. The decision in this respect should be taken after consultation with seafarers' and shipowners' representatives and subject to the approval of the competent authority. Account should be taken of factors such as the size of the ship and the distinctive cultural, religious and social needs of the seafarers.

2. Where separate mess room facilities are to be provided to seafarers, then separate mess rooms should be provided for:

(a) master and officers; and

(b) petty officers and other seafarers.

3. On ships other than passenger ships, the floor area of mess rooms for seafarers should be not less than 1.5 square metres per person of the planned seating capacity.

4. In all ships, mess rooms should be equipped with tables and appropriate seats, fixed or movable, sufficient to accommodate the greatest number of seafarers likely to use them at any one time.

5. There should be available at all times when seafarers are on board:

(a) a refrigerator, which should be conveniently situated and of sufficient capacity for the number of persons using the mess room or mess rooms;

(b) facilities for hot beverages; and

(c) cool water facilities.

6. Where available pantries are not accessible to mess rooms, adequate lockers for mess utensils and proper facilities for washing utensils should be provided.

7. The tops of tables and seats should be of damp-resistant material.

Guideline B3.1.7 – Sanitary accommodation

1. Washbasins and tub baths should be of adequate size and constructed of approved material with a smooth surface not liable to crack, flake or corrode.

2. All toilets should be of an approved pattern and provided with an ample flush of water or with some other suitable flushing means, such as air, which are available at all times and independently controllable.

3. Sanitary accommodation intended for the use of more than one person should comply with the following:

(a) floors should be of approved durable material, impervious to damp, and should be properly drained;

(b) bulkheads should be of steel or other approved material and should be watertight up to at least 23 centimetres above the level of the deck;

(c) the accommodation should be sufficiently lit, heated and ventilated;

(d) toilets should be situated convenient to, but separate from, sleeping rooms and wash rooms, without direct access from the sleeping rooms or from a passage between sleeping rooms and toilets to which there is no other access; this requirement does not apply where a toilet is located in a compartment between two sleeping rooms having a total of not more than four seafarers; and

(e) where there is more than one toilet in a compartment, they should be sufficiently screened to ensure privacy.

4. The laundry facilities provided for seafarers' use should include:

(a) washing machines;

(b) drying machines or adequately heated and ventilated drying rooms; and
(c) irons and ironing boards or their equivalent.

Guideline B3.1.8 – Hospital accommodation

1. The hospital accommodation should be designed so as to facilitate consultation and the giving of medical first aid and to help prevent the spread of infectious diseases.

2. The arrangement of the entrance, berths, lighting, ventilation, heating and water supply should be designed to ensure the comfort and facilitate the treatment of the occupants.

3. The number of hospital berths required should be prescribed by the competent authority.

4. Sanitary accommodation should be provided for the exclusive use of the occupants of the hospital accommodation, either as part of the accommodation or in close proximity thereto. Such sanitary accommodation should comprise a minimum of one toilet, one washbasin and one tub or shower.

Guideline B3.1.9 – Other facilities

1. Where separate facilities for engine department personnel to change their clothes are provided, they should be:
(a) located outside the machinery space but with easy access to it; and
(b) fitted with individual clothes lockers as well as with tubs or showers or both and washbasins having hot and cold running fresh water.

Guideline B3.1.10 – Bedding, mess utensils and miscellaneous provisions

1. Each Member should consider applying the following principles:
(a) clean bedding and mess utensils should be supplied by the shipowner to all seafarers for use on board during service on the ship, and such seafarers should be responsible for their return at times specified by the master and on completion of service in the ship;
(b) bedding should be of good quality, and plates, cups and other mess utensils should be of approved material which can be easily cleaned; and
(c) towels, soap and toilet paper for all seafarers should be provided by the shipowner.

Guideline B3.1.11 – Recreational facilities, mail and ship visit arrangements

1. Recreational facilities and services should be reviewed frequently to ensure that they are appropriate in the light of changes in the needs of seafarers resulting from technical, operational and other developments in the shipping industry.

2. Furnishings for recreational facilities should as a minimum include a bookcase and facilities for reading, writing and, where practicable, games.

3. In connection with the planning of recreation facilities, the competent authority should give consideration to the provision of a canteen.

4. Consideration should also be given to including the following facilities at no cost to the seafarer, where practicable:

(a) a smoking room;

(b) television viewing and the reception of radio broadcasts;

(c) showing of films, the stock of which should be adequate for the duration of the voyage and, where necessary, changed at reasonable intervals;

(d) sports equipment including exercise equipment, table games and deck games;

(e) where possible, facilities for swimming;

(f) a library containing vocational and other books, the stock of which should be adequate for the duration of the voyage and changed at reasonable intervals;

(g) facilities for recreational handicrafts;

(h) electronic equipment such as a radio, television, video recorders, DVD/CD player, personal computer and software and cassette recorder/player;

(i) where appropriate, the provision of bars on board for seafarers unless these are contrary to national, religious or social customs; and

(j) reasonable access to ship-to-shore telephone communications, and email and Internet facilities, where available, with any charges for the use of these services being reasonable in amount.

5. Every effort should be given to ensuring that the forwarding of seafarers' mail is as reliable and expeditious as possible. Efforts should also be considered for avoiding seafarers being required to pay additional postage when mail has to be re-addressed owing to circumstances beyond their control.

6. Measures should be considered to ensure, subject to any applicable national or international laws or regulations, that whenever possible and reasonable seafarers are expeditiously granted permission to have their partners, relatives and friends as visitors on board their ship when in port. Such measures should meet any concerns for security clearances.

7. Consideration should be given to the possibility of allowing seafarers to be accompanied by their partners on occasional voyages where this is practicable and reasonable. Such partners should carry adequate insurance cover against accident and illness; the shipowners should give every assistance to the seafarer to effect such insurance.

Guideline B3.1.12 – Prevention of noise and vibration

1. Accommodation and recreational and catering facilities should be located as far as practicable from the engines, steering gear rooms, deck winches, ventilation, heating and air-conditioning equipment and other noisy machinery and apparatus.

2. Acoustic insulation or other appropriate sound-absorbing materials should be used in the construction and finishing of bulkheads, deckheads and

decks within the sound-producing spaces as well as self-closing noise-isolating doors for machinery spaces.

3. Engine rooms and other machinery spaces should be provided, wherever practicable, with soundproof centralized control rooms for engine-room personnel. Working spaces, such as the machine shop, should be insulated, as far as practicable, from the general engine-room noise and measures should be taken to reduce noise in the operation of machinery.

4. The limits for noise levels for working and living spaces should be in conformity with the ILO international guidelines on exposure levels, including those in the ILO code of practice entitled *Ambient factors in the workplace*, 2001, and, where applicable, the specific protection recommended by the International Maritime Organization, and with any subsequent amending and supplementary instruments for acceptable noise levels on board ships. A copy of the applicable instruments in English or the working language of the ship should be carried on board and should be accessible to seafarers.

5. No accommodation or recreational or catering facilities should be exposed to excessive vibration.

Regulation 3.2 – Food and catering

Purpose: To ensure that seafarers have access to good quality food and drinking water provided under regulated hygienic conditions

1. Each Member shall ensure that ships that fly its flag carry on board and serve food and drinking water of appropriate quality, nutritional value and quantity that adequately covers the requirements of the ship and takes into account the differing cultural and religious backgrounds.

2. Seafarers on board a ship shall be provided with food free of charge during the period of engagement.

3. Seafarers employed as ships' cooks with responsibility for food preparation must be trained and qualified for their position on board ship.

Standard A3.2 – Food and catering

1. Each Member shall adopt laws and regulations or other measures to provide minimum standards for the quantity and quality of food and drinking water and for the catering standards that apply to meals provided to seafarers on ships that fly its flag, and shall undertake educational activities to promote awareness and implementation of the standards referred to in this paragraph.

2. Each Member shall ensure that ships that fly its flag meet the following minimum standards:

(a) food and drinking water supplies, having regard to the number of seafarers on board, their religious requirements and cultural practices as they pertain to food, and the duration and nature of the voyage, shall be suitable in respect of quantity, nutritional value, quality and variety;

(b) the organization and equipment of the catering department shall be such as to permit the provision to the seafarers of adequate, varied and nutritious meals prepared and served in hygienic conditions; and

(c) catering staff shall be properly trained or instructed for their positions.

3. Shipowners shall ensure that seafarers who are engaged as ships' cooks are trained, qualified and found competent for the position in accordance with requirements set out in the laws and regulations of the Member concerned.

4. The requirements under paragraph 3 of this Standard shall include a completion of a training course approved or recognized by the competent authority, which covers practical cookery, food and personal hygiene, food storage, stock control, and environmental protection and catering health and safety.

5. On ships operating with a prescribed manning of less than ten which, by virtue of the size of the crew or the trading pattern, may not be required by the competent authority to carry a fully qualified cook, anyone processing food in the galley shall be trained or instructed in areas including food and personal hygiene as well as handling and storage of food on board ship.

6. In circumstances of exceptional necessity, the competent authority may issue a dispensation permitting a non-fully qualified cook to serve in a specified ship for a specified limited period, until the next convenient port of call or for a period not exceeding one month, provided that the person to whom the dispensation is issued is trained or instructed in areas including food and personal hygiene as well as handling and storage of food on board ship.

7. In accordance with the ongoing compliance procedures under Title 5, the competent authority shall require that frequent documented inspections be carried out on board ships, by or under the authority of the master, with respect to:

(a) supplies of food and drinking water;

(b) all spaces and equipment used for the storage and handling of food and drinking water; and

(c) galley and other equipment for the preparation and service of meals.

8. No seafarer under the age of 18 shall be employed or engaged or work as a ship's cook.

Guideline B3.2 – Food and catering

Guideline B3.2.1 – Inspection, education, research and publication

1. The competent authority should, in cooperation with other relevant agencies and organizations, collect up-to-date information on nutrition and on methods of purchasing, storing, preserving, cooking and serving food, with special reference to the requirements of catering on board a ship. This information should be made available, free of charge or at reasonable cost, to manufacturers of and traders in ships' food supplies and equipment, masters, stewards and cooks, and to shipowners' and seafarers' organizations concerned. Appropriate forms of publicity, such as manuals, brochures, posters, charts or advertisements in trade journals, should be used for this purpose.

2. The competent authority should issue recommendations to avoid wastage of food, facilitate the maintenance of a proper standard of hygiene, and ensure the maximum practicable convenience in working arrangements.

3. The competent authority should work with relevant agencies and organizations to develop educational materials and on-board information concerning methods of ensuring proper food supply and catering services.

4. The competent authority should work in close cooperation with the shipowners' and seafarers' organizations concerned and with national or local authorities dealing with questions of food and health, and may where necessary utilize the services of such authorities.

Guideline B3.2.2 – Ships' cooks

1. Seafarers should only be qualified as ships' cooks if they have:

(a) served at sea for a minimum period to be prescribed by the competent authority, which could be varied to take into account existing relevant qualifications or experience;

(b) passed an examination prescribed by the competent authority or passed an equivalent examination at an approved training course for cooks.

2. The prescribed examination may be conducted and certificates granted either directly by the competent authority or, subject to its control, by an approved school for the training of cooks.

3. The competent authority should provide for the recognition, where appropriate, of certificates of qualification as ships' cooks issued by other Members, which have ratified this Convention or the Certification of Ships' Cooks Convention, 1946 (No. 69), or other approved body.

Title 4. Health protection, medical care, welfare and social security protection

Regulation 4.1 – Medical care on board ship and ashore

Purpose: To protect the health of seafarers and ensure their prompt access to medical care on board ship and ashore

1. Each Member shall ensure that all seafarers on ships that fly its flag are covered by adequate measures for the protection of their health and that they have access to prompt and adequate medical care whilst working on board.

2. The protection and care under paragraph 1 of this Regulation shall, in principle, be provided at no cost to the seafarers.

3. Each Member shall ensure that seafarers on board ships in its territory who are in need of immediate medical care are given access to the Member's medical facilities on shore.

4. The requirements for on-board health protection and medical care set out in the Code include standards for measures aimed at providing seafarers with health protection and medical care as comparable as possible to that which is generally available to workers ashore.

Standard A4.1 – Medical care on board ship and ashore

1. Each Member shall ensure that measures providing for health protection and medical care, including essential dental care, for seafarers working on board a ship that flies its flag are adopted which:

(a) ensure the application to seafarers of any general provisions on occupational health protection and medical care relevant to their duties, as well as of special provisions specific to work on board ship;

(b) ensure that seafarers are given health protection and medical care as comparable as possible to that which is generally available to workers ashore, including prompt access to the necessary medicines, medical equipment and facilities for diagnosis and treatment and to medical information and expertise;

(c) give seafarers the right to visit a qualified medical doctor or dentist without delay in ports of call, where practicable;

(d) ensure that, to the extent consistent with the Member's national law and practice, medical care and health protection services while a seafarer is on board ship or landed in a foreign port are provided free of charge to seafarers; and

(e) are not limited to treatment of sick or injured seafarers but include measures of a preventive character such as health promotion and health education programmes.

2. The competent authority shall adopt a standard medical report form for use by the ships' masters and relevant onshore and on-board medical personnel. The form, when completed, and its contents shall be kept confidential and shall only be used to facilitate the treatment of seafarers.

3. Each Member shall adopt laws and regulations establishing requirements for on-board hospital and medical care facilities and equipment and training on ships that fly its flag.

4. National laws and regulations shall as a minimum provide for the following requirements:

(a) all ships shall carry a medicine chest, medical equipment and a medical guide, the specifics of which shall be prescribed and subject to regular inspection by the competent authority; the national requirements shall take into account the type of ship, the number of persons on board and the nature, destination and duration of voyages and relevant national and international recommended medical standards;

(b) ships carrying 100 or more persons and ordinarily engaged on international voyages of more than three days' duration shall carry a qualified medical doctor who is responsible for providing medical care; national laws or regulations shall also specify which other ships shall be required to carry a medical doctor, taking into account, inter alia, such factors as the duration, nature and conditions of the voyage and the number of seafarers on board;

(c) ships which do not carry a medical doctor shall be required to have either at least one seafarer on board who is in charge of medical care and administering medicine as part of their regular duties or at least one seafarer on board competent to provide medical first aid; persons in charge of medical care on board who are not medical doctors shall have satisfactorily completed training in medical care that meets the requirements of the International Convention on Standards of Training, Certification and Watchkeeping for Seafarers, 1978, as amended ("STCW"); seafarers designated to provide medical first aid shall have satisfactorily completed training in medical first aid that meets the requirements of STCW; national laws or regulations shall specify the level of approved training required taking into account, inter alia, such factors as the duration, nature and conditions of the voyage and the number of seafarers on board; and

(d) the competent authority shall ensure by a prearranged system that medical advice by radio or satellite communication to ships at sea, including specialist advice, is available 24 hours a day; medical advice, including the onward transmission of medical messages by radio or satellite communication between a ship and those ashore giving the advice, shall be available free of charge to all ships irrespective of the flag that they fly.

Guideline B4.1 – Medical care on board ship and ashore

Guideline B4.1.1 – Provision of medical care

1. When determining the level of medical training to be provided on board ships that are not required to carry a medical doctor, the competent authority should require that:

(a) ships which ordinarily are capable of reaching qualified medical care and medical facilities within eight hours should have at least one designated seafarer with the approved medical first-aid training required by STCW which will enable such persons to take immediate, effective action in case of accidents or illnesses likely to occur on board a ship and to make use of medical advice by radio or satellite communication; and

(b) all other ships should have at least one designated seafarer with approved training in medical care required by STCW, including practical training and training in life-saving techniques such as intravenous therapy, which will enable the persons concerned to participate effectively in coordinated schemes for medical assistance to ships at sea, and to provide the sick or injured with a satisfactory standard of medical care during the period they are likely to remain on board.

2. The training referred to in paragraph 1 of this Guideline should be based on the contents of the most recent editions of the *International Medical Guide for Ships*, the *Medical First Aid Guide for Use in Accidents Involving Dangerous Goods*, the *Document for Guidance - An International Maritime Training Guide*, and the medical section of the *International Code of Signals* as well as similar national guides.

3. Persons referred to in paragraph 1 of this Guideline and such other seafarers as may be required by the competent authority should undergo, at approximately five-year intervals, refresher courses to enable them to maintain and increase their knowledge and skills and to keep up-to-date with new developments.

4. The medicine chest and its contents, as well as the medical equipment and medical guide carried on board, should be properly maintained and inspected at regular intervals, not exceeding 12 months, by responsible persons designated by the competent authority, who should ensure that the labelling, expiry dates and conditions of storage of all medicines and directions for their use are checked and all equipment functioning as required. In adopting or reviewing the ship's medical guide used nationally, and in determining the contents of the medicine chest and medical equipment, the competent authority should take into account international recommendations in this field, including the latest edition of the *International Medical Guide for Ships*, and other guides mentioned in paragraph 2 of this Guideline.

5. Where a cargo which is classified dangerous has not been included in the most recent edition of the *Medical First Aid Guide for Use in Accidents Involving Dangerous Goods*, the necessary information on the nature of the substances, the risks involved, the necessary personal protective devices, the relevant medical procedures and specific antidotes should be made available to the seafarers. Such specific antidotes and personal protective devices should be on board

whenever dangerous goods are carried. This information should be integrated with the ship's policies and programmes on occupational safety and health described in Regulation 4.3 and related Code provisions.

6. All ships should carry a complete and up-to-date list of radio stations through which medical advice can be obtained; and, if equipped with a system of satellite communication, carry an up-to-date and complete list of coast earth stations through which medical advice can be obtained. Seafarers with responsibility for medical care or medical first aid on board should be instructed in the use of the ship's medical guide and the medical section of the most recent edition of the *International Code of Signals* so as to enable them to understand the type of information needed by the advising doctor as well as the advice received.

Guideline B4.1.2 – Medical report form

1. The standard medical report form for seafarers required under Part A of this Code should be designed to facilitate the exchange of medical and related information concerning individual seafarers between ship and shore in cases of illness or injury.

Guideline B4.1.3 – Medical care ashore

1. Shore-based medical facilities for treating seafarers should be adequate for the purposes. The doctors, dentists and other medical personnel should be properly qualified.

2. Measures should be taken to ensure that seafarers have access when in port to:

(a) outpatient treatment for sickness and injury;

(b) hospitalization when necessary; and

(c) facilities for dental treatment, especially in cases of emergency.

3. Suitable measures should be taken to facilitate the treatment of seafarers suffering from disease. In particular, seafarers should be promptly admitted to clinics and hospitals ashore, without difficulty and irrespective of nationality or religious belief, and, whenever possible, arrangements should be made to ensure, when necessary, continuation of treatment to supplement the medical facilities available to them.

Guideline B4.1.4 – Medical assistance to other ships and international cooperation

1. Each Member should give due consideration to participating in international cooperation in the area of assistance, programmes and research in health protection and medical care. Such cooperation might cover:

(a) developing and coordinating search and rescue efforts and arranging prompt medical help and evacuation at sea for the seriously ill or injured on board a ship through such means as periodic ship position reporting systems, rescue coordination centres and emergency helicopter services, in conformity with the International Convention on Maritime Search and Rescue, 1979, as amended, and the *International Aeronautical and Maritime Search and Rescue (IAMSAR) Manual*;

(b) making optimum use of all ships carrying a doctor and stationing ships at sea which can provide hospital and rescue facilities;

(c) compiling and maintaining an international list of doctors and medical care facilities available worldwide to provide emergency medical care to seafarers;

(d) landing seafarers ashore for emergency treatment;

(e) repatriating seafarers hospitalized abroad as soon as practicable, in accordance with the medical advice of the doctors responsible for the case, which takes into account the seafarer's wishes and needs;

(f) arranging personal assistance for seafarers during repatriation, in accordance with the medical advice of the doctors responsible for the case, which takes into account the seafarer's wishes and needs;

(g) endeavouring to set up health centres for seafarers to:

  (i) conduct research on the health status, medical treatment and preventive health care of seafarers; and

  (ii) train medical and health service staff in maritime medicine;

(h) collecting and evaluating statistics concerning occupational accidents, diseases and fatalities of seafarers and integrating and harmonizing the statistics with any existing national system of statistics on occupational accidents and diseases covering other categories of workers;

(i) organizing international exchanges of technical information, training material and personnel, as well as international training courses, seminars and working groups;

(j) providing all seafarers with special curative and preventive health and medical services in port, or making available to them general health, medical and rehabilitation services; and

(k) arranging for the repatriation of the bodies or ashes of deceased seafarers, in accordance with the wishes of the next of kin and as soon as practicable.

2. International cooperation in the field of health protection and medical care for seafarers should be based on bilateral or multilateral agreements or consultations among Members.

Guideline B4.1.5 – Dependants of seafarers

1. Each Member should adopt measures to secure proper and sufficient medical care for the dependants of seafarers domiciled in its territory pending the development of a medical care service which would include within its scope workers generally and their dependants where such services do not exist and should inform the International Labour Office concerning the measures taken for this purpose.

Regulation 4.2 – Shipowners' liability

Purpose: To ensure that seafarers are protected from the financial consequences of sickness, injury or death occurring in connection with their employment

1. Each Member shall ensure that measures, in accordance with the Code, are in place on ships that fly its flag to provide seafarers employed on the ships with a right to material assistance and support from the shipowner with respect to the financial consequences of sickness, injury or death occurring while they are serving under a seafarers' employment agreement or arising from their employment under such agreement.

2. This Regulation does not affect any other legal remedies that a seafarer may seek.

Standard A4.2 – Shipowners' liability

1. Each Member shall adopt laws and regulations requiring that shipowners of ships that fly its flag are responsible for health protection and medical care of all seafarers working on board the ships in accordance with the following minimum standards:

(a) shipowners shall be liable to bear the costs for seafarers working on their ships in respect of sickness and injury of the seafarers occurring between the date of commencing duty and the date upon which they are deemed duly repatriated, or arising from their employment between those dates;

(b) shipowners shall provide financial security to assure compensation in the event of the death or long-term disability of seafarers due to an occupational injury, illness or hazard, as set out in national law, the seafarers' employment agreement or collective agreement;

(c) shipowners shall be liable to defray the expense of medical care, including medical treatment and the supply of the necessary medicines and therapeutic appliances, and board and lodging away from home until the sick or injured seafarer has recovered, or until the sickness or incapacity has been declared of a permanent character; and

(d) shipowners shall be liable to pay the cost of burial expenses in the case of death occurring on board or ashore during the period of engagement.

2. National laws or regulations may limit the liability of the shipowner to defray the expense of medical care and board and lodging to a period which shall not be less than 16 weeks from the day of the injury or the commencement of the sickness.

3. Where the sickness or injury results in incapacity for work the shipowner shall be liable:

(a) to pay full wages as long as the sick or injured seafarers remain on board or until the seafarers have been repatriated in accordance with this Convention; and

(b) to pay wages in whole or in part as prescribed by national laws or regulations or as provided for in collective agreements from the time when the seafarers are repatriated or landed until their recovery or, if earlier, until they are entitled to cash benefits under the legislation of the Member concerned.

4. National laws or regulations may limit the liability of the shipowner to pay wages in whole or in part in respect of a seafarer no longer on board to a period which shall not be less than 16 weeks from the day of the injury or the commencement of the sickness.

5. National laws or regulations may exclude the shipowner from liability in respect of:

(a) injury incurred otherwise than in the service of the ship;

(b) injury or sickness due to the wilful misconduct of the sick, injured or deceased seafarer; and

(c) sickness or infirmity intentionally concealed when the engagement is entered into.

6. National laws or regulations may exempt the shipowner from liability to defray the expense of medical care and board and lodging and burial expenses in so far as such liability is assumed by the public authorities.

7. Shipowners or their representatives shall take measures for safeguarding property left on board by sick, injured or deceased seafarers and for returning it to them or to their next of kin.

Guideline B4.2 – Shipowners' liability

1. The payment of full wages required by Standard A4.2, paragraph 3(a), may be exclusive of bonuses.

2. National laws or regulations may provide that a shipowner shall cease to be liable to bear the costs of a sick or injured seafarer from the time at which that seafarer can claim medical benefits under a scheme of compulsory sickness insurance, compulsory accident insurance or workers' compensation for accidents.

3. National laws or regulations may provide that burial expenses paid by the shipowner shall be reimbursed by an insurance institution in cases in which funeral benefit is payable in respect of the deceased seafarer under laws or regulations relating to social insurance or workers' compensation.

Regulation 4.3 – Health and safety protection and accident prevention

Purpose: To ensure that seafarers' work environment on board ships promotes occupational safety and health

1. Each Member shall ensure that seafarers on ships that fly its flag are provided with occupational health protection and live, work and train on board ship in a safe and hygienic environment.

2. Each Member shall develop and promulgate national guidelines for the management of occupational safety and health on board ships that fly its flag, after consultation with representative shipowners' and seafarers' organizations and taking

into account applicable codes, guidelines and standards recommended by international organizations, national administrations and maritime industry organizations.

3. Each Member shall adopt laws and regulations and other measures addressing the matters specified in the Code, taking into account relevant international instruments, and set standards for occupational safety and health protection and accident prevention on ships that fly its flag.

Standard A4.3 – Health and safety protection and accident prevention

1. The laws and regulations and other measures to be adopted in accordance with Regulation 4.3, paragraph 3, shall include the following subjects:

(a) the adoption and effective implementation and promotion of occupational safety and health policies and programmes on ships that fly the Member's flag, including risk evaluation as well as training and instruction of seafarers;

(b) reasonable precautions to prevent occupational accidents, injuries and diseases on board ship, including measures to reduce and prevent the risk of exposure to harmful levels of ambient factors and chemicals as well as the risk of injury or disease that may arise from the use of equipment and machinery on board ships;

(c) on-board programmes for the prevention of occupational accidents, injuries and diseases and for continuous improvement in occupational safety and health protection, involving seafarers' representatives and all other persons concerned in their implementation, taking account of preventive measures, including engineering and design control, substitution of processes and procedures for collective and individual tasks, and the use of personal protective equipment; and

(d) requirements for inspecting, reporting and correcting unsafe conditions and for investigating and reporting on-board occupational accidents.

2. The provisions referred to in paragraph 1 of this Standard shall:

(a) take account of relevant international instruments dealing with occupational safety and health protection in general and with specific risks, and address all matters relevant to the prevention of occupational accidents, injuries and diseases that may be applicable to the work of seafarers and particularly those which are specific to maritime employment;

(b) clearly specify the obligation of shipowners, seafarers and others concerned to comply with the applicable standards and with the ship's occupational safety and health policy and programme with special attention being paid to the safety and health of seafarers under the age of 18;

(c) specify the duties of the master or a person designated by the master, or both, to take specific responsibility for the implementation of and compliance with the ship's occupational safety and health policy and programme; and

(d) specify the authority of the ship's seafarers appointed or elected as safety representatives to participate in meetings of the ship's safety committee. Such a committee shall be established on board a ship on which there are five or more seafarers.

3. The laws and regulations and other measures referred to in Regulation 4.3, paragraph 3, shall be regularly reviewed in consultation with the representatives of the shipowners' and seafarers' organizations and, if necessary, revised to take account of changes in technology and research in order to facilitate continuous improvement in occupational safety and health policies and programmes and to provide a safe occupational environment for seafarers on ships that fly the Member's flag.

4. Compliance with the requirements of applicable international instruments on the acceptable levels of exposure to workplace hazards on board ships and on the development and implementation of ships' occupational safety and health policies and programmes shall be considered as meeting the requirements of this Convention.

5. The competent authority shall ensure that:

(a) occupational accidents, injuries and diseases are adequately reported, taking into account the guidance provided by the International Labour Organization with respect to the reporting and recording of occupational accidents and diseases;

(b) comprehensive statistics of such accidents and diseases are kept, analysed and published and, where appropriate, followed up by research into general trends and into the hazards identified; and

(c) occupational accidents are investigated.

6. Reporting and investigation of occupational safety and health matters shall be designed to ensure the protection of seafarers' personal data, and shall take account of the guidance provided by the International Labour Organization on this matter.

7. The competent authority shall cooperate with shipowners' and seafarers' organizations to take measures to bring to the attention of all seafarers information concerning particular hazards on board ships, for instance, by posting official notices containing relevant instructions.

8. The competent authority shall require that shipowners conducting risk evaluation in relation to management of occupational safety and health refer to appropriate statistical information from their ships and from general statistics provided by the competent authority.

Guideline B4.3 – Health and safety protection and accident prevention

Guideline B4.3.1 – Provisions on occupational accidents, injuries and diseases

1. The provisions required under Standard A4.3 should take into account the ILO code of practice entitled *Accident prevention on board ship at sea and in port*, 1996, and subsequent versions and other related ILO and other international standards and guidelines and codes of practice regarding occupational safety and health protection, including any exposure levels that they may identify.

2. The competent authority should ensure that the national guidelines for the management of occupational safety and health address the following matters, in particular:

(a) general and basic provisions;

(b) structural features of the ship, including means of access and asbestos-related risks;

(c) machinery;

(d) the effects of the extremely low or high temperature of any surfaces with which seafarers may be in contact;

(e) the effects of noise in the workplace and in shipboard accommodation;

(f) the effects of vibration in the workplace and in shipboard accommodation;

(g) the effects of ambient factors, other than those referred to in subparagraphs (e) and (f), in the workplace and in shipboard accommodation, including tobacco smoke;

(h) special safety measures on and below deck;

(i) loading and unloading equipment;

(j) fire prevention and fire-fighting;

(k) anchors, chains and lines;

(l) dangerous cargo and ballast;

(m) personal protective equipment for seafarers;

(n) work in enclosed spaces;

(o) physical and mental effects of fatigue;

(p) the effects of drug and alcohol dependency;

(q) HIV/AIDS protection and prevention; and

(r) emergency and accident response.

3. The assessment of risks and reduction of exposure on the matters referred to in paragraph 2 of this Guideline should take account of the physical occupational health effects, including manual handling of loads, noise and vibration, the chemical and biological occupational health effects, the mental occupational health effects, the physical and mental health effects of fatigue, and occupational accidents. The necessary measures should take due account of the preventive principle according to which, among other things, combating risk at the source, adapting work to the individual, especially as regards the design of workplaces, and replacing the dangerous by the non-dangerous or the less dangerous, have precedence over personal protective equipment for seafarers.

4. In addition, the competent authority should ensure that the implications for health and safety are taken into account, particularly in the following areas:

(a) emergency and accident response;

(b) the effects of drug and alcohol dependency; and

(c) HIV/AIDS protection and prevention.

Guideline B4.3.2 – Exposure to noise

1. The competent authority, in conjunction with the competent international bodies and with representatives of shipowners' and seafarers' organizations concerned, should review on an ongoing basis the problem of noise on board ships with the objective of improving the protection of seafarers, in so far as practicable, from the adverse effects of exposure to noise.

2. The review referred to in paragraph 1 of this Guideline should take account of the adverse effects of exposure to excessive noise on the hearing, health and comfort of seafarers and the measures to be prescribed or recommended to reduce shipboard noise to protect seafarers. The measures to be considered should include the following:

(a) instruction of seafarers in the dangers to hearing and health of prolonged exposure to high noise levels and in the proper use of noise protection devices and equipment;

(b) provision of approved hearing protection equipment to seafarers where necessary; and

(c) assessment of risk and reduction of exposure levels to noise in all accommodation and recreational and catering facilities, as well as engine rooms and other machinery spaces.

Guideline B4.3.3 – Exposure to vibration

1. The competent authority, in conjunction with the competent international bodies and with representatives of shipowners' and seafarers' organizations concerned, and taking into account, as appropriate, relevant international standards, should review on an ongoing basis the problem of vibration on board ships with the objective of improving the protection of seafarers, in so far as practicable, from the adverse effects of vibration.

2. The review referred to in paragraph 1 of this Guideline should cover the effect of exposure to excessive vibration on the health and comfort of seafarers and the measures to be prescribed or recommended to reduce shipboard vibration to protect seafarers. The measures to be considered should include the following:

(a) instruction of seafarers in the dangers to their health of prolonged exposure to vibration;

(b) provision of approved personal protective equipment to seafarers where necessary; and

(c) assessment of risks and reduction of exposure to vibration in all accommodation and recreational and catering facilities by adopting measures in accordance with the guidance provided by the ILO code of practice entitled *Ambient factors in the workplace*, 2001, and any subsequent revisions, taking account of the difference between exposure in those areas and in the workplace.

Guideline B4.3.4 – Obligations of shipowners

1. Any obligation on the shipowner to provide protective equipment or other accident prevention safeguards should, in general, be accompanied by pro-

visions requiring their use by seafarers and by a requirement for seafarers to comply with the relevant accident prevention and health protection measures.

2. Account should also be taken of Articles 7 and 11 of the Guarding of Machinery Convention, 1963 (No. 119), and the corresponding provisions of the Guarding of Machinery Recommendation, 1963 (No. 118), under which the obligation to ensure compliance with the requirement that machinery in use is properly guarded, and its use without appropriate guards prevented, rests on the employer, while there is an obligation on the worker not to use machinery without the guards being in position nor to make inoperative the guards provided.

Guideline B4.3.5 – Reporting and collection of statistics

1. All occupational accidents and occupational injuries and diseases should be reported so that they can be investigated and comprehensive statistics can be kept, analysed and published, taking account of protection of the personal data of the seafarers concerned. Reports should not be limited to fatalities or to accidents involving the ship.

2. The statistics referred to in paragraph 1 of this Guideline should record the numbers, nature, causes and effects of occupational accidents and occupational injuries and diseases, with a clear indication, as applicable, of the department on board a ship, the type of accident and whether at sea or in port.

3. Each Member should have due regard to any international system or model for recording accidents to seafarers which may have been established by the International Labour Organization.

Guideline B4.3.6 – Investigations

1. The competent authority should undertake investigations into the causes and circumstances of all occupational accidents and occupational injuries and diseases resulting in loss of life or serious personal injury, and such other cases as may be specified in national laws or regulations.

2. Consideration should be given to including the following as subjects of investigation:

(a) working environment, such as working surfaces, layout of machinery, means of access, lighting and methods of work;

(b) incidence in different age groups of occupational accidents and occupational injuries and diseases;

(c) special physiological or psychological problems created by the shipboard environment;

(d) problems arising from physical stress on board a ship, in particular as a consequence of increased workload;

(e) problems arising from and effects of technical developments and their influence on the composition of crews; and

(f) problems arising from any human failures.

Guideline B4.3.7 – National protection and prevention programmes

1. In order to provide a sound basis for measures to promote occupational safety and health protection and prevention of accidents, injuries and diseases which are due to particular hazards of maritime employment, research should be undertaken into general trends and into such hazards as are revealed by statistics.

2. The implementation of protection and prevention programmes for the promotion of occupational safety and health should be so organized that the competent authority, shipowners and seafarers or their representatives and other appropriate bodies may play an active role, including through such means as information sessions, on-board guidelines on maximum exposure levels to potentially harmful ambient workplace factors and other hazards or outcomes of a systematic risk evaluation process. In particular, national or local joint occupational safety and health protection and accident prevention committees or ad hoc working parties and on-board committees, on which shipowners' and seafarers' organizations concerned are represented, should be established.

3. Where such activity takes place at company level, the representation of seafarers on any safety committee on board that shipowner's ships should be considered.

Guideline B4.3.8 – Content of protection and prevention programmes

1. Consideration should be given to including the following in the functions of the committees and other bodies referred to in Guideline B4.3.7, paragraph 2:

(a) the preparation of national guidelines and policies for occupational safety and health management systems and for accident prevention provisions, rules and manuals;

(b) the organization of occupational safety and health protection and accident prevention training and programmes;

(c) the organization of publicity on occupational safety and health protection and accident prevention, including films, posters, notices and brochures; and

(d) the distribution of literature and information on occupational safety and health protection and accident prevention so that it reaches seafarers on board ships.

2. Relevant provisions or recommendations adopted by the appropriate national authorities or organizations or international organizations should be taken into account by those preparing texts of occupational safety and health protection and accident prevention measures or recommended practices.

3. In formulating occupational safety and health protection and accident prevention programmes, each Member should have due regard to any code of practice concerning the safety and health of seafarers which may have been published by the International Labour Organization.

Guideline B4.3.9 – Instruction in occupational safety and health protection and the prevention of occupational accidents

1. The curriculum for the training referred to in Standard A4.3, paragraph 1(a), should be reviewed periodically and brought up to date in the light of development in types and sizes of ships and in their equipment, as well as changes in manning practices, nationality, language and the organization of work on board ships.

2. There should be continuous occupational safety and health protection and accident prevention publicity. Such publicity might take the following forms:

(a) educational audiovisual material, such as films, for use in vocational training centres for seafarers and where possible shown on board ships;

(b) display of posters on board ships;

(c) inclusion in periodicals read by seafarers of articles on the hazards of maritime employment and on occupational safety and health protection and accident prevention measures; and

(d) special campaigns using various publicity media to instruct seafarers, including campaigns on safe working practices.

3. The publicity referred to in paragraph 2 of this Guideline should take account of the different nationalities, languages and cultures of seafarers on board ships.

Guideline B4.3.10 – Safety and health education of young seafarers

1. Safety and health regulations should refer to any general provisions on medical examinations before and during employment and on the prevention of accidents and the protection of health in employment, which may be applicable to the work of seafarers. Such regulations should specify measures which will minimize occupational dangers to young seafarers in the course of their duties.

2. Except where a young seafarer is recognized as fully qualified in a pertinent skill by the competent authority, the regulations should specify restrictions on young seafarers undertaking, without appropriate supervision and instruction, certain types of work presenting special risk of accident or of detrimental effect on their health or physical development, or requiring a particular degree of maturity, experience or skill. In determining the types of work to be restricted by the regulations, the competent authority might consider in particular work involving:

(a) the lifting, moving or carrying of heavy loads or objects;

(b) entry into boilers, tanks and cofferdams;

(c) exposure to harmful noise and vibration levels;

(d) operating hoisting and other power machinery and tools, or acting as signallers to operators of such equipment;

(e) handling mooring or tow lines or anchoring equipment;

(f) rigging;

(g) work aloft or on deck in heavy weather;

(h) nightwatch duties;

(i) servicing of electrical equipment;

(j) exposure to potentially harmful materials, or harmful physical agents such as dangerous or toxic substances and ionizing radiations;

(k) the cleaning of catering machinery; and

(l) the handling or taking charge of ships' boats.

3. Practical measures should be taken by the competent authority or through the appropriate machinery to bring to the attention of young seafarers information concerning the prevention of accidents and the protection of their health on board ships. Such measures could include adequate instruction in courses, official accident prevention publicity intended for young persons and professional instruction and supervision of young seafarers.

4. Education and training of young seafarers both ashore and on board ships should include guidance on the detrimental effects on their health and well-being of the abuse of alcohol and drugs and other potentially harmful substances, and the risk and concerns relating to HIV/AIDS and of other health risk related activities.

Guideline B4.3.11 – International cooperation

1. Members, with the assistance as appropriate of intergovernmental and other international organizations, should endeavour, in cooperation with each other, to achieve the greatest possible uniformity of action for the promotion of occupational safety and health protection and prevention of accidents.

2. In developing programmes for promoting occupational safety and health protection and prevention of accidents under Standard A4.3, each Member should have due regard to relevant codes of practice published by the International Labour Organization and the appropriate standards of international organizations.

3. Members should have regard to the need for international cooperation in the continuous promotion of activity related to occupational safety and health protection and prevention of occupational accidents. Such cooperation might take the form of:

(a) bilateral or multilateral arrangements for uniformity in occupational safety and health protection and accident prevention standards and safeguards;

(b) exchange of information on particular hazards affecting seafarers and on means of promoting occupational safety and health protection and preventing accidents;

(c) assistance in testing of equipment and inspection according to the national regulations of the flag State;

(d) collaboration in the preparation and dissemination of occupational safety and health protection and accident prevention provisions, rules or manuals;

(e) collaboration in the production and use of training aids; and

(f) joint facilities for, or mutual assistance in, the training of seafarers in occupational safety and health protection, accident prevention and safe working practices.

Regulation 4.4 – Access to shore-based welfare facilities

Purpose: To ensure that seafarers working on board a ship have access to shore-based facilities and services to secure their health and well-being

1. Each Member shall ensure that shore-based welfare facilities, where they exist, are easily accessible. The Member shall also promote the development of welfare facilities, such as those listed in the Code, in designated ports to provide seafarers on ships that are in its ports with access to adequate welfare facilities and services.

2. The responsibilities of each Member with respect to shore-based facilities, such as welfare, cultural, recreational and information facilities and services, are set out in the Code.

Standard A4.4 – Access to shore-based welfare facilities

1. Each Member shall require, where welfare facilities exist on its territory, that they are available for the use of all seafarers, irrespective of nationality, race, colour, sex, religion, political opinion or social origin and irrespective of the flag State of the ship on which they are employed or engaged or work.

2. Each Member shall promote the development of welfare facilities in appropriate ports of the country and determine, after consultation with the shipowners' and seafarers' organizations concerned, which ports are to be regarded as appropriate.

3. Each Member shall encourage the establishment of welfare boards which shall regularly review welfare facilities and services to ensure that they are appropriate in the light of changes in the needs of seafarers resulting from technical, operational and other developments in the shipping industry.

Guideline B4.4 – Access to shore-based welfare facilities

Guideline B4.4.1 – Responsibilities of Members

1. Each Member should:

(a) take measures to ensure that adequate welfare facilities and services are provided for seafarers in designated ports of call and that adequate protection is provided to seafarers in the exercise of their profession; and

(b) take into account, in the implementation of these measures, the special needs of seafarers, especially when in foreign countries and when entering war zones, in respect of their safety, health and spare-time activities.

2. Arrangements for the supervision of welfare facilities and services should include participation by representative shipowners' and seafarers' organizations concerned.

3. Each Member should take measures designed to expedite the free circulation among ships, central supply agencies and welfare establishments of welfare materials such as films, books, newspapers and sports equipment for use by seafarers on board their ships and in welfare centres ashore.

4. Members should cooperate with one another in promoting the welfare of seafarers at sea and in port. Such cooperation should include the following:

(a) consultations among competent authorities aimed at the provision and improvement of seafarers' welfare facilities and services, both in port and on board ships;

(b) agreements on the pooling of resources and the joint provision of welfare facilities in major ports so as to avoid unnecessary duplication;

(c) organization of international sports competitions and encouragement of the participation of seafarers in sports activities; and

(d) organization of international seminars on the subject of welfare of seafarers at sea and in port.

Guideline B4.4.2 – Welfare facilities and services in ports

1. Each Member should provide or ensure the provision of such welfare facilities and services as may be required, in appropriate ports of the country.

2. Welfare facilities and services should be provided, in accordance with national conditions and practice, by one or more of the following:

(a) public authorities;

(b) shipowners' and seafarers' organizations concerned under collective agreements or other agreed arrangements; and

(c) voluntary organizations.

3. Necessary welfare and recreational facilities should be established or developed in ports. These should include:

(a) meeting and recreation rooms as required;

(b) facilities for sports and outdoor facilities, including competitions;

(c) educational facilities; and

(d) where appropriate, facilities for religious observances and for personal counselling.

4. These facilities may be provided by making available to seafarers in accordance with their needs facilities designed for more general use.

5. Where large numbers of seafarers of different nationalities require facilities such as hotels, clubs and sports facilities in a particular port, the competent authorities or bodies of the countries of origin of the seafarers and of the flag States, as well as the international associations concerned, should consult and cooperate with the competent authorities and bodies of the country in which the port is situated and with one another, with a view to the pooling of resources and to avoiding unnecessary duplication.

6. Hotels or hostels suitable for seafarers should be available where there is need for them. They should provide facilities equal to those found in a good-class hotel, and should wherever possible be located in good surroundings away from the immediate vicinity of the docks. Such hotels or hostels should be properly supervised, the prices charged should be reasonable in amount and, where necessary and possible, provision should be made for accommodating seafarers' families.

7. These accommodation facilities should be open to all seafarers, irrespective of nationality, race, colour, sex, religion, political opinion or social origin and irrespective of the flag State of the ship on which they are employed or engaged or work. Without in any way infringing this principle, it may be necessary in certain ports to provide several types of facilities, comparable in standard but adapted to the customs and needs of different groups of seafarers.

8. Measures should be taken to ensure that, as necessary, technically competent persons are employed full time in the operation of seafarers' welfare facilities and services, in addition to any voluntary workers.

Guideline B4.4.3 – Welfare boards

1. Welfare boards should be established, at the port, regional and national levels, as appropriate. Their functions should include:

(a) keeping under review the adequacy of existing welfare facilities and monitoring the need for the provision of additional facilities or the withdrawal of under-utilized facilities; and

(b) assisting and advising those responsible for providing welfare facilities and ensuring coordination between them.

2. Welfare boards should include among their members representatives of shipowners' and seafarers' organizations, the competent authorities and, where appropriate, voluntary organizations and social bodies.

3. As appropriate, consuls of maritime States and local representatives of foreign welfare organizations should, in accordance with national laws and regulations, be associated with the work of port, regional and national welfare boards.

Guideline B4.4.4 – Financing of welfare facilities

1. In accordance with national conditions and practice, financial support for port welfare facilities should be made available through one or more of the following:

(a) grants from public funds;

(b) levies or other special dues from shipping sources;

(c) voluntary contributions from shipowners, seafarers, or their organizations; and

(d) voluntary contributions from other sources.

2. Where welfare taxes, levies and special dues are imposed, they should be used only for the purposes for which they are raised.

Guideline B4.4.5 – Dissemination of information and facilitation measures

1. Information should be disseminated among seafarers concerning facilities open to the general public in ports of call, particularly transport, welfare, entertainment and educational facilities and places of worship, as well as facilities provided specifically for seafarers.

2. Adequate means of transport at moderate prices should be available at any reasonable time in order to enable seafarers to reach urban areas from convenient locations in the port.

3. All suitable measures should be taken by the competent authorities to make known to shipowners and to seafarers entering port any special laws and customs, the contravention of which may jeopardize their freedom.

4. Port areas and access roads should be provided by the competent authorities with adequate lighting and signposting and regular patrols for the protection of seafarers.

Guideline B4.4.6 – Seafarers in a foreign port

1. For the protection of seafarers in foreign ports, measures should be taken to facilitate:

(a) access to consuls of their State of nationality or State of residence; and

(b) effective cooperation between consuls and the local or national authorities.

2. Seafarers who are detained in a foreign port should be dealt with promptly under due process of law and with appropriate consular protection.

3. Whenever a seafarer is detained for any reason in the territory of a Member, the competent authority should, if the seafarer so requests, immediately inform the flag State and the State of nationality of the seafarer. The competent authority should promptly inform the seafarer of the right to make such a request. The State of nationality of the seafarer should promptly notify the seafarer's next of kin. The competent authority should allow consular officers of these States immediate access to the seafarer and regular visits thereafter so long as the seafarer is detained.

4. Each Member should take measures, whenever necessary, to ensure the safety of seafarers from aggression and other unlawful acts while ships are in their territorial waters and especially in approaches to ports.

5. Every effort should be made by those responsible in port and on board a ship to facilitate shore leave for seafarers as soon as possible after a ship's arrival in port.

Regulation 4.5 – Social security

Purpose: To ensure that measures are taken with a view to providing seafarers with access to social security protection

1. Each Member shall ensure that all seafarers and, to the extent provided for in its national law, their dependants have access to social security protection in accordance with the Code without prejudice however to any more favourable conditions referred to in paragraph 8 of article 19 of the Constitution.

2. Each Member undertakes to take steps, according to its national circumstances, individually and through international cooperation, to achieve progressively comprehensive social security protection for seafarers.

3. Each Member shall ensure that seafarers who are subject to its social security legislation, and, to the extent provided for in its national law, their dependants, are entitled to benefit from social security protection no less favourable than that enjoyed by shoreworkers.

Standard A4.5 – Social security

1. The branches to be considered with a view to achieving progressively comprehensive social security protection under Regulation 4.5 are: medical care, sickness benefit, unemployment benefit, old-age benefit, employment injury benefit, family benefit, maternity benefit, invalidity benefit and survivors' benefit, complementing the protection provided for under Regulations 4.1, on medical care, and 4.2, on shipowners' liability, and under other titles of this Convention.

2. At the time of ratification, the protection to be provided by each Member in accordance with Regulation 4.5, paragraph 1, shall include at least three of the nine branches listed in paragraph 1 of this Standard.

3. Each Member shall take steps according to its national circumstances to provide the complementary social security protection referred to in paragraph 1 of this Standard to all seafarers ordinarily resident in its territory. This responsibility could be satisfied, for example, through appropriate bilateral or multilateral agreements or contribution-based systems. The resulting protection shall be no less favourable than that enjoyed by shoreworkers resident in their territory.

4. Notwithstanding the attribution of responsibilities in paragraph 3 of this Standard, Members may determine, through bilateral and multilateral agreements and through provisions adopted in the framework of regional economic integration organizations, other rules concerning the social security legislation to which seafarers are subject.

5. Each Member's responsibilities with respect to seafarers on ships that fly its flag shall include those provided for by Regulations 4.1 and 4.2 and the related provisions of the Code, as well as those that are inherent in its general obligations under international law.

6. Each Member shall give consideration to the various ways in which comparable benefits will, in accordance with national law and practice, be provided to seafarers in the absence of adequate coverage in the branches referred to in paragraph 1 of this Standard.

7. The protection under Regulation 4.5, paragraph 1, may, as appropriate, be contained in laws or regulations, in private schemes or in collective bargaining agreements or in a combination of these.

8. To the extent consistent with their national law and practice, Members shall cooperate, through bilateral or multilateral agreements or other arrangements, to ensure the maintenance of social security rights, provided through contributory or non-contributory schemes, which have been acquired, or are in the course of acquisition, by all seafarers regardless of residence.

9. Each Member shall establish fair and effective procedures for the settlement of disputes.

10. Each Member shall at the time of ratification specify the branches for which protection is provided in accordance with paragraph 2 of this Standard. It shall subsequently notify the Director-General of the International Labour Office when it provides social security protection in respect of one or more other branches stated in paragraph 1 of this Standard. The Director-General shall maintain a register of this information and shall make it available to all interested parties.

11. The reports to the International Labour Office pursuant to article 22 of the Constitution, shall also include information regarding steps taken in accordance with Regulation 4.5, paragraph 2, to extend protection to other branches.

Guideline B4.5 – Social security

1. The protection to be provided at the time of ratification in accordance with Standard A4.5, paragraph 2, should at least include the branches of medical care, sickness benefit and employment injury benefit.

2. In the circumstances referred to in Standard A4.5, paragraph 6, comparable benefits may be provided through insurance, bilateral and multilateral agreements or other effective means, taking into consideration the provisions of relevant collective bargaining agreements. Where such measures are adopted, seafarers covered by such measures should be advised of the means by which the various branches of social security protection will be provided.

3. Where seafarers are subject to more than one national legislation covering social security, the Members concerned should cooperate in order to determine by mutual agreement which legislation is to apply, taking into account such factors as the type and level of protection under the respective legislations which is more favourable to the seafarer concerned as well as the seafarer's preference.

4. The procedures to be established under Standard A4.5, paragraph 9, should be designed to cover all disputes relevant to the claims of the seafarers concerned, irrespective of the manner in which the coverage is provided.

5. Each Member which has national seafarers, non-national seafarers or both serving on ships that fly its flag should provide the social security protection in the Convention as applicable, and should periodically review the branches of social security protection in Standard A4.5, paragraph 1, with a view to identifying any additional branches appropriate for the seafarers concerned.

6. The seafarers' employment agreement should identify the means by which the various branches of social security protection will be provided to the seafarer by the shipowner as well as any other relevant information at the disposal of the shipowner, such as statutory deductions from the seafarers' wages and shipowners' contributions which may be made in accordance with the requirements of identified authorized bodies pursuant to relevant national social security schemes.

7. The Member whose flag the ship flies should, in effectively exercising its jurisdiction over social matters, satisfy itself that the shipowners' responsibilities concerning social security protection are met, including making the required contributions to social security schemes.

TITLE 5. COMPLIANCE AND ENFORCEMENT

1. The Regulations in this Title specify each Member's responsibility to fully implement and enforce the principles and rights set out in the Articles of this Convention as well as the particular obligations provided for under its Titles 1, 2, 3 and 4.

2. Paragraphs 3 and 4 of Article VI, which permit the implementation of Part A of the Code through substantially equivalent provisions, do not apply to Part A of the Code in this Title.

3. In accordance with paragraph 2 of Article VI, each Member shall implement its responsibilities under the Regulations in the manner set out in the corresponding Standards of Part A of the Code, giving due consideration to the corresponding Guidelines in Part B of the Code.

4. The provisions of this Title shall be implemented bearing in mind that seafarers and shipowners, like all other persons, are equal before the law and are entitled to the equal protection of the law and shall not be subject to discrimination in their access to courts, tribunals or other dispute resolution mechanisms. The provisions of this Title do not determine legal jurisdiction or a legal venue.

Regulation 5.1 – Flag State responsibilities

Purpose: To ensure that each Member implements its responsibilities under this Convention with respect to ships that fly its flag

Regulation 5.1.1 – General principles

1. Each Member is responsible for ensuring implementation of its obligations under this Convention on ships that fly its flag.

2. Each Member shall establish an effective system for the inspection and certification of maritime labour conditions, in accordance with Regulations 5.1.3 and 5.1.4 ensuring that the working and living conditions for seafarers on ships that fly its flag meet, and continue to meet, the standards in this Convention.

3. In establishing an effective system for the inspection and certification of maritime labour conditions, a Member may, where appropriate, authorize public institutions or other organizations (including those of another Member, if the latter agrees) which it recognizes as competent and independent to carry out inspections or to issue certificates or to do both. In all cases, the Member shall remain fully responsible for the inspection and certification of the working and living conditions of the seafarers concerned on ships that fly its flag.

4. A maritime labour certificate, complemented by a declaration of maritime labour compliance, shall constitute prima facie evidence that the ship has been duly inspected by the Member whose flag it flies and that the requirements of this Convention relating to working and living conditions of the seafarers have been met to the extent so certified.

5. Information about the system referred to in paragraph 2 of this Regulation, including the method used for assessing its effectiveness, shall be included in the Member's reports to the International Labour Office pursuant to article 22 of the Constitution.

Standard A5.1.1 – General principles

1. Each Member shall establish clear objectives and standards covering the administration of its inspection and certification systems, as well as adequate overall procedures for its assessment of the extent to which those objectives and standards are being attained.

2. Each Member shall require all ships that fly its flag to have a copy of this Convention available on board.

Guideline B5.1.1 – General principles

1. The competent authority should make appropriate arrangements to promote effective cooperation between public institutions and other organizations, referred to in Regulations 5.1.1 and 5.1.2, concerned with seafarers' shipboard working and living conditions.

2. In order to better ensure cooperation between inspectors and shipowners, seafarers and their respective organizations, and to maintain or improve seafarers' working and living conditions, the competent authority should consult the representatives of such organizations at regular intervals as to the best means of attaining these ends. The manner of such consultation should be determined by the competent authority after consulting with shipowners' and seafarers' organizations.

Regulation 5.1.2 – Authorization of recognized organizations

1. The public institutions or other organizations referred to in paragraph 3 of Regulation 5.1.1 ("recognized organizations") shall have been recognized by the competent authority as meeting the requirements in the Code regarding competency and independence. The inspection or certification functions which the recognized organizations may be authorized to carry out shall come within the scope of the activities that are expressly mentioned in the Code as being carried out by the competent authority or a recognized organization.

2. The reports referred to in paragraph 5 of Regulation 5.1.1 shall contain information regarding any recognized organization, the extent of authorizations given and the arrangements made by the Member to ensure that the authorized activities are carried out completely and effectively.

Standard A5.1.2 – Authorization of recognized organizations

1. For the purpose of recognition in accordance with paragraph 1 of Regulation 5.1.2, the competent authority shall review the competency and independence of the organization concerned and determine whether the organization has demonstrated, to the extent necessary for carrying out the activities covered by the authorization conferred on it, that the organization:

(a) has the necessary expertise in the relevant aspects of this Convention and an appropriate knowledge of ship operations, including the minimum requirements for seafarers to work on a ship, conditions of employment, accommodation, recreational facilities, food and catering, accident prevention, health protection, medical care, welfare and social security protection;

(b) has the ability to maintain and update the expertise of its personnel;

(c) has the necessary knowledge of the requirements of this Convention as well as of applicable national laws and regulations and relevant international instruments; and

(d) is of the appropriate size, structure, experience and capability commensurate with the type and degree of authorization.

2. Any authorizations granted with respect to inspections shall, as a minimum, empower the recognized organization to require the rectification of deficiencies that it identifies in seafarers' working and living conditions and to carry out inspections in this regard at the request of a port State.

3. Each Member shall establish:

(a) a system to ensure the adequacy of work performed by recognized organizations, which includes information on all applicable national laws and regulations and relevant international instruments; and

(b) procedures for communication with and oversight of such organizations.

4. Each Member shall provide the International Labour Office with a current list of any recognized organizations authorized to act on its behalf and it shall keep this list up to date. The list shall specify the functions that the recognized organizations have been authorized to carry out. The Office shall make the list publicly available.

Guideline B5.1.2 – Authorization of recognized organizations

1. The organization seeking recognition should demonstrate the technical, administrative and managerial competence and capacity to ensure the provision of timely service of satisfactory quality.

2. In evaluating the capability of an organization, the competent authority should determine whether the organization:

(a) has adequate technical, managerial and support staff;

(b) has sufficient qualified professional staff to provide the required service, representing an adequate geographical coverage;

(c) has proven ability to provide a timely service of satisfactory quality; and

(d) is independent and accountable in its operations.

3. The competent authority should conclude a written agreement with any organization that it recognizes for purposes of an authorization. The agreement should include the following elements:

(a) scope of application;

(b) purpose;

(c) general conditions;

(d) the execution of functions under authorization;

(e) legal basis of the functions under authorization;

(f) reporting to the competent authority;

(g) specification of the authorization from the competent authority to the recognized organization; and

(h) the competent authority's supervision of activities delegated to the recognized organization.

4. Each Member should require the recognized organizations to develop a system for qualification of staff employed by them as inspectors to ensure the timely updating of their knowledge and expertise.

5. Each Member should require the recognized organizations to maintain records of the services performed by them such that they are able to demonstrate achievement of the required standards in the items covered by the services.

6. In establishing the oversight procedures referred to in Standard A5.1.2, paragraph 3(b), each Member should take into account the *Guidelines for the Authorization of Organizations Acting on Behalf of the Administration*, adopted in the framework of the International Maritime Organization.

Regulation 5.1.3 – Maritime labour certificate and declaration of maritime labour compliance

1. This Regulation applies to ships of:

(a) 500 gross tonnage or over, engaged in international voyages; and

(b) 500 gross tonnage or over, flying the flag of a Member and operating from a port, or between ports, in another country.

For the purpose of this Regulation, "international voyage" means a voyage from a country to a port outside such a country.

2. This Regulation also applies to any ship that flies the flag of a Member and is not covered by paragraph 1 of this Regulation, at the request of the shipowner to the Member concerned.

3. Each Member shall require ships that fly its flag to carry and maintain a maritime labour certificate certifying that the working and living conditions of seafarers on the ship, including measures for ongoing compliance to be included in the declaration of maritime labour compliance referred to in paragraph 4 of this Regulation, have been inspected and meet the requirements of national laws or regulations or other measures implementing this Convention.

4. Each Member shall require ships that fly its flag to carry and maintain a declaration of maritime labour compliance stating the national requirements implementing this Convention for the working and living conditions for seafarers and setting out the measures adopted by the shipowner to ensure compliance with the requirements on the ship or ships concerned.

5. The maritime labour certificate and the declaration of maritime labour compliance shall conform to the model prescribed by the Code.

6. Where the competent authority of the Member or a recognized organization duly authorized for this purpose has ascertained through inspection that a ship that flies the Member's flag meets or continues to meet the standards of this Convention, it shall issue or renew a maritime labour certificate to that effect and maintain a publicly available record of that certificate.

7. Detailed requirements for the maritime labour certificate and the declaration of maritime labour compliance, including a list of the matters that must be inspected and approved, are set out in Part A of the Code.

Standard A5.1.3 – Maritime labour certificate and declaration of maritime labour compliance

1. The maritime labour certificate shall be issued to a ship by the competent authority, or by a recognized organization duly authorized for this purpose, for a period which shall not exceed five years. A list of matters that must be inspected and found to meet national laws and regulations or other measures implementing the requirements of this Convention regarding the working and living conditions of seafarers on ships before a maritime labour certificate can be issued is found in Appendix A5-I.

2. The validity of the maritime labour certificate shall be subject to an intermediate inspection by the competent authority, or by a recognized organization duly authorized for this purpose, to ensure continuing compliance with the national requirements implementing this Convention. If only one intermediate inspection is carried out and the period of validity of the certificate is five years, it shall take place between the second and third anniversary dates of the certificate. Anniversary date means the day and month of each year which will correspond to the date of expiry of the maritime labour certificate. The scope and depth of the intermediate inspection shall be equal to an inspection for renewal of the certificate. The certificate shall be endorsed following satisfactory intermediate inspection.

3. Notwithstanding paragraph 1 of this Standard, when the renewal inspection has been completed within three months before the expiry of the existing maritime labour certificate, the new maritime labour certificate shall be valid from the date of completion of the renewal inspection for a period not exceeding five years from the date of expiry of the existing certificate.

4. When the renewal inspection is completed more than three months before the expiry date of the existing maritime labour certificate, the new maritime labour certificate shall be valid for a period not exceeding five years starting from the date of completion of the renewal inspection.

5. A maritime labour certificate may be issued on an interim basis:

(a) to new ships on delivery;

(b) when a ship changes flag; or

(c) when a shipowner assumes responsibility for the operation of a ship which is new to that shipowner.

6. An interim maritime labour certificate may be issued for a period not exceeding six months by the competent authority or a recognized organization duly authorized for this purpose.

7. An interim maritime labour certificate may only be issued following verification that:

(a) the ship has been inspected, as far as reasonable and practicable, for the matters listed in Appendix A5-I, taking into account verification of items under subparagraphs (b), (c) and (d) of this paragraph;

(b) the shipowner has demonstrated to the competent authority or recognized organization that the ship has adequate procedures to comply with this Convention;

(c) the master is familiar with the requirements of this Convention and the responsibilities for implementation; and

(d) relevant information has been submitted to the competent authority or recognized organization to produce a declaration of maritime labour compliance.

8. A full inspection in accordance with paragraph 1 of this Standard shall be carried out prior to expiry of the interim certificate to enable issue of the full-term maritime labour certificate. No further interim certificate may be issued following the initial six months referred to in paragraph 6 of this Standard. A declaration of maritime labour compliance need not be issued for the period of validity of the interim certificate.

9. The maritime labour certificate, the interim maritime labour certificate and the declaration of maritime labour compliance shall be drawn up in the form corresponding to the models given in Appendix A5-II.

10. The declaration of maritime labour compliance shall be attached to the maritime labour certificate. It shall have two parts:

(a) Part I shall be drawn up by the competent authority which shall: (i) identify the list of matters to be inspected in accordance with paragraph 1 of this Standard; (ii) identify the national requirements embodying the relevant provisions of this Convention by providing a reference to the relevant national legal provisions as well as, to the extent necessary, concise information on the main content of the national requirements; (iii) refer to ship-type specific requirements under national legislation; (iv) record any substantially equivalent provisions adopted pursuant to paragraph 3 of Article VI; and (v) clearly indicate any exemption granted by the competent authority as provided in Title 3; and

(b) Part II shall be drawn up by the shipowner and shall identify the measures adopted to ensure ongoing compliance with the national requirements between inspections and the measures proposed to ensure that there is continuous improvement.

The competent authority or recognized organization duly authorized for this purpose shall certify Part II and shall issue the declaration of maritime labour compliance.

11. The results of all subsequent inspections or other verifications carried out with respect to the ship concerned and any significant deficiencies found during any such verification shall be recorded, together with the date when the deficiencies were found to have been remedied. This record, accompanied by an English-language translation where it is not in English, shall, in accordance with national laws or regulations, be inscribed upon or appended to the declaration of maritime labour compliance or made available in some other way to seafarers, flag State inspectors, authorized officers in port States and shipowners' and seafarers' representatives.

12. A current valid maritime labour certificate and declaration of maritime labour compliance, accompanied by an English-language translation where it is not in English, shall be carried on the ship and a copy shall be posted in a conspicuous place on board where it is available to the seafarers. A copy shall be made available in accordance with national laws and regulations, upon request, to seafarers, flag State inspectors, authorized officers in port States, and shipowners' and seafarers' representatives.

13. The requirement for an English-language translation in paragraphs 11 and 12 of this Standard does not apply in the case of a ship not engaged in an international voyage.

14. A certificate issued under paragraph 1 or 5 of this Standard shall cease to be valid in any of the following cases:

(a) if the relevant inspections are not completed within the periods specified under paragraph 2 of this Standard;

(b) if the certificate is not endorsed in accordance with paragraph 2 of this Standard;

(c) when a ship changes flag;

(d) when a shipowner ceases to assume the responsibility for the operation of a ship; and

(e) when substantial changes have been made to the structure or equipment covered in Title 3.

15. In the case referred to in paragraph 14(c), (d) or (e) of this Standard, a new certificate shall only be issued when the competent authority or recognized organization issuing the new certificate is fully satisfied that the ship is in compliance with the requirements of this Standard.

16. A maritime labour certificate shall be withdrawn by the competent authority or the recognized organization duly authorized for this purpose by the flag State, if there is evidence that the ship concerned does not comply with the requirements of this Convention and any required corrective action has not been taken.

17. When considering whether a maritime labour certificate should be withdrawn in accordance with paragraph 16 of this Standard, the competent authority or the recognized organization shall take into account the seriousness or the frequency of the deficiencies.

Guideline B5.1.3 – Maritime labour certificate and declaration of maritime labour compliance

1. The statement of national requirements in Part I of the declaration of maritime labour compliance should include or be accompanied by references to the legislative provisions relating to seafarers' working and living conditions in each of the matters listed in Appendix A5-I. Where national legislation precisely follows the requirements stated in this Convention, a reference may be all that is necessary. Where a provision of the Convention is implemented through substantial equivalence as provided under Article VI, paragraph 3, this provision should be identified and a concise explanation should be provided. Where an exemption is granted by the competent authority as provided in Title 3, the particular provision or provisions concerned should be clearly indicated.

2. The measures referred to in Part II of the declaration of maritime labour compliance, drawn up by the shipowner, should, in particular, indicate the occasions on which ongoing compliance with particular national requirements will be verified, the persons responsible for verification, the records to be taken, as well as the procedures to be followed where non-compliance is noted. Part II may take a number of forms. It could make reference to other more comprehensive documentation covering policies and procedures relating to other aspects of the maritime sector, for example documents required by the *International Safety Management (ISM) Code* or the information required by Regulation 5 of the SOLAS Convention, Chapter XI-1 relating to the ship's Continuous Synopsis Record.

3. The measures to ensure ongoing compliance should include general international requirements for the shipowner and master to keep themselves informed of the latest advances in technology and scientific findings concerning workplace design, taking into account the inherent dangers of seafarers' work, and to inform the seafarers' representatives accordingly, thereby guaranteeing a better level of protection of the seafarers' working and living conditions on board.

4. The declaration of maritime labour compliance should, above all, be drafted in clear terms designed to help all persons concerned, such as flag State inspectors, authorized officers in port States and seafarers, to check that the requirements are being properly implemented.

5. An example of the kind of information that might be contained in a declaration of maritime labour compliance is given in Appendix B5-I.

6. When a ship changes flag as referred to in Standard A5.1.3, paragraph 14(c), and where both States concerned have ratified this Convention, the Member whose flag the ship was formerly entitled to fly should, as soon as possible, transmit to the competent authority of the other Member copies of the maritime labour certificate and the declaration of maritime labour compliance carried by the ship before the change of flag and, if applicable, copies of the relevant inspection reports if the competent authority so requests within three months after the change of flag has taken place.

Regulation 5.1.4 – Inspection and enforcement

1. Each Member shall verify, through an effective and coordinated system of regular inspections, monitoring and other control measures, that ships that fly its flag comply with the requirements of this Convention as implemented in national laws and regulations.

2. Detailed requirements regarding the inspection and enforcement system referred to in paragraph 1 of this Regulation are set out in Part A of the Code.

Standard A5.1.4 – Inspection and enforcement

1. Each Member shall maintain a system of inspection of the conditions for seafarers on ships that fly its flag which shall include verification that the measures relating to working and living conditions as set out in the declaration of maritime labour compliance, where applicable, are being followed, and that the requirements of this Convention are met.

2. The competent authority shall appoint a sufficient number of qualified inspectors to fulfil its responsibilities under paragraph 1 of this Standard. Where recognized organizations have been authorized to carry out inspections, the Member shall require that personnel carrying out the inspection are qualified to undertake these duties and shall provide them with the necessary legal authority to perform their duties.

3. Adequate provision shall be made to ensure that the inspectors have the training, competence, terms of reference, powers, status and independence necessary or desirable so as to enable them to carry out the verification and ensure the compliance referred to in paragraph 1 of this Standard.

4. Inspections shall take place at the intervals required by Standard A5.1.3, where applicable. The interval shall in no case exceed three years.

5. If a Member receives a complaint which it does not consider manifestly unfounded or obtains evidence that a ship that flies its flag does not conform to the requirements of this Convention or that there are serious deficiencies in the implementation of the measures set out in the declaration of maritime labour compliance, the Member shall take the steps necessary to investigate the matter and ensure that action is taken to remedy any deficiencies found.

6. Adequate rules shall be provided and effectively enforced by each Member in order to guarantee that inspectors have the status and conditions of service to ensure that they are independent of changes of government and of improper external influences.

7. Inspectors, issued with clear guidelines as to the tasks to be performed and provided with proper credentials, shall be empowered:

(a) to board a ship that flies the Member's flag;

(b) to carry out any examination, test or inquiry which they may consider necessary in order to satisfy themselves that the standards are being strictly observed; and

(c) to require that any deficiency is remedied and, where they have grounds to believe that deficiencies constitute a serious breach of the requirements of this

Convention (including seafarers' rights), or represent a significant danger to seafarers' safety, health or security, to prohibit a ship from leaving port until necessary actions are taken.

8. Any action taken pursuant to paragraph 7(c) of this Standard shall be subject to any right of appeal to a judicial or administrative authority.

9. Inspectors shall have the discretion to give advice instead of instituting or recommending proceedings when there is no clear breach of the requirements of this Convention that endangers the safety, health or security of the seafarers concerned and where there is no prior history of similar breaches.

10. Inspectors shall treat as confidential the source of any grievance or complaint alleging a danger or deficiency in relation to seafarers' working and living conditions or a violation of laws and regulations and give no intimation to the shipowner, the shipowner's representative or the operator of the ship that an inspection was made as a consequence of such a grievance or complaint.

11. Inspectors shall not be entrusted with duties which might, because of their number or nature, interfere with effective inspection or prejudice in any way their authority or impartiality in their relations with shipowners, seafarers or other interested parties. In particular, inspectors shall:

(a) be prohibited from having any direct or indirect interest in any operation which they are called upon to inspect; and

(b) subject to appropriate sanctions or disciplinary measures, not reveal, even after leaving service, any commercial secrets or confidential working processes or information of a personal nature which may come to their knowledge in the course of their duties.

12. Inspectors shall submit a report of each inspection to the competent authority. One copy of the report in English or in the working language of the ship shall be furnished to the master of the ship and another copy shall be posted on the ship's notice board for the information of the seafarers and, upon request, sent to their representatives.

13. The competent authority of each Member shall maintain records of inspections of the conditions for seafarers on ships that fly its flag. It shall publish an annual report on inspection activities within a reasonable time, not exceeding six months, after the end of the year.

14. In the case of an investigation pursuant to a major incident, the report shall be submitted to the competent authority as soon as practicable, but not later than one month following the conclusion of the investigation.

15. When an inspection is conducted or when measures are taken under this Standard, all reasonable efforts shall be made to avoid a ship being unreasonably detained or delayed.

16. Compensation shall be payable in accordance with national laws and regulations for any loss or damage suffered as a result of the wrongful exercise of the inspectors' powers. The burden of proof in each case shall be on the complainant.

17. Adequate penalties and other corrective measures for breaches of the requirements of this Convention (including seafarers' rights) and for obstructing

inspectors in the performance of their duties shall be provided for and effectively enforced by each Member.

Guideline B5.1.4 – Inspection and enforcement

1. The competent authority and any other service or authority wholly or partly concerned with the inspection of seafarers' working and living conditions should have the resources necessary to fulfil their functions. In particular:

(a) each Member should take the necessary measures so that duly qualified technical experts and specialists may be called upon, as needed, to assist in the work of inspectors; and

(b) inspectors should be provided with conveniently situated premises, equipment and means of transport adequate for the efficient performance of their duties.

2. The competent authority should develop a compliance and enforcement policy to ensure consistency and otherwise guide inspection and enforcement activities related to this Convention. Copies of this policy should be provided to all inspectors and relevant law-enforcement officials and should be made available to the public and shipowners and seafarers.

3. The competent authority should establish simple procedures to enable it to receive information in confidence concerning possible breaches of the requirements of this Convention (including seafarers' rights) presented by seafarers directly or by representatives of the seafarers, and permit inspectors to investigate such matters promptly, including:

(a) enabling masters, seafarers or representatives of the seafarers to request an inspection when they consider it necessary; and

(b) supplying technical information and advice to shipowners and seafarers and organizations concerned as to the most effective means of complying with the requirements of this Convention and of bringing about a continual improvement in seafarers' on-board conditions.

4. Inspectors should be fully trained and sufficient in numbers to secure the efficient discharge of their duties with due regard to:

(a) the importance of the duties which the inspectors have to perform, in particular the number, nature and size of ships subject to inspection and the number and complexity of the legal provisions to be enforced;

(b) the resources placed at the disposal of the inspectors; and

(c) the practical conditions under which inspections must be carried out in order to be effective.

5. Subject to any conditions for recruitment to the public service which may be prescribed by national laws and regulations, inspectors should have qualifications and adequate training to perform their duties and where possible should have a maritime education or experience as a seafarer. They should have adequate knowledge of seafarers' working and living conditions and of the English language.

6. Measures should be taken to provide inspectors with appropriate further training during their employment.

7. All inspectors should have a clear understanding of the circumstances in which an inspection should be carried out, the scope of the inspection to be carried out in the various circumstances referred to and the general method of inspection.

8. Inspectors provided with proper credentials under the national law should at a minimum be empowered:

(a) to board ships freely and without previous notice; however, when commencing the ship inspection, inspectors should provide notification of their presence to the master or person in charge and, where appropriate, to the seafarers or their representatives;

(b) to question the master, seafarer or any other person, including the shipowner or the shipowner's representative, on any matter concerning the application of the requirements under laws and regulations, in the presence of any witness that the person may have requested;

(c) to require the production of any books, log books, registers, certificates or other documents or information directly related to matters subject to inspection, in order to verify compliance with the national laws and regulations implementing this Convention;

(d) to enforce the posting of notices required under the national laws and regulations implementing this Convention;

(e) to take or remove, for the purpose of analysis, samples of products, cargo, drinking water, provisions, materials and substances used or handled;

(f) following an inspection, to bring immediately to the attention of the shipowner, the operator of the ship or the master, deficiencies which may affect the health and safety of those on board ship;

(g) to alert the competent authority and, if applicable, the recognized organization to any deficiency or abuse not specifically covered by existing laws or regulations and submit proposals to them for the improvement of the laws or regulations; and

(h) to notify the competent authority of any occupational injuries or diseases affecting seafarers in such cases and in such manner as may be prescribed by laws and regulations.

9. When a sample referred to in paragraph 8(e) of this Guideline is being taken or removed, the shipowner or the shipowner's representative, and where appropriate a seafarer, should be notified or should be present at the time the sample is taken or removed. The quantity of such a sample should be properly recorded by the inspector.

10. The annual report published by the competent authority of each Member, in respect of ships that fly its flag, should contain:

(a) a list of laws and regulations in force relevant to seafarers' working and living conditions and any amendments which have come into effect during the year;

(b) details of the organization of the system of inspection;

(c) statistics of ships or other premises subject to inspection and of ships and other premises actually inspected;

(d) statistics on all seafarers subject to its national laws and regulations;

(e) statistics and information on violations of legislation, penalties imposed and cases of detention of ships; and

(f) statistics on reported occupational injuries and diseases affecting seafarers.

Regulation 5.1.5 – On-board complaint procedures

1. Each Member shall require that ships that fly its flag have on-board procedures for the fair, effective and expeditious handling of seafarer complaints alleging breaches of the requirements of this Convention (including seafarers' rights).

2. Each Member shall prohibit and penalize any kind of victimization of a seafarer for filing a complaint.

3. The provisions in this Regulation and related sections of the Code are without prejudice to a seafarer's right to seek redress through whatever legal means the seafarer considers appropriate.

Standard A5.1.5 – On-board complaint procedures

1. Without prejudice to any wider scope that may be given in national laws or regulations or collective agreements, the on-board procedures may be used by seafarers to lodge complaints relating to any matter that is alleged to constitute a breach of the requirements of this Convention (including seafarers' rights).

2. Each Member shall ensure that, in its laws or regulations, appropriate on board complaint procedures are in place to meet the requirements of Regulation 5.1.5. Such procedures shall seek to resolve complaints at the lowest level possible. However, in all cases, seafarers shall have a right to complain directly to the master and, where they consider it necessary, to appropriate external authorities.

3. The on-board complaint procedures shall include the right of the seafarer to be accompanied or represented during the complaints procedure, as well as safeguards against the possibility of victimization of seafarers for filing complaints. The term "victimization" covers any adverse action taken by any person with respect to a seafarer for lodging a complaint which is not manifestly vexatious or maliciously made.

4. In addition to a copy of their seafarers' employment agreement, all seafarers shall be provided with a copy of the on-board complaint procedures applicable on the ship. This shall include contact information for the competent authority in the flag State and, where different, in the seafarers' country of residence, and the name of a person or persons on board the ship who can, on a confidential basis, provide seafarers with impartial advice on their complaint and otherwise assist them in following the complaint procedures available to them on board the ship.

Guideline B5.1.5 – On-board complaint procedures

1. Subject to any relevant provisions of an applicable collective agreement, the competent authority should, in close consultation with shipowners' and seafarers' organizations, develop a model for fair, expeditious and well-documented on-board complaint-handling procedures for all ships that fly the Member's flag. In developing these procedures the following matters should be considered:

(a) many complaints may relate specifically to those individuals to whom the complaint is to be made or even to the master of the ship. In all cases seafarers should also be able to complain directly to the master and to make a complaint externally; and

(b) in order to help avoid problems of victimization of seafarers making complaints about matters under this Convention, the procedures should encourage the nomination of a person on board who can advise seafarers on the procedures available to them and, if requested by the complainant seafarer, also attend any meetings or hearings into the subject matter of the complaint.

2. At a minimum the procedures discussed during the consultative process referred to in paragraph 1 of this Guideline should include the following:

(a) complaints should be addressed to the head of the department of the seafarer lodging the complaint or to the seafarer's superior officer;

(b) the head of department or superior officer should then attempt to resolve the matter within prescribed time limits appropriate to the seriousness of the issues involved;

(c) if the head of department or superior officer cannot resolve the complaint to the satisfaction of the seafarer, the latter may refer it to the master, who should handle the matter personally;

(d) seafarers should at all times have the right to be accompanied and to be represented by another seafarer of their choice on board the ship concerned;

(e) all complaints and the decisions on them should be recorded and a copy provided to the seafarer concerned;

(f) if a complaint cannot be resolved on board, the matter should be referred ashore to the shipowner, who should be given an appropriate time limit for resolving the matter, where appropriate, in consultation with the seafarers concerned or any person they may appoint as their representative; and

(g) in all cases seafarers should have a right to file their complaints directly with the master and the shipowner and competent authorities.

Regulation 5.1.6 – Marine casualties

1. Each Member shall hold an official inquiry into any serious marine casualty, leading to injury or loss of life, that involves a ship that flies its flag. The final report of an inquiry shall normally be made public.

2. Members shall cooperate with each other to facilitate the investigation of serious marine casualties referred to in paragraph 1 of this Regulation.

Standard A5.1.6 – Marine casualties

(No provisions)

Guideline B5.1.6 – Marine casualties

(No provisions)

Regulation 5.2 – Port State responsibilities

Purpose: To enable each Member to implement its responsibilities under this Convention regarding international cooperation in the implementation and enforcement of the Convention standards on foreign ships

Regulation 5.2.1 – Inspections in port

1. Every foreign ship calling, in the normal course of its business or for operational reasons, in the port of a Member may be the subject of inspection in accordance with paragraph 4 of Article V for the purpose of reviewing compliance with the requirements of this Convention (including seafarers' rights) relating to the working and living conditions of seafarers on the ship.

2. Each Member shall accept the maritime labour certificate and the declaration of maritime labour compliance required under Regulation 5.1.3 as prima facie evidence of compliance with the requirements of this Convention (including seafarers' rights). Accordingly, the inspection in its ports shall, except in the circumstances specified in the Code, be limited to a review of the certificate and declaration.

3. Inspections in a port shall be carried out by authorized officers in accordance with the provisions of the Code and other applicable international arrangements governing port State control inspections in the Member. Any such inspection shall be limited to verifying that the matter inspected is in conformity with the relevant requirements set out in the Articles and Regulations of this Convention and in Part A only of the Code.

4. Inspections that may be carried out in accordance with this Regulation shall be based on an effective port State inspection and monitoring system to help ensure that the working and living conditions for seafarers on ships entering a port of the Member concerned meet the requirements of this Convention (including seafarers' rights).

5. Information about the system referred to in paragraph 4 of this Regulation, including the method used for assessing its effectiveness, shall be included in the Member's reports pursuant to article 22 of the Constitution.

Standard A5.2.1 – Inspections in port

1. Where an authorized officer, having come on board to carry out an inspection and requested, where applicable, the maritime labour certificate and the declaration of maritime labour compliance, finds that:

(a) the required documents are not produced or maintained or are falsely maintained or that the documents produced do not contain the information required by this Convention or are otherwise invalid; or

(b) there are clear grounds for believing that the working and living conditions on the ship do not conform to the requirements of this Convention; or

(c) there are reasonable grounds to believe that the ship has changed flag for the purpose of avoiding compliance with this Convention; or

(d) there is a complaint alleging that specific working and living conditions on the ship do not conform to the requirements of this Convention;

a more detailed inspection may be carried out to ascertain the working and living conditions on board the ship. Such inspection shall in any case be carried out where the working and living conditions believed or alleged to be defective could constitute a clear hazard to the safety, health or security of seafarers or where the authorized officer has grounds to believe that any deficiencies constitute a serious breach of the requirements of this Convention (including seafarers' rights).

2. Where a more detailed inspection is carried out on a foreign ship in the port of a Member by authorized officers in the circumstances set out in subparagraph (a), (b) or (c) of paragraph 1 of this Standard, it shall in principle cover the matters listed in Appendix A5-III.

3. In the case of a complaint under paragraph 1(d) of this Standard, the inspection shall generally be limited to matters within the scope of the complaint, although a complaint, or its investigation, may provide clear grounds for a detailed inspection in accordance with paragraph 1(b) of this Standard. For the purpose of paragraph 1(d) of this Standard, "complaint" means information submitted by a seafarer, a professional body, an association, a trade union or, generally, any person with an interest in the safety of the ship, including an interest in safety or health hazards to seafarers on board.

4. Where, following a more detailed inspection, the working and living conditions on the ship are found not to conform to the requirements of this Convention, the authorized officer shall forthwith bring the deficiencies to the attention of the master of the ship, with required deadlines for their rectification. In the event that such deficiencies are considered by the authorized officer to be significant, or if they relate to a complaint made in accordance with paragraph 3 of this Standard, the authorized officer shall bring the deficiencies to the attention of the appropriate seafarers' and shipowners' organizations in the Member in which the inspection is carried out, and may:

(a) notify a representative of the flag State;

(b) provide the competent authorities of the next port of call with the relevant information.

5. The Member in which the inspection is carried out shall have the right to transmit a copy of the officer's report, which must be accompanied by any reply received from the competent authorities of the flag State within the prescribed deadline, to the Director-General of the International Labour Office with a view to such action as may be considered appropriate and expedient in order to ensure that a

record is kept of such information and that it is brought to the attention of parties which might be interested in availing themselves of relevant recourse procedures.

6. Where, following a more detailed inspection by an authorized officer, the ship is found not to conform to the requirements of this Convention and:

(a) the conditions on board are clearly hazardous to the safety, health or security of seafarers; or

(b) the non-conformity constitutes a serious or repeated breach of the requirements of this Convention (including seafarers' rights);

the authorized officer shall take steps to ensure that the ship shall not proceed to sea until any non-conformities that fall within the scope of subparagraph (a) or (b) of this paragraph have been rectified, or until the authorized officer has accepted a plan of action to rectify such non-conformities and is satisfied that the plan will be implemented in an expeditious manner. If the ship is prevented from sailing, the authorized officer shall forthwith notify the flag State accordingly and invite a representative of the flag State to be present, if possible, requesting the flag State to reply within a prescribed deadline. The authorized officer shall also inform forthwith the appropriate shipowners' and seafarers' organizations in the port State in which the inspection was carried out.

7. Each Member shall ensure that its authorized officers are given guidance, of the kind indicated in Part B of the Code, as to the kinds of circumstances justifying detention of a ship under paragraph 6 of this Standard.

8. When implementing their responsibilities under this Standard, each Member shall make all possible efforts to avoid a ship being unduly detained or delayed. If a ship is found to be unduly detained or delayed, compensation shall be paid for any loss or damage suffered. The burden of proof in each case shall be on the complainant.

Guideline B5.2.1 – Inspections in port

1. The competent authority should develop an inspection policy for authorized officers carrying out inspections under Regulation 5.2.1. The objective of the policy should be to ensure consistency and to otherwise guide inspection and enforcement activities related to the requirements of this Convention (including seafarers' rights). Copies of this policy should be provided to all authorized officers and should be available to the public and shipowners and seafarers.

2. When developing a policy relating to the circumstances warranting a detention of the ship under Standard A5.2.1, paragraph 6, of the competent authority should consider that, with respect to the breaches referred to in Standard A5.2.1, paragraph 6(b), the seriousness could be due to the nature of the deficiency concerned. This would be particularly relevant in the case of the violation of fundamental rights and principles or seafarers' employment and social rights under Articles III and IV. For example, the employment of a person who is under age should be considered as a serious breach even if there is only one such person on board. In other cases, the number of different defects found during a particular inspection should be taken into account: for example, several instances of defects relating to accommodation or food and catering which do not threaten safety or

health might be needed before they should be considered as constituting a serious breach.

3. Members should cooperate with each other to the maximum extent possible in the adoption of internationally agreed guidelines on inspection policies, especially those relating to the circumstances warranting the detention of a ship.

Regulation 5.2.2 – Onshore seafarer complaint-handling procedures

1. Each Member shall ensure that seafarers on ships calling at a port in the Member's territory who allege a breach of the requirements of this Convention (including seafarers' rights) have the right to report such a complaint in order to facilitate a prompt and practical means of redress.

Standard A5.2.2 – Onshore seafarer complaint-handling procedures

1. A complaint by a seafarer alleging a breach of the requirements of this Convention (including seafarers' rights) may be reported to an authorized officer in the port at which the seafarer's ship has called. In such cases, the authorized officer shall undertake an initial investigation.

2. Where appropriate, given the nature of the complaint, the initial investigation shall include consideration of whether the on-board complaint procedures provided under Regulation 5.1.5 have been explored. The authorized officer may also conduct a more detailed inspection in accordance with Standard A5.2.1.

3. The authorized officer shall, where appropriate, seek to promote a resolution of the complaint at the ship-board level.

4. In the event that the investigation or the inspection provided under this Standard reveals a non-conformity that falls within the scope of paragraph 6 of Standard A5.2.1, the provisions of that paragraph shall be applied.

5. Where the provisions of paragraph 4 of this Standard do not apply, and the complaint has not been resolved at the ship-board level, the authorized officer shall forthwith notify the flag State, seeking, within a prescribed deadline, advice and a corrective plan of action.

6. Where the complaint has not been resolved following action taken in accordance with paragraph 5 of this Standard, the port State shall transmit a copy of the authorized officer's report to the Director-General. The report must be accompanied by any reply received within the prescribed deadline from the competent authority of the flag State. The appropriate shipowners' and seafarers' organizations in the port State shall be similarly informed. In addition, statistics and information regarding complaints that have been resolved shall be regularly submitted by the port State to the Director-General. Both such submissions are provided in order that, on the basis of such action as may be considered appropriate and expedient, a record is kept of such information and is brought to the attention of parties, including shipowners' and seafarers' organizations, which might be interested in availing themselves of relevant recourse procedures.

7. Appropriate steps shall be taken to safeguard the confidentiality of complaints made by seafarers.

Guideline B5.2.2 – Onshore seafarer complaint-handling procedures

1. Where a complaint referred to in Standard A5.2.2 is dealt with by an authorized officer, the officer should first check whether the complaint is of a general nature which concerns all seafarers on the ship, or a category of them, or whether it relates only to the individual case of the seafarer concerned.

2. If the complaint is of a general nature, consideration should be given to undertaking a more detailed inspection in accordance with Standard A5.2.1.

3. If the complaint relates to an individual case, an examination of the results of any on-board complaint procedures for the resolution of the complaint concerned should be undertaken. If such procedures have not been explored, the authorized officer should suggest that the complainant take advantage of any such procedures available. There should be good reasons for considering a complaint before any on-board complaint procedures have been explored. These would include the inadequacy of, or undue delay in, the internal procedures or the complainant's fear of reprisal for lodging a complaint.

4. In any investigation of a complaint, the authorized officer should give the master, the shipowner and any other person involved in the complaint a proper opportunity to make known their views.

5. In the event that the flag State demonstrates, in response to the notification by the port State in accordance with paragraph 5 of Standard A5.2.2, that it will handle the matter, and that it has in place effective procedures for this purpose and has submitted an acceptable plan of action, the authorized officer may refrain from any further involvement with the complaint.

Regulation 5.3 – Labour-supplying responsibilities

Purpose: To ensure that each Member implements its responsibilities under this Convention as pertaining to seafarer recruitment and placement and the social protection of its seafarers

1. Without prejudice to the principle of each Member's responsibility for the working and living conditions of seafarers on ships that fly its flag, the Member also has a responsibility to ensure the implementation of the requirements of this Convention regarding the recruitment and placement of seafarers as well as the social security protection of seafarers that are its nationals or are resident or are otherwise domiciled in its territory, to the extent that such responsibility is provided for in this Convention.

2. Detailed requirements for the implementation of paragraph 1 of this Regulation are found in the Code.

3. Each Member shall establish an effective inspection and monitoring system for enforcing its labour-supplying responsibilities under this Convention.

4. Information about the system referred to in paragraph 3 of this Regulation, including the method used for assessing its effectiveness, shall be included in the Member's reports pursuant to article 22 of the Constitution.

Standard A5.3 – Labour-supplying responsibilities

1. Each Member shall enforce the requirements of this Convention applicable to the operation and practice of seafarer recruitment and placement services established on its territory through a system of inspection and monitoring and legal proceedings for breaches of licensing and other operational requirements provided for in Standard A1.4.

Guideline B5.3 – Labour-supplying responsibilities

1. Private seafarer recruitment and placement services established in the Member's territory and securing the services of a seafarer for a shipowner, wherever located, should be required to assume obligations to ensure the proper fulfilment by shipowners of the terms of their employment agreements concluded with seafarers.

APPENDIX A5-I

The working and living conditions of seafarers that must be inspected and approved by the flag State before certifying a ship in accordance with Standard A5.1.3, paragraph 1:

Minimum age

Medical certification

Qualifications of seafarers

Seafarers' employment agreements

Use of any licensed or certified or regulated private recruitment and placement service

Hours of work or rest

Manning levels for the ship

Accommodation

On-board recreational facilities

Food and catering

Health and safety and accident prevention

On-board medical care

On-board complaint procedures

Payment of wages

Appendix A5-II

Maritime Labour Certificate

(Note: This Certificate shall have a Declaration of Maritime Labour Compliance attached)

Issued under the provisions of Article V and Title 5 of the Maritime Labour Convention, 2006 (referred to below as "the Convention") under the authority of the Government of:

....

(full designation of the State whose flag the ship is entitled to fly)

by ....

(full designation and address of the competent authority or recognized organization duly authorized under the provisions of the Convention)

Particulars of the ship

Name of ship ....

Distinctive number or letters ....

Port of registry ....

Date of registry ....

Gross tonnage [1] ....

IMO number ....

Type of ship ....

Name and address of the shipowner [2] ....

....

....

[1] For ships covered by the tonnage measurement interim scheme adopted by the IMO, the gross tonnage is that which is included in the REMARKS column of the International Tonnage Certificate (1969). See Article II(1)(c) of the Convention.

[2] *Shipowner* means the owner of the ship or another organization or person, such as the manager, agent or bareboat charterer, who has assumed the responsibility for the operation of the ship from the owner and who, on assuming such responsibility, has agreed to take over the duties and responsibilities imposed on shipowners in accordance with this Convention, regardless of whether any other organizations or persons fulfil certain of the duties or responsibilities on behalf of the shipowner. See Article II(1)(j) of the Convention.

This is to certify:

1. That this ship has been inspected and verified to be in compliance with the requirements of the Convention, and the provisions of the attached Declaration of Maritime Labour Compliance.

2. That the seafarers' working and living conditions specified in Appendix A5-I of the Convention were found to correspond to the abovementioned country's national requirements implementing the Convention. These national requirements are summarized in the Declaration of Maritime Labour Compliance, Part I.

This Certificate is valid until .... subject to inspections in accordance with Standards A5.1.3 and A5.1.4 of the Convention.

This Certificate is valid only when the Declaration of Maritime Labour Compliance issued

at .... on .... is attached.

Completion date of the inspection on which this Certificate is based was ....

Issued at .... on ....

Signature of the duly authorized official issuing the Certificate

(Seal or stamp of issuing authority, as appropriate)

Endorsements for mandatory intermediate inspection and, if required, any additional inspection

This is to certify that the ship was inspected in accordance with Standards A5.1.3 and A5.1.4 of the Convention and that the seafarers' working and living conditions specified in Appendix A5-I of the Convention were found to correspond to the abovementioned country's national requirements implementing the Convention.

Intermediate inspection:
(to be completed between the second and third anniversary dates)

Signed ....
(Signature of authorized official)

Place ....

Date ....
(Seal or stamp of the authority, as appropriate)

Additional endorsements (if required)

This is to certify that the ship was the subject of an additional inspection for the purpose of verifying that the ship continued to be in compliance with the national requirements implementing the Convention, as required by Standard A3.1, paragraph 3, of the Convention (re-registration or substantial alteration of accommodation) or for other reasons.

Additional inspection:
(if required)

Signed ....
(Signature of authorized official)

Place ....

Date ....
(Seal or stamp of the authority, as appropriate)

Additional inspection:
(if required)

Signed ....
(Signature of authorized official)

Place ....

Date ....
(Seal or stamp of the authority,
as appropriate)

Additional inspection:
(if required)

Signed ....
(Signature of authorized official)

Place ....

Date ....
(Seal or stamp of the authority,
as appropriate)

Maritime Labour Convention, 2006

Declaration of Maritime Labour Compliance – Part I

(Note: This Declaration must be attached to the ship's Maritime Labour Certificate)

Issued under the authority of: .... *(insert name of competent authority as defined in Article II, paragraph 1(a), of the Convention)*

With respect to the provisions of the Maritime Labour Convention, 2006, the following referenced ship:

Name of ship	IMO number	Gross tonnage

is maintained in accordance with Standard A5.1.3 of the Convention.

The undersigned declares, on behalf of the abovementioned competent authority, that:

(a) the provisions of the Maritime Labour Convention are fully embodied in the national requirements referred to below;

(b) these national requirements are contained in the national provisions referenced below; explanations concerning the content of those provisions are provided where necessary;

(c) the details of any substantial equivalencies under Article VI, paragraphs 3 and 4, are provided <under the corresponding national requirement listed below> <in the section provided for this purpose below> *(strike out the statement which is not applicable)*;

(d) any exemptions granted by the competent authority in accordance with Title 3 are clearly indicated in the section provided for this purpose below; and

(e) any ship-type specific requirements under national legislation are also referenced under the requirements concerned.

1. Minimum age (Regulation 1.1)
2. Medical certification (Regulation 1.2)
3. Qualifications of seafarers (Regulation 1.3) ....
4. Seafarers' employment agreements (Regulation 2.1) ....
5. Use of any licensed or certified or regulated private recruitment and placement service (Regulation 1.4) ....
6. Hours of work or rest (Regulation 2.3) ....
7. Manning levels for the ship (Regulation 2.7) ....
8. Accommodation (Regulation 3.1) ....
9. On-board recreational facilities (Regulation 3.1) ....
10. Food and catering (Regulation 3.2) ....
11. Health and safety and accident prevention (Regulation 4.3) ....
12. On-board medical care (Regulation 4.1) ....

13. On-board complaint procedures (Regulation 5.1.5) ....

14. Payment of wages (Regulation 2.2) ....

Name: ....

Title: ....

Signature: ....

Place: ....

Date: ....

(Seal or stamp of the authority, as appropriate)

Substantial equivalencies

(Note: Strike out the statement which is not applicable)

The following substantial equivalencies, as provided under Article VI, paragraphs 3 and 4, of the Convention, except where stated above, are noted *(insert description if applicable)*:

....

....

No equivalency has been granted.

Name: ....

Title: ....

Signature: ....

Place: ....

Date: ....

(Seal or stamp of the authority, as appropriate)

Exemptions

(Note: Strike out the statement which is not applicable)

The following exemptions granted by the competent authority as provided in Title 3 of the Convention are noted:

....

....

No exemption has been granted.

Name: ....

Title: ....

Signature: ....

Place: ....

Date: ....

(Seal or stamp of the authority,
as appropriate)

Declaration of Maritime Labour Compliance – Part II

Measures adopted to ensure ongoing compliance between inspections

The following measures have been drawn up by the shipowner, named in the Maritime Labour Certificate to which this Declaration is attached, to ensure ongoing compliance between inspections:

(State below the measures drawn up to ensure compliance with each of the items in Part I)

1. Minimum age (Regulation 1.1) ☐

   ....

2. Medical certification (Regulation 1.2) ☐

   ....

3. Qualifications of seafarers (Regulation 1.3) ☐

   ....

4. Seafarers' employment agreements (Regulation 2.1) ☐

   ....

5. Use of any licensed or certified or regulated private recruitment and placement service (Regulation 1.4) ☐

   ....

6. Hours of work or rest (Regulation 2.3) ☐

   ....

7. Manning levels for the ship (Regulation 2.7) ☐

   ....

8. Accommodation (Regulation 3.1) ☐

   ....

9. On-board recreational facilities (Regulation 3.1) ☐

   ....

10. Food and catering (Regulation 3.2) ☐

    ....

11. Health and safety and accident prevention (Regulation 4.3) ☐

    ....

12. On-board medical care (Regulation 4.1) ☐

    ....

13. On-board complaint procedures (Regulation 5.1.5) ☐

    ....

14. Payment of wages (Regulation 2.2) ☐

    ....

I hereby certify that the above measures have been drawn up to ensure ongoing compliance, between inspections, with the requirements listed in Part I.

Name of shipowner: [1] ....

....

Company address: ....

....

Name of the authorized signatory: ....

....

Title: ....

Signature of the authorized signatory:

....

Date: ....

(Stamp or seal of the shipowner)[1]

The above measures have been reviewed by *(insert name of competent authority or duly recognized organization)* and, following inspection of the ship, have been determined as meeting the purposes set out under Standard A5.1.3, paragraph 10(b), regarding measures to ensure initial and ongoing compliance with the requirements set out in Part I of this Declaration.

Name: ....

Title: ....

Address: ....

....

....

Signature: ....

Place: ....

Date: ....

(Seal or stamp of the authority, as appropriate)

---

[1] *Shipowner* means the owner of the ship or another organization or person, such as the manager, agent or bareboat charterer, who has assumed the responsibility for the operation of the ship from the owner and who, on assuming such responsibility, has agreed to take over the duties and responsibilities imposed on shipowners in accordance with this Convention, regardless of whether any other organizations or persons fulfil certain of the duties or responsibilities on behalf of the shipowner. See Article II(1)(j) of the Convention.

Interim Maritime Labour Certificate

Issued under the provisions of Article V and Title 5 of the
Maritime Labour Convention, 2006
(referred to below as "the Convention")
under the authority of the Government of:

....

(full designation of the State whose flag the ship is entitled to fly)

by ....

(full designation and address of the competent authority or recognized organization duly authorized under the provisions of the Convention)

Particulars of the ship

Name of ship ....

Distinctive number or letters ....

Port of registry ....

Date of registry ....

Gross tonnage [1] ....

IMO number ....

Type of ship ....

Name and address of the shipowner [2] ....

....

This is to certify, for the purposes of Standard A5.1.3, paragraph 7, of the Convention, that:

(a) this ship has been inspected, as far as reasonable and practicable, for the matters listed in Appendix A5-I to the Convention, taking into account verification of items under (b), (c) and (d) below;

(b) the shipowner has demonstrated to the competent authority or recognized organization that the ship has adequate procedures to comply with the Convention;

(c) the master is familiar with the requirements of the Convention and the responsibilities for implementation; and

(d) relevant information has been submitted to the competent authority or recognized organization to produce a Declaration of Maritime Labour Compliance.

---

[1] For ships covered by the tonnage measurement interim scheme adopted by the IMO, the gross tonnage is that which is included in the REMARKS column of the International Tonnage Certificate (1969). See Article II(1)(c) of the Convention.

[2] *Shipowner* means the owner of the ship or another organization or person, such as the manager, agent or bareboat charterer, who has assumed the responsibility for the operation of the ship from the owner and who, on assuming such responsibility, has agreed to take over the duties and responsibilities imposed on shipowners in accordance with this Convention, regardless of whether any other organizations or persons fulfil certain of the duties or responsibilities on behalf of the shipowner. See Article II(1)(j) of the Convention.

This Certificate is valid until .... subject to inspections in accordance with Standards A5.1.3 and A5.1.4.

Completion date of the inspection referred to under (a) above was ....

Issued at .... on ....

Signature of the duly authorized official
issuing the interim certificate ....

(Seal or stamp of issuing authority, as appropriate)

Appendix A5-III

General areas that are subject to a detailed inspection by an authorized officer in a port of a Member carrying out a port State inspection pursuant to Standard A5.2.1:

Minimum age

Medical certification

Qualifications of seafarers

Seafarers' employment agreements

Use of any licensed or certified or regulated private recruitment and placement service

Hours of work or rest

Manning levels for the ship

Accommodation

On-board recreational facilities

Food and catering

Health and safety and accident prevention

On-board medical care

On-board complaint procedures

Payment of wages

APPENDIX B5-I – EXAMPLE OF A NATIONAL DECLARATION

See Guideline B5.1.3, paragraph 5

Maritime Labour Convention, 2006

Declaration of Maritime Labour Compliance – Part I

(Note: This Declaration must be attached to the ship's Maritime Labour Certificate)

Issued under the authority of: **The Ministry of Maritime Transport of Xxxxxx**

With respect to the provisions of the Maritime Labour Convention, 2006, the following referenced ship:

Name of ship	IMO number	Gross tonnage
M.S. EXAMPLE	12345	1,000

is maintained in accordance with Standard A5.1.3 of the Convention.

The undersigned declares, on behalf of the abovementioned competent authority, that:

(a) the provisions of the Maritime Labour Convention are fully embodied in the national requirements referred to below;

(b) these national requirements are contained in the national provisions referenced below; explanations concerning the content of those provisions are provided where necessary;

(c) the details of any substantial equivalencies under Article VI, paragraphs 3 and 4, are provided <under the corresponding national requirement listed below> <in the section provided for this purpose below> *(strike out the statement which is not applicable)*;

(d) any exemptions granted by the competent authority in accordance with Title 3 are clearly indicated in the section provided for this purpose below; and

(e) any ship-type specific requirements under national legislation are also referenced under the requirements concerned.

1. Minimum age (Regulation 1.1)

   Shipping Law, No. 123 of 1905, as amended ("Law"), Chapter X; Shipping Regulations ("Regulations"), 2006, Rules 1111-1222.

   Minimum ages are those referred to in the Convention.

   "Night" means 9 p.m. to 6 a.m. unless the Ministry of Maritime Transport ("Ministry") approves a different period.

   Examples of hazardous work restricted to 18-year-olds or over are listed in Schedule A hereto. In the case of cargo ships, no one under 18 may work in the areas marked on the ship's plan (to be attached to this Declaration) as "hazardous area".

2. **Medical certification (Regulation 1.2)**

Law, Chapter XI; Regulations, Rules 1223-1233.

Medical certificates shall conform to the STCW requirements, where applicable; in other cases, the STCW requirements are applied with any necessary adjustments.

Qualified opticians on list approved by Ministry may issue certificates concerning eyesight.

Medical examinations follow the ILO/WHO Guidelines referred to in Guideline B1.2.1

....

....

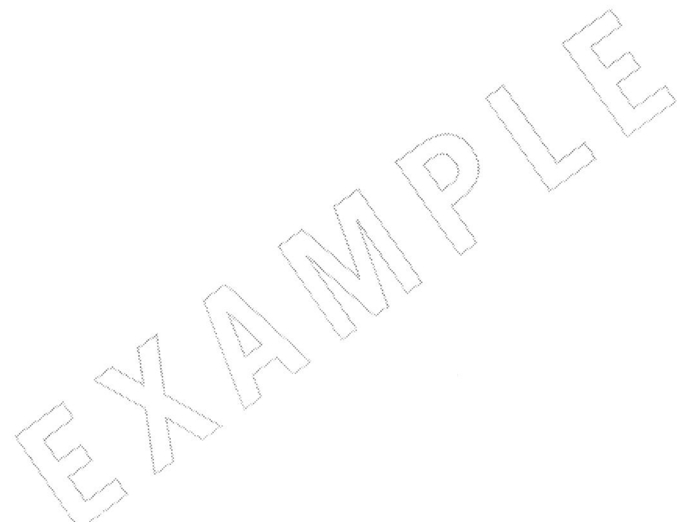

Declaration of Maritime Labour Compliance – Part II

Measures adopted to ensure ongoing compliance between inspections

The following measures have been drawn up by the shipowner, named in the Maritime Labour Certificate to which this Declaration is attached, to ensure ongoing compliance between inspections:

(State below the measures drawn up to ensure compliance with each of the items in Part I)

1. Minimum age (Regulation 1.1) [X]

   Date of birth of each seafarer is noted against his/her name on the crew list.

   The list is checked at the beginning of each voyage by the master or officer acting on his or her behalf ("competent officer"), who records the date of such verification.

   Each seafarer under 18 receives, at the time of engagement, a note prohibiting him/her from performing night work or the work specifically listed as hazardous (see Part I, section 1, above) and any other hazardous work, and requiring him/her to consult the competent officer in case of doubt. A copy of the note, with the seafarer's signature under "received and read", and the date of signature, is kept by the competent officer.

2. Medical certification (Regulation 1.2) 

   The medical certificates are kept in strict confidence by the competent officer, together with a list, prepared under the competent officer's responsibility and stating for each seafarer on board: the functions of the seafarer, the date of the current medical certificate(s) and the health status noted on the certificate concerned.

   In any case of possible doubt as to whether the seafarer is medically fit for a particular function or functions, the competent officer consults the seafarer's doctor or another qualified practitioner and records a summary of the practitioner's conclusions, as well as the practitioner's name and telephone number and the date of the consultation.

....

....

RESOLUTIONS ADOPTED BY THE INTERNATIONAL LABOUR CONFERENCE AT ITS 94TH (MARITIME) SESSION (Geneva, February 2006)

I

Resolution concerning the promotion of the Maritime Labour Convention, 2006[1]

The General Conference of the International Labour Organization,

Having adopted the Maritime Labour Convention, 2006,

Noting that the success of the Convention will depend upon its being widely ratified and the effective implementation of its requirements,

Mindful that the core mandate of the Organization is to promote decent working and living conditions,

Confirming the resolution concerning technical cooperation to strengthen the capacities of the national administrations responsible for maritime labour inspection, adopted by the Preparatory Technical Maritime Conference of the International Labour Organization (Geneva, 13-24 September 2004);

Invites the Governing Body of the International Labour Office to request the Director-General to give due priority in the allocation of resources to conducting the outstanding tripartite work required for effective implementation of the Convention,

Further invites the Governing Body to request the Director-General to give due priority in the allocation of the resources of the Organization's technical cooperation programme to promoting the ratification of the Convention and to assisting countries which request assistance in its implementation in such areas as:

- technical assistance for Members, including on capacity building for national administrations and the drafting of national legislation to meet the requirements of the Convention;

[1] Adopted on 22 February 2006.

- the development of training materials for inspectors and other staff;
- the training of inspectors;
- the development of promotional materials and advocacy tools for the Convention; and
- national and regional seminars, as well as workshops on the Convention.

II

Resolution concerning the promotion of opportunities for women seafarers[1]

The General Conference of the International Labour Organization,

Having adopted the Maritime Labour Convention, 2006,

Recalling the resolution concerning women seafarers adopted by the 29th Session of the Joint Maritime Commission,

Noting the findings of the Office's report *Women seafarers: Global employment policies and practices*,

Mindful of the mandate of the Organization to promote equality of opportunity for women and men;

Invites the Governing Body of the International Labour Office to request the Director-General to give due priority in the use of resources to examining measures which can further promote career opportunities and appropriate working and living conditions for women seafarers.

III

Resolution concerning the Joint IMO/ILO Ad Hoc Expert Working Group on Liability and Compensation regarding Claims for Death, Personal Injury and Abandonment of Seafarers[1]

The General Conference of the International Labour Organization,

Having adopted the Maritime Labour Convention, 2006,

Noting and commending the work undertaken by the Joint IMO/ILO Ad Hoc Working Group, which has the potential to make a significant contribution to ensuring decent work for seafarers,

Noting also that the Joint IMO/ILO Ad Hoc Working Group found that there was a gap in the international legal regime addressing this issue,

Considering that the text in the Convention does not address many of the provisions set out in the Guidelines on Shipowners' Responsibilities in respect of Contractual Claims for Personal Injury to or Death of Seafarers and the Guidelines on Provision of Financial Security in Cases of Abandonment

---

[1] Adopted on 22 February 2006.

of Seafarers, which have been adopted by both the Assembly of the International Maritime Organization and the Governing Body of the International Labour Office;

Believes that the Joint Ad Hoc Working Group should continue its work,

Recommends to both organizations that the way forward would be for the Joint Ad Hoc Working Group to develop a standard accompanied by guidelines, which could be included in the Maritime Labour Convention or another existing instrument, at a later date.

IV

Resolution concerning the development of guidelines for port State control[1]

The General Conference of the International Labour Organization,

Having adopted the Maritime Labour Convention, 2006,

Considering that this Convention aims to establish a new pillar of international legislation for the shipping industry,

Mindful of the core mandate of the Organization to promote decent working and living conditions,

Noting paragraphs 4 and 7 of Article V, and Regulation 5.2.1, Standard A5.2.1, Guideline B5.2.1 of the above Convention, which provide for port State responsibilities and control under the term of "no more favourable treatment",

Noting that the success of the Convention will depend, among others, upon the uniform and harmonized implementation of port State responsibilities in accordance with its relevant provisions,

Considering that, given the global nature of the shipping industry, it is important for port State control officers to receive proper guidelines for the performance of their duties,

Recognizing the work done by the IMO in this area, and the importance the international community attaches to cooperation between international agencies;

Invites the Governing Body of the International Labour Office to request the Director-General to convene a tripartite expert meeting to develop suitable guidance for port State control officers and to request that the Office utilizes the technical expertise of the IMO in this area.

V

Resolution concerning the development of international standards of medical fitness for crew members and other seafarers[1]

The General Conference of the International Labour Organization,

Having adopted the Maritime Labour Convention, 2006,

[1] Adopted on 22 February 2006.

Considering that this Convention aims to establish a new pillar of international legislation for the shipping industry,

Noting that resolution 9 of the International Convention on Standards of Training, Certification and Watchkeeping for Seafarers (STCW) 1978, as amended in 1995, invited the International Maritime Organization, in cooperation with the International Labour Organization and the World Health Organization, to develop international standards of medical fitness for seafarers,

Noting also the existing ILO/WHO Guidelines for Conducting Pre-sea and Periodic Medical Fitness Examinations for Seafarers (ILO/WHO/D.2/1997),

Recognizing the importance of seafarers being medically fit so as not to endanger their own health and safety or that of others,

Recognizing also the importance of easily understood and globally implementable medical fitness standards for seafarers in ensuring safe, environmentally sound and efficient shipping;

Invites the Governing Body of the International Labour Office to request the Director-General, in cooperation with the International Maritime Organization and the World Health Organization, to consider whether a review of the existing ILO/WHO Guidelines for Conducting Pre-Sea and Periodic Medical Fitness Examinations for Seafarers (ILO/WHO/D.2/1997) is necessary, taking into consideration whether different standards are appropriate for seafarers according to the duties they have to perform on board, and to report their recommendations to the Organization for further consideration and action as appropriate.

VI

Resolution concerning the promotion of the Seafarers' Identity Documents Convention (Revised), 2003 (No. 185)[1]

The General Conference of the International Labour Organization,

Having adopted the Maritime Labour Convention, 2006,

Having also adopted the Seafarers' Identity Documents Convention (Revised), 2003 (No. 185), at the 91st Session of the International Labour Conference,

Recalling that the 91st Session of the International Labour Conference adopted a resolution concerning decent work for seafarers, which noted, inter alia, that access to shore facilities, shore leave and facilitation of transit are vital elements of seafarers' general well-being and, therefore, to the realization of decent work for seafarers,

Mindful that the core mandate of the Organization is to promote decent working and living conditions,

[1] Adopted on 22 February 2006.

Noting the continued difficulty that seafarers experience in being able to enjoy shore leave in certain countries;

Urges the Governing Body of the International Labour Office to request the Director-General to contact all member States and remind them of the importance of the speedy ratification and implementation of ILO Convention No. 185 and to invite member States to promote decent work for seafarers and, in this regard, to permit seafarers to enjoy shore leave within their territory;

Calls for the Governing Body to remain seized of this issue.

VII

Resolution concerning information on occupational groups[1]

The General Conference of the International Labour Organization,

Having adopted the Maritime Labour Convention, 2006,

Noting that many of the maritime instruments consolidated within the Maritime Labour Convention contained different definitions of the term "seafarer",

Considering the need for clarity over the issue of the definition in the Convention,

Recognizing that situations may arise in which a Member may have doubts as to whether or not certain categories of persons who undertake periods of work on board a ship should be regarded as seafarers for the purpose of the Convention,

Recognizing also that there is need for clarification on this subject to help to provide uniformity in the application in the rights and obligations provided by the Convention,

Noting that Article II, paragraph 1(f), of the Convention provides that:

"*Seafarer* means any person who is employed or engaged or works in any capacity on board a ship to which this Convention applies",

Noting also that Article II, paragraph 3, provides that:

"In the event of doubt as to whether any categories of persons are to be regarded as seafarers for the purpose of this Convention, the question shall be determined by the competent authority in each Member after consultation with the shipowners' and seafarers' organizations concerned with this question";

Decides that the International Labour Organization should seek to ensure uniform implementation of the Convention and invites member States to maintain the intent of Article II, paragraph 1(f), through the application of Annex 1.

---

[1] Adopted on 22 February 2006.

Annex

Maritime Labour Convention, 2006

Information on occupational groups

General

The Convention recognizes in Article II, paragraph 3, that there may be doubts whether a particular category or categories of persons who may perform work on board a ship covered by the Convention should be regarded as seafarers for the purpose of the Convention.

This Annex has therefore been adopted by the General Conference of the International Labour Organization to assist administrations in resolving any difficulties that might arise.

There are persons who principally work onshore, but who occasionally spend a short period working on a ship. These may not be seafarers. There are persons who regularly spend a short period on a ship. These may be seafarers. In both cases, their work may or may not be directly concerned with the routine business of the ship.

Persons who might not be determined to be seafarers include harbour pilots and portworkers, as well as certain specialist staff such as guest entertainers, ship inspectors, superintendents and repair technicians.

Persons who regularly spend more than short periods aboard, even where they perform tasks that are not normally regarded as maritime tasks, may still be regarded as seafarers for the purpose of this Convention regardless of their position on board. For example, repair and maintenance squads and specialist ship staff engaged to work at sea on particular ships may well be regarded as seafarers and entitled to be covered by the rights and obligations provided for in this Convention.

The Convention provides seafarers with significant rights and benefits covering their working and living conditions that might not always be available to them in their home countries. Therefore, in resolving doubts about whether particular persons are seafarers, account should also be taken of the extent to which their national legal and social system provides protection for their labour standards comparable to that provided for under the Convention.

Categories

An administration may have doubts about designating a particular category of persons working on board as a seafarer under Article II, paragraph 1(f), because:

(i) the nature of their work is not part of the routine business of the ship (for example, scientists, researchers, divers, specialist offshore technicians, etc.);

(ii) although trained and qualified in maritime skills, the persons concerned perform key specialist functions that are not part of the routine business of the ship (for example, harbour pilots, inspectors or superintendents);

(iii) the work they perform is occasional and short term, with their principal place of employment being onshore (for example, guest entertainers, repair technicians, surveyors or portworkers).

A person or category of persons should not automatically be excluded from the definition of seafarers solely on account of falling within one or more of the categories listed above. These lists are simply illustrative of situations where doubts may arise.

Special factors in the situation may lead the administration to determine when a person is or is not a seafarer.

Criteria

In considering how to resolve such doubts, the following issues should be considered:

(i) the duration of the stay on board of the persons concerned;
(ii) the frequency of periods of work spent on board;
(iii) the location of the person's principal place of work;
(iv) the purpose of the person's work on board;
(v) the protection that would normally be available to the persons concerned with regard to their labour and social conditions to ensure they are comparable to that provided for under the Convention.

VIII

Resolution concerning seafarers' welfare[1]

The General Conference of the International Labour Organization,

Having adopted the Maritime Labour Convention, 2006,

Recalling the resolution concerning seafarers' welfare adopted by the 29th Session of the Joint Maritime Commission,

Mindful that the core mandate of the Organization is to promote decent working and living conditions and that seafarers' welfare facilities are important in this regard,

Considering that, given the global nature of the shipping industry, seafarers need special protection and that the provision of and access to seafarers' welfare facilities is important in this regard,

Noting that, because of the structural changes in the industry, seafarers have fewer opportunities to go ashore and, as a consequence, welfare facilities and services for seafarers are needed more than at any time,

Recognizing the vital role of the voluntary organizations and their expertise in providing welfare facilities,

Noting also that the new security regime and the denial of shore leave mean that seafarers may not be able to take advantage of welfare facilities provided for them in ports,

Noting further that the port facilities in certain countries are making excessive charges or imposing unreasonable procedures in order for seafarers to leave the ship and visit welfare facilities provided for them in ports,

Recognizing also that many governments rely solely on voluntary or charitable organizations and in many cases transfer their responsibilities to regional/local governmental bodies in order to maintain such welfare facilities and services for seafarers;

Requests the Governing Body of the International Labour Office to invite the Director-General to take all necessary measures to strongly encourage member States to ensure that seafarers on ships in their ports are able to secure access to seafarers' welfare facilities,

Requests also that the Director-General propose to the Governing Body to convene a tripartite meeting of experts to examine the provision of and difficulties in securing access to seafarers' welfare facilities.

[1] Adopted on 22 February 2006.

IX

Resolution concerning maintenance of the Joint Maritime Commission[1]

The General Conference of the International Labour Organization,

Having adopted the Maritime Labour Convention, 2006,

Noting the long history of the Joint Maritime Commission (JMC) and the important contribution it has made in addressing key issues within the shipping industry and thereby ensuring that ILO activities remain relevant to the realities of the shipping industry,

Noting also that the important contribution made by the JMC was recognized by the Governing Body of the International Labour Office at its 280th Session when it agreed to establish a JMC Subcommittee on Wages of Seafarers, which should meet every two years, without budgetary implications for the Office, in order to review the ILO minimum basic wage for an able seafarer,

Recognizing the unique role played by the JMC in promoting social dialogue within the shipping industry and that social dialogue is one of the four pillars of decent work,

Recognizing also that the adoption of the Maritime Labour Convention is of great importance in terms of regulating maritime labour standards and that there will also be a need, in the future, for the ILO to address other aspects of decent work in the shipping industry,

Considering that, given the global nature of the shipping industry, seafarers need special protection and that the JMC plays an important role in this regard;

Requests the Governing Body of the International Labour Office to ensure that this important body is adequately funded and resourced,

Invites the Director-General to ensure that adequate resources are provided for activities relating to the maritime sector within the International Labour Organization so that the continued relevance of the ILO to the sector can be maintained in the future.

X

Resolution concerning addressing the human element through international cooperation between United Nations specialized agencies[1]

The General Conference of the International Labour Organization,

Having adopted the Maritime Labour Convention, 2006,

Noting the significance of issues related to the human element in shipping,

[1] Adopted on 22 February 2006.

Mindful of the core mandate of the Organization to promote decent working and living conditions,

Recalling the resolution on this issue adopted by the 29th Session of the Joint Maritime Commission,

Recalling the cooperation agreement between the International Labour Office and the International Maritime Organization and how well it has functioned over time and the beneficial results which have resulted from the establishment of joint bodies,

Considering that the human element is multifaceted and can only be addressed in a holistic manner, and that such an endeavour would come within the core competencies of the International Labour Office and the International Maritime Organization;

Invites the Governing Body of the International Labour Office to request the Director-General to give due priority in the use of resources to promoting the role of the human element in shipping and to work with the International Maritime Organization to establish a Joint IMO/ILO Working Group on the Human Element.

XI

Resolution concerning recruitment and retention of seafarers[1]

The General Conference of the International Labour Organization,

Having adopted the Maritime Labour Convention, 2006,

Mindful that the core mandate of the Organization is to promote decent work,

Being aware that shipping is the engine of the globalized economy and carries around 90 per cent of world trade in terms of tonnage, and that the shipping industry and the smooth transportation of goods are essential to world trade, which will require the availability of a sufficient number of suitably qualified seafarers,

Being aware also that ships are crewed by suitably trained seafarers who have a crucial role in achieving safe, secure and efficient shipping on clean oceans and that it is fundamental to the sustainable operation of this strategic sector that it is able to continue to attract an adequate number of quality new entrants,

Noting that there is a projected shortage of suitably qualified seafarers, that many essential shore-based shipping positions require trained seafarers and that filling some of these positions with suitably qualified seafarers is essential to overall maritime safety,

[1] Adopted on 22 February 2006.

Noting also that traditional maritime countries are going through a process of industrial change and have lost substantial parts of their maritime skills base,

Noting further that there is a need for proper career paths for officers and ratings alike,

Considers that, while there is a need to improve the image of the shipping industry, there is also a need to improve the conditions of employment and of work and opportunities for many seafarers,

Considers also that issues such as access to shore leave and security from attack by pirates and armed robbers need to be addressed,

Considers further that all flag States should encourage operators of ships which fly their flag to provide training berths for new seafarers and for cadets,

Recognizes that the recruitment and retention of seafarers in a global labour market is a complex issue, which involves a social, political and economic dimension and, where appropriate, the provision of suitable policies by governments and industry alike,

Believes that the International Labour Office is well placed to undertake work in this area and invites the Director-General to request the Governing Body to convene a tripartite meeting of experts to examine the issues and propose a set of suitable policy recommendations.

XII

Resolution concerning the effects on the industry of piracy and armed robbery[1]

The General Conference of the International Labour Organization,

Having adopted the Maritime Labour Convention, 2006,

Mindful that the core mandate of the Organization is to promote decent working and living conditions,

Noting the continued incidence of cases of piracy and armed robbery in many parts of the world and the increasing violence directed against seafarers that is associated with such attacks, as well as the trend to hold seafarers hostage against the payment of a ransom,

Noting also the impact that this is having on seafarers and that it has been agreed that, given the global nature of the shipping industry, seafarers need special protection,

Being aware of the work undertaken by the International Labour Organization in this area,

[1] Adopted on 22 February 2006.

Being aware also of the concern the United Nations General Assembly has expressed in various resolutions on the law of the sea in recent years at the continuing problem of transnational organized crime and threats to maritime safety and security, including piracy, armed robbery at sea and smuggling, and noting the deplorable loss of life, injuries to seafarers and adverse impact on international trade resulting from such activities;

Urges the Governing Body of the International Labour Office to request the Director-General to work closely with the International Maritime Organization and the United Nations in encouraging all member States to ensure that adequate measures are introduced to prevent such attacks and to ensure the safety and security of seafarers in their waters and off their coastlines,

Calls for the Governing Body to remain seized of this issue.

XIII
Resolution concerning the development of guidelines for flag State inspection[1]

The General Conference of the International Labour Organization,

Having adopted the Maritime Labour Convention, 2006,

Considering that this Convention aims to establish a new pillar of international legislation for the shipping industry,

Noting paragraphs 1, 2 and 3 of Article V, and Regulation 5.1.1, Standard A5.1.1, Guideline B5.1.1 of the above Convention, which provide for flag State responsibilities, inspection and certification of maritime labour conditions,

Noting that the success of the Convention will depend, among others, upon the uniform and harmonized implementation of flag State responsibilities in accordance with its relevant provisions,

Considering that, given the global nature of the shipping industry, it is important for flag State inspectors to receive proper guidelines for the performance of their duties;

Invites the Governing Body of the International Labour Office to request the Director-General to give due priority, through tripartite meetings of experts, to developing suitable guidance for flag State inspection.

XIV

Resolution concerning occupational safety and health[1]

The General Conference of the International Labour Organization,

Having adopted the Maritime Labour Convention, 2006,

[1] Adopted on 22 February 2006.

Mindful that the core mandate of the Organization is to promote decent working and living conditions and a global strategy on occupational safety and health,

Recognizing that the occupational safety and health of seafarers and the risks they face on board vessels are inextricably linked to the effective implementation of the International Safety Management (ISM) Code of the International Maritime Organization, which endeavours to ensure the safe management of ships,

Noting the importance of a culture of safety on board ships, addressed by the provisions contained in the ILO code of practice on accident prevention on board ship at sea and in port,

Emphasizing the need to promote the establishment of shipboard safety committees and to appoint crew safety representatives;

Urges the Governing Body of the International Labour Office to allocate resources for the promotion of awareness of the health, safety and accident prevention provisions contained in Title 4 of the Maritime Labour Convention,

Requests the Director-General to invite the Governing Body to convene a tripartite expert working group on seafarers' occupational safety and health, to consider how best to undertake this work.

XV

Resolution concerning search and rescue capability[1]

The General Conference of the International Labour Organization,

Having adopted the Maritime Labour Convention, 2006,

Recognizing the need for the comprehensive coverage of a prompt and efficient search and rescue service to aid seafarers in distress,

Further recognizing the problem faced by the governments of developing countries in fulfilling the requirements of the International Maritime Organization (IMO) Search and Rescue Convention, 1979, and the need for the governments of the developed world to contribute to the IMO Search and Rescue Fund;

Urges governments to assist developing countries by sharing technology, expertise and resources to facilitate adequate training both ashore and on board ships and to develop the necessary infrastructure to enable a swift and effective response to accidents at sea,

Invites the Governing Body of the International Labour Office to request the Office to work closely with the IMO to minimize hazards to seafarers' occupational health by promoting the Search and Rescue Convention.

[1] Adopted on 22 February 2006.

XVI

Resolution concerning social security[1]

The General Conference of the International Labour Organization,

Having adopted the Maritime Labour Convention, 2006,

Noting the Declaration of Philadelphia of 1944 concerning the aims and purposes of the International Labour Organization, which include the extension of social security measures to provide a basic income to all in need of such protection and comprehensive medical care,

Noting also that the principal aim of the Organization is the achievement of decent work for all and that social protection is one of the four pillars of the ILO's Decent Work Agenda,

Noting further that the provision of social protection and the other pillars of decent work are mutually reinforcing in addressing poverty reduction, which is one of the principal aims of the Millennium Development Goals,

Being aware of the considerable work undertaken by the Organization to enhance the coverage and effectiveness of social protection for all,

Noting that the Maritime Labour Convention, 2006, requires that member States provide seafarers with social security protection no less favourable than that enjoyed by shoreworkers resident in their territory,

Recalling that the Social Security (Minimum Standards) Convention, 1952 (No. 102), establishes the framework for the promotion of social protection by the Organization,

Considering that, although Article 77 of ILO Convention No. 102 expressly excludes seafarers and sea fishers from the application of that Convention, the ILO should not exclude these sectors from the ongoing work of the Organization to secure effective social protection for all,

Considering also that, given the global nature of the shipping industry, seafarers need special protection;

Invites the Director-General of the International Labour Office to promote the provision of effective social protection and social security for seafarers,

Suggests that such work could be facilitated by an inventory on the provision of social protection and social security for seafarers,

Further invites the Director-General to propose to the Governing Body that such a document be prepared by the Office and discussed at a future tripartite meeting of experts.

---

[1] Adopted on 22 February 2006.

XVII

Resolution concerning the practical implementation of the issue of certificates on entry into force[1]

The General Conference of the International Labour Organization,

Having adopted the Maritime Labour Convention, 2006,

Recalling Article VIII, paragraph 3, concerning the entry into force 12 months after the date on which the required number of ratifications have been registered,

Noting that flag States and recognized organizations would not be in a position to recruit, train and have in place a sufficient number of inspectors until there is a good degree of confidence as to the probable date of entry into force,

Noting that even when a sufficient number of inspectors is in place to ensure a continuing level of inspection and enforcement, it will not be possible to review, inspect and certify all the ships (possibly 40,000 ships) required to carry a maritime labour certificate and declaration of maritime labour compliance within the 12 months before entry into force,

Noting also that should this certification effort be accomplished notwithstanding, these inspectors will be largely idle until the next peak of inspections two years after entry into force,

Recognizing the practical difficulties in providing a maritime labour certificate and a declaration of maritime labour compliance to all ships immediately following entry into force;

Requests governments to develop plans, which will ensure the phasing in of certification requirements starting with bulk carriers and passenger ships no later than 12 months after the date on which there have been registered ratifications by at least 30 Members with a total share in the world gross tonnage of ships of at least 33 per cent,

Requests further that, during a period of one year following the initial entry into force of the Convention, Members (both flag and port States) give due consideration to allowing ships to continue to operate without the certificate and declaration referred to, provided that their inspectors have no evidence that the ships do not conform to the requirements of the Convention.

---

[1] Adopted on 22 February 2006.

THE MARITIME LABOUR CONVENTION, 2006: FREQUENTLY ASKED QUESTIONS[1]

1. What is the Maritime Labour Convention, 2006?

It is an important new international labour Convention that was adopted by the International Labour Conference of the International Labour Organization (ILO), under article 19 of its Constitution at a maritime session in February 2006 in Geneva, Switzerland. It sets out seafarers' rights to decent conditions of work and helps to create conditions of fair competition for shipowners. It is intended to be globally applicable, easily understandable, readily updatable and uniformly enforced. The Maritime Labour Convention, 2006, has been designed to become a global legal instrument that, once it enters into force, will be the the "fourth pillar" of the international regulatory regime for quality shipping, complementing the key Conventions of the International Maritime Organization (IMO) such as the International Convention for the Safety of Life at Sea, 1974, as amended (SOLAS), the International Convention on Standards of Training, Certification and Watchkeeping, 1978, as amended (STCW) and the International Convention for the Prevention of Pollution from Ships, 73/78 (MARPOL).

2. Why is it also sometimes called the *consolidated* Maritime Labour Convention, 2006?

The Maritime Labour Convention, 2006, contains a comprehensive set of global standards, based on those that are already found in 68 maritime labour instruments (Conventions and Recommendations), adopted by the ILO since 1920. The new Convention brings almost all of the existing maritime labour instruments together in a single new Convention that uses a new format with some updating, where necessary, to reflect modern conditions and language. The Convention "consolidates" the

[1] These questions and answers are intended to provide a quick overview of the Maritime Labour Convention, 2006, to persons unfamiliar with the new Convention. They do not purport to provide interpretations of any provisions and should not in any way be treated as a substitute for the actual provisions of the Convention. The text is based on a previous document entitled *Proposed consolidated maritime labour Convention: Frequently asked questions*, which was a background document to the International Labour Confernece, 94th (Maritime) Session, February 2006.

existing international law on all these matters. The Conventions addressing the seafarers' identity documents were recently revised in 2003 (Convention Nos. 108 and 185) and are not included in the new Convention. In addition, the Seafarers' Pension Convention, 1946 (No. 71) and one Convention (The Minimum Age (Trimmers and Stokers) Convention, 1921 (No. 15)), which is no longer relevant to the sector, are not consolidated by the Maritime Labour Convention, 2006.

3. When will the Maritime Labour Convention, 2006, come into force and what will happen to the existing Conventions?

The Convention will enter into force:

> ...12 months after the date on which there have been registered ratifications by at least 30 Members with a total share in the world gross tonnage of ships of 33 per cent.

This is a much higher than the usual ratification level (for ILO Conventions) and it uses a new formula that is intended to assure greater actual impact of the Convention. It reflects the fact that the enforcement and compliance system established under the Convention needs widespread international cooperation in order to be effective. Since many of the obligations under the Convention are directed to shipowners and flag States it is important that ILO Members with a strong maritme interest and a high level of tonnage operating under their legal jurisdiction ratify the Convention.

The existing ILO maritime labour Conventions will be gradually phased out as ILO Member States that have ratified those Conventions ratify the new Convention, but there will be a transitional period when some parallel Conventions will be in force. Countries that ratify the Maritime Labour Convention, 2006, will no longer be bound by the existing Conventions when the new Convention comes into force for them. Countries that do not ratify the new Convention will remain bound by the existing Conventions they have ratified, but those Conventions will be closed to further ratification.

4. Why was a new Convention needed?

The decision by the ILO to move forward to create this major new maritime labour Convention was the result of a joint resolution in 2001 by the international seafarers' and shipowners' organizations, later supported by governments. They pointed out that the shipping industry is "the world's first genuinely global industry" which "requires an international regulatory response of an appropriate kind - global standards applicable to the entire industry". The industry called on the ILO to develop "an instrument which brings together into a consolidated text as much of the existing body of ILO instruments as it proves possible to achieve" as a matter of priority "in order to improve the relevance of those standards to the needs of all the stakeholders of the maritime sector". It was felt that the very large number of the existing maritime Conventions, many of which are very detailed, made it difficult for governments to ratify and to enforce all of the standards. Many of the standards were out of date and did not reflect contemporary working and living conditions on board ships. In addition, there was a need to develop a more effective enforcement and compliance system that would help to eliminate substandard ships and that would work within the well-established international system for enforcement of the international standards for ship safety and security and environmental protection that have been adopted by the International Maritime Organization (IMO).

5. Does the new Convention deal with any new subjects?

The Convention is organized into three main parts: the Articles coming first set out the broad principles and obligations. This is followed by the more detailed Regulations and Code (with two parts: Parts A and B) provisions. The Regulations and the Standards (Part A) and Guidelines (Part B) in the Code are integrated and organized into general areas of concern under five Titles:

Title 1: Minimum requirements for seafarers to work on a ship

Title 2: Conditions of employment

Title 3: Accommodation, recreational facilities, food and catering

Title 4: Health protection, medical care, welfare and social security protection

Title 5: Compliance and enforcement.

These five Titles essentially cover the same subject matter as the existing 68 maritime labour instruments, updating them where necessary. It occasionally contains new subjects, particularly in the area of occupational safety and health to meet current health concerns, such as the effects of noise and vibration on workers or other workplace risks. The provisions relating to flag State inspections, the use of "recognized organizations" and the potential for inspections in foreign ports (port State control) in Title 5 are based on existing maritime labour Conventions; however, the new Convention builds upon them to develop a more effective approach to these important issues, consistent with other international maritime Conventions that establish standards for quality shipping with respect to issues such as ship safety and security and protection of the marine environment.

6. Why do we need effective international standards for seafarers' conditions of work?

In ships flying the flags of countries that do not exercise effective jurisdiction and control over them, as required by international law, seafarers often have to work under unacceptable conditions, to the detriment of their well-being, health and safety and the safety of the ships on which they work. Since seafarers' working lives are spent outside the home country and their employers are also often not based in their country, effective international standards are necessary for this sector. Of course these standards must also be implemented at a national level, particularly by governments that have a ship registry and authorize ships to fly their countries' flags. This is already well recognized in connection with ensuring the safety and security of ships and protecting the marine environment. It is also important to understand that there are many flag States and shipowners that take pride in providing the seafarers on their ships with decent conditions of work. These countries and shipowners face unfair competition in that they pay the price of being undercut by shipowners which operate substandard ships.

7. Are the standards in the new Convention lower than existing maritime labour standards?

No, the aim is to maintain the standards in the current maritime labour Conventions at their present level, while leaving each country greater discretion in the formulation of their national laws establishing that level of protection.

8. How will the Maritime Labour Convention, 2006, protect more of the world's seafarers?

The Convention aims to achieve worldwide protection for all seafarers. It seeks to meet this goal in a number of ways. It is estimated that there are over 1.2 million people working at sea in the world. Until now it had not been clear that all of these people, particularly for example, those that work on board ships but are not directly involved in navigating or operating the ship, such as many personnel that work on passenger ships, would be considered seafarers. The new Convention clearly defines a seafarer as any person who is employed or engaged or works in any capacity on board a ship that is covered by the Convention. Except for a few specific exclusions and areas where flexibility is provided for national authorities to exempt smaller ships (200 gross tonnage and below) that do not go on international voyages from some aspects of the Convention, the Convention *applies* to all ships (and to the seafarers on those ships) whether publicly or privately owned that are ordinarily engaged in commercial activities.

The Convention does *not apply* to:

- ships which navigate exclusively in inland waters or waters within, or closely adjacent to, sheltered waters or areas where port regulations apply;
- ships engaged in fishing;
- ships of traditional build such as dhows and junks;
- warships or naval auxiliaries.

Many existing maritime labour Conventions have a low ratification level. The new Convention has been designed specifically to address this problem. More protection of seafarers will be achieved by the early ratification and national-level implementation of the new Convention by the vast majority of ILO nations active in the maritime sector, as is the case of the key Conventions of the International Maritime Organization (IMO): SOLAS, STCW and MARPOL.

9. How does the new Convention make it easier for countries to ratify it and to implement its requirements?

Both the Constitution of the ILO and many ILO instruments seek to take account of national circumstances and provide for some flexibility in application of Conventions, with a view to gradually improving protection of workers, by taking into account the specific situation in some sectors and the diversity of national circumstances. Flexibility is usually based on principles of **tripartism**, **transparency** and **accountability**. When flexibility with respect to a Convention is exercised by a government it usually involves consultation with the workers' and employers' organizations concerned, with any determinations that are made reported to the ILO by the government concerned. This is seen as a necessary and important approach to ensuring that all countries, irrespective of national circumstances, can engage with the international legal system and that international obligations are respected and implemented, to the extent possible, while also making efforts to improve conditions. This is particularly important for an international industry such as shipping.

The Maritime Labour Convention, 2006, generally follows this approach as well as also providing for additional flexibility, relevant to the sector, at a national level. The Convention seeks to be "firm on rights and flexible on implementation". A major obstacle to the ratification of existing maritime labour Conventions is the excessive detail in many of them. The new Convention sets out the basic rights of seafarers to decent work in firm statements, but leaves a large measure of flexibility to ratifying countries as to how they will implement these standards for decent work in their national laws.

The areas of *flexibility* in the Convention include the following:

- the "Seafarers Employment and Social Rights" set out in Article IV are to be fully implemented, "in accordance with the requirements of this Convention" (in accordance with the relevant provisions of the Articles, Regulations and Part A of the Code); however, unless specified otherwise in the Convention, national implementation may be achieved through national laws or regulations, through applicable collective bargaining agreements or through other measures or in practice;
- implementation of the mandatory standards in Part A of the Code (other than Title 5) may also be achieved through measures which are "substantially equivalent";
- many of the prescriptive or detailed requirements in existng Conventions which had created difficulties for some governments interested in ratifying the Convention are now found in the Guidelines, which are in Part B of the Code. The provisions of Part B of the Code are not mandatory and are not subject to port State inspections, however governments are required to give "due consideration" to their content when implementing their obligations;
- the requirements of the Convention, other than the ship certification system, will apply to most ships (it does not apply to fishing vessels, ships of traditional build or warships); however, the application of details in the Code may be relaxed for some smaller ships - 200 gross tonnage (GT) and below - that do not go on international voyages. This determination would be made in consultation with shipowners' and seafarers' organizations concerned;
- all ships covered by the Convention would be subject to the inspection system developed by the flag State but the certification system is only mandatory for ships of 500 GT and above that are engaged in international voyages (or are operating between ports in a foreign country). The certification system will certify that the ship is being operated in conformity with the Convention's requirements as implemented in the laws or regulations of the flag State concerned (in the case of other ships, the shipowners can also request their flag State to include their ships in the certification system so as to avoid or reduce the likelihood of their being inspected in foreign ports);

- the Convention expressly recognizes that some flag States may make use of recognized organizations such as classification societies to carry out aspects of the ship certification system on their behalf;
- provisions affecting ship construction and equipment (Title 3) will not apply to ships constructed before the Convention comes into force for the country concerned. Smaller ships (200 gross tonnage and below) may be exempted from specific accommodation requirements;
- specific allowance is made for making determinations at a national level through consultation with shipowners' and seafarers' organizations "in case of doubt" as to the application of the Convention to categories of persons or ships or a particular ship. A Resolution was adopted along with the Convention which provides guidance to national authorities on the question of who would be considered "seafarers" in this context;
- provision is made for the situation of countries that may not have national organizations of shipowners or seafarers to consult;
- provision is made for national circumstances and for bilateral, multilateral and other arrangements in connection with social security coverage.

10. Will the shipowners' duties and responsibilities cover seafarers whose work does not relate to the navigation or safe operation of the ship?

Yes, shipowners (or ship operators) have the overall responsibility as employers with respect to all seafarers working on their ships. It is understood that they could make arrangements with persons who may also have responsibility for the employment of particular seafarers, enabling the shipowners to recover the costs involved, for example.

11. Why is the new Convention likely to achieve the aim of near universal ratification?

Because the Convention was adopted by a record vote of 314 in favour and none against (two countries abstained for reasons unrelated to the substance of the Convention), after nearly two weeks of detailed review by over 1,000 participants drawn from 106 countries. This almost unprecedented level of support reflects the lengthy tripartite consultation exercise and the unswerving support that has been shown for it by the governments and workers and employers who have worked together since 2001 to develop the Convention text. It will also achieve near universal ratification because of its blend of firmness on rights and flexibility with respect to approaches to implementation of the more technical requirements and because of the advantages it gives to the ships of countries that ratify it.

12. What will be the advantages for ships of ratifying countries?

The ships of ratifying countries that provide decent conditions of work for their seafarers will have protection against unfair competition from substandard ships and will benefit from a system of certification, avoiding or reducing the likelihood of lengthy delays related to inspections in foreign ports.

13. How will the Maritime Labour Convention, 2006, improve compliance and enforcement?

The Maritime Labour Convention, 2006, aims to establish a continuous "compliance awareness" at every stage, from the national systems of protection up to the international system. This starts with the individual **seafarers**, who - under the Convention - have to be properly informed of their rights and of the remedies available in case of alleged non-compliance with the requirements of the Convention and whose right to make complaints, both on board ship and ashore, is recognized in the Convention. It continues with the **shipowners**. Those that own or operate ships of 500 gross tonnage and above, engaged in international voyages or voyages between foreign ports, are required to develop and carry out plans for ensuring that the applicable national laws, regulations or other measures to implement the Convention are actually being complied with. The **masters** of these ships are then responsible for carrying out the shipowners' stated plans, and for keeping proper records to evidence implementation of the requirements of the Convention. As part of its updated responsibilities for the labour inspections for ships above 500 gross tonnage that are engaged in international voyages or voyages between foreign ports, the **flag State** (or recognized organization on its behalf) will review the shipowners' plans and verify and certify that they are actually in place and being implemented. Ships will then be required to carry a **maritime labour certificate** and a **declaration of maritime labour compliance** on board. Flag States will also be expected to ensure that national laws and regulations implementing the Convention's standards are respected on smaller ships that are not covered by the certification system. Flag States will carry out periodic quality assessments of the effectiveness of their national systems of compliance, and their **reports to the ILO under article 22** of the Constitution will need to provide information on their inspection and certification systems, including on their methods of quality assessment. This general inspection system in the flag State (which is founded on ILO Convention No. 178) is complemented by procedures to be followed in countries that are also or even primarily the source of the world's supply of seafarers, which will similarly be reporting under article 22 of the ILO Constitution. The system is further reinforced by voluntary measures for inspections in **foreign ports (port State control)**.

14. What are the maritime labour certificate and the declaration of maritime labour compliance?

The Appendices to the Convention contain key model documents: a **maritime labour certificate** and a **declaration of maritime labour compliance**. The certificate would be issued by the flag State to a ship that flies its flag, once the State (or a recognized organization that has been authorized to carry out the inspections), has verified that the labour conditions on the ship comply with national laws and regulations implementing the Convention. The certificate would be valid for five years subject to periodic inspections by the flag State. The declaration is attached to the certificate and summarizes the national laws or regulations implementing an agreed-upon list of 14 areas of the maritime standards and setting out the shipowner's or operator's plan for ensuring that the national requirements implementing the Convention will be maintained on the ship between inspections. The lists of the 14 areas that *must* be certified by the flag State and that *may* be inspected, if an inspection occurs, in a foreign port are also set out in the Appendices to the Convention.

15. What is meant by "no more favourable treatment" for ships of non-ratifying countries?

These words appear in Article V, paragraph 7, of the Convention. The idea, which is also found in IMO Conventions, is that ships must not be placed at a disadvantage because their country has ratified the new Convention. The practical consequence comes out clearly in the port State control provisions of Title 5 of the Convention, under which ships of all countries (irrespective of ratification) will be subject to inspection in any country that has ratified the Convention, and to possible detention if they do not meet the minimum standards of the new Convention.

16. How will respect for the new Convention actually be enforced?

The new Convention is intended to achieve more compliance by operators and owners of ships and to strengthen enforcement of standards through mechanisms which operate at all levels. For example, it contains provisions for:

- complaint procedures available to seafarers;
- shipowners' and shipmasters' supervision of conditions on their ships;
- flag States' jurisdiction and control over their ships;
- port State inspections of foreign ships.

By requiring ratifying Members not only to implement the Convention in the national laws but also to document their implementation, the Convention should also enhance the effectiveness of the supervision carried out at the international level, especially by the competent bodies of the ILO.

17. How will the new Convention be kept more up to date than the existing Conventions?

The part of the Convention which is expected to need updating from time to time, namely the two-part Code relating to the technical and detailed implementation of the basic obligations under the Convention, can be amended under an accelerated procedure ("tacit acceptance") (provided for in Article XV) enabling changes to come into effect, for all or almost all ratifying countries, within three to four years from when they are proposed.

18. Will ratifying Members be bound by all new amendments?

A ratifying Member will not be bound by an amendment to the Code entering into effect in accordance with Article XV of the Convention if it expresses formal disagreement within a period of normally two years. Amendments under Article XIV, which lays down a procedure to be followed in the case of amendments to the basic provisions, i.e. the Articles and Regulations, can only take effect for countries that ratify the amendment concerned.

19. How do the amendment procedures differ from those in the IMO Conventions?

Both types of amendment procedure - under Article XIV for the Convention as a whole, and Article XV for amendments only to the Code - are based to a certain extent on procedures that are already well established in another agency of the United Nations, the International Maritime Organization (IMO). However, the Article XIV *express ratification* procedure is closer to the present ILO procedure for revising Conventions. The accelerated or *tacit acceptance* procedure under Article XV follows the IMO procedures especially with respect to the submission of amendments to Member States and their entry into effect; the main difference relates to the adoption of amendments: here (unlike under the IMO procedures) non-ratifying Members play a role and amendments have to be approved by the International Labour Conference, open to all ILO Members.

20. What are the novel features of the new Convention?

There are several novel features as far as the ILO is concerned. The whole structure of the new Convention differs from that of traditional ILO Conventions. It consists of the basic provisions, i.e. the **Articles** and **Regulations**, followed by a **two-part Code** and divided into **five Titles**, one of which is devoted to compliance and enforcement. The Regulations and the Code, which contains **Standards** and **Guidelines**, are organized under the five Titles.

Title 1: Minimum requirements for seafarers to work on a ship

Title 2: Conditions of employment

Title 3: Accommodation, recreational facilities, food and catering

Title 4: Health protection, medical care, welfare and social security protection

Title 5: Compliance and enforcement.

There is also an **Explanatory note** to further assist Members implementing the Convention. The Convention also uses a new **"vertically integrated"** format with a numbering system that links the Regulations, Standards and Guidelines. Each Regulation also has a "plain language" purpose clause. For example:

Regulation 1.2 – Medical certificate

Purpose: To ensure that all seafarers are medically fit to perform their duties at sea

1. Seafarers shall not work on a ship unless they are certified as medically fit to perform their duties.

...

Standard A1.2 – Medical certificate

1. The competent authority shall require that, prior to beginning work on a ship, seafarers hold a valid medical certificate attesting that they are medically fit to perform the duties they are to carry out at sea.

...

Guideline B1.2 – Medical certificate

Guideline B1.2.1 – International Guidelines...

Other innovations are the amendment procedures and the system for the certification of ships. However, most of these novel features are based on those of the instruments of other organizations, especially the IMO. One unique feature relates to the special status of the non-mandatory Part B of the Code and its relationship with the mandatory Part A.

21. What is meant by the special status of Part B of the Code and why is it needed?

The status of Part B of the Code is based on the idea of firmness on principle and rights combined with flexibility in implementation. Without this innovation the new Convention could never aspire to wide-scale ratification: many of the provisions of existing maritime labour Conventions, which relate to the method of implementing basic seafarers' rights (rather than to the content of those rights), have been transferred to the non-mandatory Part B Guidelines of the Code. Their placement in the mandatory Regulations and Part A (Standards) could have resulted in clear obstacles to ratification.

The special status is reflected in the following agreed set of questions and answers:

Is Part B of the Code mandatory?
Answer: No.

Can Part B be ignored by ratifying Members?
Answer: No.

Is implementation of Part B verified by port State inspectors?
Answer: No.

Does the ratifying Member have to follow the guidance in Part B?
Answer: No, but if it does not follow the guidance it may - vis-à-vis the competent bodies of the International Labour Organization - need to justify the way in which it has implemented the corresponding mandatory provisions of the consolidated Convention.

22. Since Part B is not mandatory, why is it part of the Convention and not the subject of an international labour Recommendation?

Part A and Part B of the Code are interrelated. The provisions of Part B, called Guidelines, while not mandatory, are helpful and sometimes essential for a proper understanding of the Regulations and the mandatory Standards in Part A. In some cases, the mandatory Standards in Part A are so generally worded it may be difficult to implement them without the guidance in the corresponding provisions of Part B.

23. Can an ILO Convention legally contain non-mandatory provisions?

There is no reason why mandatory provisions should not be complemented by non-mandatory ones. There are precedents in international labour Conventions where the non-mandatory "should" is used rather than the mandatory "shall".

24. Why does there sometimes appear to be some duplication between the Regulations and Part A of the Code of the Convention?

The Regulations, which will be approved by parliaments or legislatures during the national ratification processes, not only set out the basic rights of seafarers but also govern the content of the Code, including its possible future content after amendment under the accelerated procedure. Every provision of Part A of the Code must come within the general scope of the Articles or Regulations to be valid. This requirement sometimes leads to a measure of duplication.

25. Will the Convention also require ratifying countries to apply the ILO's core human rights Conventions or other Conventions mentioned in the new Convention?

No, but they will - under Article III of the Convention - have to satisfy themselves that their laws and regulations respect, in the context of the Convention, the fundamental rights, such as freedom of association, that are embodied in the core Conventions (there would be no requirement concerning the actual provisions of those Conventions).

The fact that other international Conventions are referred to in the Preamble or other parts of the Convention does not create a legal obligation, with respect to those Conventions, for a country that ratifies the Maritime Labour Convention, 2006.

PART B

SEAFARERS' IDENTITY DOCUMENTS

SEAFARERS' IDENTITY DOCUMENTS CONVENTION (REVISED), 2003 (No. 185)

Convention revising the Seafarers' Identity Documents Convention, 1958

Adopted: 19 June 2003

The General Conference of the International Labour Organization,

Having been convened at Geneva by the Governing Body of the International Labour Office, and having met in its Ninety-first Session on 3 June 2003, and

Mindful of the continuing threat to the security of passengers and crews and the safety of ships, to the national interest of States and to individuals, and

Mindful also of the core mandate of the Organization, which is to promote decent conditions of work, and

Considering that, given the global nature of the shipping industry, seafarers need special protection, and

Recognizing the principles embodied in the Seafarers' Identity Documents Convention, 1958, concerning the facilitation of entry by seafarers into the territory of Members, for the purposes of shore leave, transit, transfer or repatriation, and

Noting the Convention on the Facilitation of International Maritime Traffic, 1965, as amended, of the International Maritime Organization, in particular, Standards 3.44 and 3.45, and

Noting further that United Nations General Assembly Resolution A/RES/57/219 (Protection of human rights and fundamental freedoms while countering terrorism) affirms that States must ensure that any measure taken to combat terrorism complies with their obligations under international law, in particular international human rights, refugee and humanitarian law, and

Being aware that seafarers work and live on ships involved in international trade and that access to shore facilities and shore leave are vital elements of seafarers' general well-being and, therefore, to the achievement of safer shipping and cleaner oceans, and

Being aware also that the ability to go ashore is essential for joining a ship and leaving after the agreed period of service, and

Noting the amendments to the International Convention for the Safety of Life at Sea, 1974, as amended, concerning special measures to enhance maritime safety and security, that were adopted by the International Maritime Organization Diplomatic Conference on 12 December 2002, and

Having decided upon the adoption of certain proposals with regard to the improved security of seafarers' identification, which is the seventh item on the agenda of the session, and

Having decided that these proposals shall take the form of an international Convention revising the Seafarers' Identity Documents Convention, 1958,

adopts this nineteenth day of June of the year two thousand and three, the following Convention, which may be cited as the Seafarers' Identity Documents Convention (Revised), 2003.

Article 1

Scope

1. For the purposes of this Convention, the term "seafarer" means any person who is employed or is engaged or works in any capacity on board a vessel, other than a ship of war, ordinarily engaged in maritime navigation.

2. In the event of any doubt whether any categories of persons are to be regarded as seafarers for the purpose of this Convention, the question shall be determined in accordance with the provisions of this Convention by the competent authority of the State of nationality or permanent residence of such persons after consulting with the shipowners' and seafarers' organizations concerned.

3. After consulting the representative organizations of fishing-vessel owners and persons working on board fishing vessels, the competent authority may apply the provisions of this Convention to commercial maritime fishing.

Article 2

Issuance of seafarers' identity documents

1. Each Member for which this Convention is in force shall issue to each of its nationals who is a seafarer and makes an application to that effect a seafarers' identity document conforming to the provisions of Article 3 of this Convention.

2. Unless otherwise provided for in this Convention, the issuance of seafarers' identity documents may be subject to the same conditions as those prescribed by national laws and regulations for the issuance of travel documents.

3. Each Member may also issue seafarers' identity documents referred to in paragraph 1 to seafarers who have been granted the status of permanent resident in its territory. Permanent residents shall in all cases travel in conformity with the provisions of Article 6, paragraph 7.

4. Each Member shall ensure that seafarers' identity documents are issued without undue delay.

5. Seafarers shall have the right to an administrative appeal in the case of a rejection of their application.

6. This Convention shall be without prejudice to the obligations of each Member under international arrangements relating to refugees and stateless persons.

Article 3

CONTENT AND FORM

1. The seafarers' identity document covered by this Convention shall conform - in its content - to the model set out in Annex I hereto. The form of the document and the materials used in it shall be consistent with the general specifications set out in the model, which shall be based on the criteria set out below. Provided that any amendment is consistent with the following paragraphs, Annex I may, where necessary, be amended in accordance with Article 8 below, in particular to take account of technological developments. The decision to adopt the amendment shall specify when the amendment will enter into effect, taking account of the need to give Members sufficient time to make any necessary revisions of their national seafarers' identity documents and procedures.

2. The seafarers' identity document shall be designed in a simple manner, be made of durable material, with special regard to conditions at sea and be machine-readable. The materials used shall:

(a) prevent tampering with the document or falsification, as far as possible, and enable easy detection of alterations; and

(b) be generally accessible to governments at the lowest cost consistent with reliably achieving the purpose set out in (a) above.

3. Members shall take into account any available guidelines developed by the International Labour Organization on standards of the technology to be used which will facilitate the use of a common international standard.

4. The seafarers' identity document shall be no larger than a normal passport.

5. The seafarers' identity document shall contain the name of the issuing authority, indications enabling rapid contact with that authority, the date and place of issue of the document, and the following statements:

(a) this document is a seafarers' identity document for the purpose of the Seafarers' Identity Documents Convention (Revised), 2003, of the International Labour Organization; and

(b) this document is a stand-alone document and not a passport.

6. The maximum validity of a seafarers' identity document shall be determined in accordance with the laws and regulations of the issuing State and shall in no case exceed ten years, subject to renewal after the first five years.

7. Particulars about the holder included in the seafarer's identity document shall be restricted to the following:

(a) full name (first and last names where applicable);

(b) sex;

(c) date and place of birth;

(d) nationality;

(e) any special physical characteristics that may assist identification;

(f) digital or original photograph; and

(g) signature.

8. Notwithstanding paragraph 7 above, a template or other representation of a biometric of the holder which meets the specification provided for in Annex I shall also be required for inclusion in the seafarers' identity document, provided that the following preconditions are satisfied:

(a) the biometric can be captured without any invasion of privacy of the persons concerned, discomfort to them, risk to their health or offence against their dignity;

(b) the biometric shall itself be visible on the document and it shall not be possible to reconstitute it from the template or other representation;

(c) the equipment needed for the provision and verification of the biometric is user-friendly and is generally accessible to governments at low cost;

(d) the equipment for the verification of the biometric can be conveniently and reliably operated in ports and in other places, including on board ship, where verification of identity is normally carried out by the competent authorities; and

(e) the system in which the biometric is to be used (including the equipment, technologies and procedures for use) provides results that are uniform and reliable for the authentication of identity.

9. All data concerning the seafarer that are recorded on the document shall be visible. Seafarers shall have convenient access to machines enabling them to inspect any data concerning them that is not eye-readable. Such access shall be provided by or on behalf of the issuing authority.

10. The content and form of the seafarers' identity document shall take into account the relevant international standards cited in Annex I.

Article 4

National electronic database

1. Each Member shall ensure that a record of each seafarers' identity document issued, suspended or withdrawn by it is stored in an electronic database. The necessary measures shall be taken to secure the database from interference or unauthorized access.

2. The information contained in the record shall be restricted to details which are essential for the purposes of verifying a seafarers' identity document or the status of a seafarer and which are consistent with the seafarer's right to privacy and which meet all applicable data protection requirements. The details are set out in Annex II hereto, which may be amended in the manner provided for in Article 8 below, taking account of the need to give Members sufficient time to make any necessary revisions of their national database systems.

3. Each Member shall put in place procedures which will enable any seafarer to whom it has issued a seafarers' identity document to examine and check

the validity of all the data held or stored in the electronic database which relate to that individual and to provide for correction if necessary, at no cost to the seafarer concerned.

4. Each Member shall designate a permanent focal point for responding to inquiries, from the immigration or other competent authorities of all Members of the Organization, concerning the authenticity and validity of the seafarers' identity document issued by its authority. Details of the permanent focal point shall be communicated to the International Labour Office, and the Office shall maintain a list which shall be communicated to all Members of the Organization.

5. The details referred to in paragraph 2 above shall at all times be immediately accessible to the immigration or other competent authorities in member States of the Organization, either electronically or through the focal point referred to in paragraph 4 above.

6. For the purposes of this Convention, appropriate restrictions shall be established to ensure that no data - in particular, photographs - are exchanged, unless a mechanism is in place to ensure that applicable data protection and privacy standards are adhered to.

7. Members shall ensure that the personal data on the electronic database shall not be used for any purpose other than verification of the seafarers' identity document.

Article 5

Quality control and evaluations

1. Minimum requirements concerning processes and procedures for the issue of seafarers' identity documents, including quality-control procedures, are set out in Annex III to this Convention. These minimum requirements establish mandatory results that must be achieved by each Member in the administration of its system for issuance of seafarers' identity documents.

2. Processes and procedures shall be in place to ensure the necessary security for:

(a) the production and delivery of blank seafarers' identity documents;

(b) the custody, handling and accountability for blank and completed seafarers' identity documents;

(c) the processing of applications, the completion of the blank seafarers' identity documents into personalized seafarers' identity documents by the authority and unit responsible for issuing them and the delivery of the seafarers' identity documents;

(d) the operation and maintenance of the database; and

(e) the quality control of procedures and periodic evaluations.

3. Subject to paragraph 2 above, Annex III may be amended in the manner provided for in Article 8, taking account of the need to give Members sufficient time to make any necessary revisions to their processes and procedures.

4. Each Member shall carry out an independent evaluation of the administration of its system for issuing seafarers' identity documents, including quality-control procedures, at least every five years. Reports on such evaluations, subject to the removal of any confidential material, shall be provided to the Director-General of the International Labour Office with a copy to the representative organizations of shipowners and seafarers in the Member concerned. This reporting requirement shall be without prejudice to the obligations of Members under article 22 of the Constitution of the International Labour Organisation.

5. The International Labour Office shall make these evaluation reports available to Members. Any disclosure, other than those authorized by this Convention, shall require the consent of the reporting Member.

6. The Governing Body of the International Labour Office, acting on the basis of all relevant information in accordance with arrangements made by it, shall approve a list of Members which fully meet the minimum requirements referred to in paragraph 1 above.

7. The list must be available to Members of the Organization at all times and be updated as appropriate information is received. In particular, Members shall be promptly notified where the inclusion of any Member on the list is contested on solid grounds in the framework of the procedures referred to in paragraph 8.

8. In accordance with procedures established by the Governing Body, provision shall be made for Members which have been or may be excluded from the list, as well as interested governments of ratifying Members and representative shipowners' and seafarers' organizations, to make their views known to the Governing Body, in accordance with the arrangements referred to above and to have any disagreements fairly and impartially settled in a timely manner.

9. The recognition of seafarers' identity documents issued by a Member is subject to its compliance with the minimum requirements referred to in paragraph 1 above.

Article 6

FACILITATION OF SHORE LEAVE AND TRANSIT AND TRANSFER OF SEAFARERS

1. Any seafarer who holds a valid seafarers' identity document issued in accordance with the provisions of this Convention by a Member for which the Convention is in force shall be recognized as a seafarer within the meaning of the Convention unless clear grounds exist for doubting the authenticity of the seafarers' identity document.

2. The verification and any related inquiries and formalities needed to ensure that the seafarer for whom entry is requested pursuant to paragraphs 3 to 6 or 7 to 9 below is the holder of a seafarers' identity document issued in accordance with the requirements of this Convention shall be at no cost to the seafarers or shipowners.

Shore leave

3. Verification and any related inquiries and formalities referred to in paragraph 2 above shall be carried out in the shortest possible time provided that reasonable advance notice of the holder's arrival was received by the competent

authorities. The notice of the holder's arrival shall include the details specified in section 1 of Annex II.

4. Each Member for which this Convention is in force shall, in the shortest possible time, and unless clear grounds exist for doubting the authenticity of the seafarers' identity document, permit the entry into its territory of a seafarer holding a valid seafarer's identity document, when entry is requested for temporary shore leave while the ship is in port.

5. Such entry shall be allowed provided that the formalities on arrival of the ship have been fulfilled and the competent authorities have no reason to refuse permission to come ashore on grounds of public health, public safety, public order or national security.

6. For the purpose of shore leave seafarers shall not be required to hold a visa. Any Member which is not in a position to fully implement this requirement shall ensure that its laws and regulations or practice provide arrangements that are substantially equivalent.

Transit and transfer

7. Each Member for which this Convention is in force shall, in the shortest possible time, also permit the entry into its territory of seafarers holding a valid seafarers' identity document supplemented by a passport, when entry is requested for the purpose of:

(a) joining their ship or transferring to another ship;

(b) passing in transit to join their ship in another country or for repatriation; or any other purpose approved by the authorities of the Member concerned.

8. Such entry shall be allowed unless clear grounds exist for doubting the authenticity of the seafarers' identity document, provided that the competent authorities have no reason to refuse entry on grounds of public health, public safety, public order or national security.

9. Any Member may, before permitting entry into its territory for one of the purposes specified in paragraph 7 above, require satisfactory evidence, including documentary evidence of a seafarer's intention and ability to carry out that intention. The Member may also limit the seafarer's stay to a period considered reasonable for the purpose in question.

Article 7

CONTINUOUS POSSESSION AND WITHDRAWAL

1. The seafarers' identity document shall remain in the seafarer's possession at all times, except when it is held for safekeeping by the master of the ship concerned, with the seafarer's written consent.

2. The seafarers' identity document shall be promptly withdrawn by the issuing State if it is ascertained that the seafarer no longer meets the conditions for its issue under this Convention. Procedures for suspending or withdrawing seafarers' identity documents shall be drawn up in consultation with the representative shipowners' and seafarers' organizations and shall include procedures for administrative appeal.

Article 8

AMENDMENT OF THE ANNEXES

1. Subject to the relevant provisions of this Convention, amendments to the Annexes may be made by the International Labour Conference, acting on the advice of a duly constituted tripartite maritime body of the International Labour Organization. The decision shall require a majority of two-thirds of the votes cast by the delegates present at the Conference, including at least half the Members that have ratified this Convention.

2. Any Member that has ratified this Convention may give written notice to the Director-General within six months of the date of the adoption of such an amendment that it shall not enter into force for that Member, or shall only enter into force at a later date upon subsequent written notification.

Article 9

TRANSITIONAL PROVISION

Any Member which is a party to the Seafarers' Identity Documents Convention, 1958, and which is taking measures, in accordance with article 19 of the Constitution of the International Labour Organisation, with a view to ratification of this Convention may notify the Director-General of its intention to apply the present Convention provisionally. A seafarers' identity document issued by such a Member shall be treated for the purposes of this Convention as a seafarers' identity document issued under it provided that the requirements of Articles 2 to 5 of this Convention are fulfilled and that the Member concerned accepts seafarers' identity documents issued under this Convention.

FINAL PROVISIONS

Article 10

This Convention revises the Seafarers' Identity Documents Convention, 1958.

Article 11

The formal ratifications of this Convention shall be communicated to the Director-General of the International Labour Office for registration.

Article 12

1. This Convention shall be binding only upon those Members of the International Labour Organization whose ratifications have been registered with the Director-General.

2. It shall come into force six months after the date on which the ratifications of two Members have been registered with the Director-General.

3. Thereafter, this Convention shall come into force for any Member six months after the date on which its ratification has been registered.

Article 13

1. A Member which has ratified this Convention may denounce it after the expiration of ten years from the date on which the Convention first comes into

force, by an act communicated to the Director-General for registration. Such denunciation shall take effect twelve months after the date on which it is registered.

2. Each Member which has ratified this Convention and which does not, within the year following the expiration of the period of ten years mentioned in the preceding paragraph, exercise the right of denunciation provided for in this Article, shall be bound for another period of ten years and, thereafter, may denounce this Convention at the expiration of each period of ten years under the terms provided for in this Article.

Article 14

1. The Director-General shall notify all Members of the registration of all ratifications, declarations and acts of denunciation communicated by the Members.

2. When notifying the Members of the registration of the second ratification of this Convention, the Director-General shall draw the attention of the Members to the date upon which the Convention shall come into force.

3. The Director-General shall notify all Members of the registration of any amendments made to the Annexes in accordance with Article 8, as well as of notifications relating thereto.

Article 15

The Director-General of the International Labour Office shall communicate to the Secretary-General of the United Nations, for registration in accordance with article 102 of the Charter of the United Nations, full particulars of all ratifications, declarations and acts of denunciation registered by the Director-General in accordance with the provisions of the preceding Articles.

Article 16

At such times as it may consider necessary, the Governing Body of the International Labour Office shall present to the General Conference a report on the working of this Convention and shall examine the desirability of placing on the agenda of the Conference the question of its revision in whole or in part, taking account also of the provisions of Article 8.

Article 17

1. Should the Conference adopt a new Convention revising this Convention in whole or in part, then, unless the new Convention otherwise provides:

(a) the ratification by a Member of the new revising Convention shall *ipso jure* involve the immediate denunciation of this Convention, notwithstanding the provisions of Article 13, if and when the new revising Convention shall have come into force;

(b) as from the date when the new revising Convention comes into force, this Convention shall cease to be open to ratification by the Members.

2. This Convention shall in any case remain in force in its actual form and content for those Members which have ratified it but have not ratified the revising Convention.

Article 18

The English and French versions of the text of this Convention are equally authoritative.

Annex I

MODEL FOR SEAFARERS' IDENTITY DOCUMENT

The seafarers' identity document, whose form and content are set out below, shall consist of good-quality materials which, as far as practicable, having regard to considerations such as cost, are not easily accessible to the general public. The document shall have no more space than is necessary to contain the information provided for by the Convention.

It shall contain the name of the issuing State and the following statement:

"This document is a seafarers' identity document for the purpose of the Seafarers' Identity Documents Convention (Revised), 2003, of the International Labour Organization. This document is a stand-alone document and not a passport."

The data page(s) of the document indicated in **bold** below shall be protected by a laminate or overlay, or by applying an imaging technology and substrate material that provide an equivalent resistance to substitution of the portrait and other biographical data.

The materials used, dimensions and placement of data shall conform to the International Civil Aviation Organization (ICAO) specifications as contained in Document 9303 Part 3 (2nd edition, 2002) or Document 9303 Part 1 (5th edition, 2003).

Other security features shall include at least one of the following features:

Watermarks, ultraviolet security features, use of special inks, special colour designs, perforated images, holograms, laser engraving, micro-printing, and heat-sealed lamination.

Data to be entered on the data page(s) of the seafarers' identity document shall be restricted to:

I. Issuing authority:

II. Telephone number(s), email and web site of the authority:

III. Date and place of issue:

Digital or original photograph of seafarer

(a) Full name of seafarer: ....

(b) Sex: ....

(c) Date and place of birth: ....

(d) Nationality: ....

(e) Any special physical characteristics of seafarer that may assist identification:

....

(f) Signature: ....

(g) Date of expiry: ....

(h) Type or designation of document: ....

(i) Unique document number: ....

(j) Personal identification number (optional): ....

(k) Biometric template based on a fingerprint printed as numbers in a bar code conforming to a standard to be developed:

....

(l) A machine-readable zone conforming to ICAO specifications in Document 9303 specified above.

....

IV. Official seal or stamp of the issuing authority.

Explanation of data:

The captions on fields on the data page(s) above may be translated into the language(s) of the issuing State. If the national language is other than English, French or Spanish, the captions shall also be entered in one of these languages.

The Roman alphabet should be used for all entries in this document.

The information listed above shall have the following characteristics:

I. Issuing authority: ISO code for the issuing State and the name and full address of the office issuing the seafarers' identity document as well as the name and position of the person authorizing the issue.

II. The telephone number, email and web site shall correspond to the links to the focal point referred to in the Convention.

III. Date and place of issue: the date shall be written in two-digit Arabic numerals in the form day/month/year - e.g. 31/12/03; the place shall be written in the same way as on the national passport.

Size of the portrait photograph: as in ICAO Document 9303 specified above

(a) Full name of seafarer: where applicable, family name shall be written first, followed by the seafarer's other names;

(b) Sex: specify "M" for male or "F" for female;

(c) Date and place of birth: the date shall be written in two-digit Arabic numerals in the form day/month/year; the place shall be written in the same way as on the national passport;

(d) Statement of nationality: specify nationality;

(e) Special physical characteristics: any evident characteristics assisting identification;

(f) Signature of seafarer;

(g) Date of expiry: in two-digit Arabic numerals in the form day/month/year;

(h) Type or designation of document: character code for document type, written in capitals in the Roman alphabet (S);

(i) Unique document number: country code (see I above) followed by an alphanumeric book inventory number of no more than nine characters;

(j) Personal identification number: optional personal identification number of the seafarer; identification number of no more than 14 alphanumeric characters;

(k) Biometric template: precise specification to be developed;

(l) Machine-readable zone: according to ICAO Document 9303 specified above.

Annex II

ELECTRONIC DATABASE

The details to be provided for each record in the electronic database to be maintained by each Member in accordance with Article 4, paragraphs 1, 2, 6 and 7 of this Convention shall be restricted to:

Section 1

1. Issuing authority named on the identity document.
2. Full name of seafarer as written on the identity document.
3. Unique document number of the identity document.
4. Date of expiry or suspension or withdrawal of the identity document.

Section 2

1. Biometric template appearing on the identity document.
2. Photograph.
3. Details of all inquiries made concerning the seafarers' identity document.

Annex III

Requirements and recommended procedures and practices concerning the issuance of seafarers' identity documents

This Annex sets out minimum requirements relating to procedures to be adopted by each Member in accordance with Article 5 of this Convention, with respect to the issuance of seafarers' identity documents (referred to below as "SIDs"), including quality-control procedures.

Part A lists the mandatory results that must be achieved, as a minimum, by each Member, in implementing a system of issuance of SIDs.

Part B recommends procedures and practices for achieving those results. Part B is to be given full consideration by Members, but is not mandatory.

Part A. Mandatory results

1. Production and delivery of blank SIDs

Processes and procedures are in place to ensure the necessary security for the production and delivery of blank SIDs, including the following:

- (a) *all blank SIDs are of uniform quality and meet the specifications in content and form as contained in Annex I;*
- (b) *the materials used for production are protected and controlled;*
- (c) *blank SIDs are protected, controlled, identified and tracked during the production and delivery processes;*
- (d) *producers have the means of properly meeting their obligations in relation to the production and delivery of blank SIDs;*
- (e) *the transport of the blank SIDs from the producer to the issuing authority is secure.*

2. Custody, handling and accountability for blank and completed SIDs

Processes and procedures are in place to ensure the necessary security for the custody, handling and accountability for blank and completed SIDs, including the following:

- (a) *the custody and handling of blank and completed SIDs is controlled by the issuing authority;*
- (b) *blank, completed and voided SIDs, including those used as specimens, are protected, controlled, identified and tracked;*
- (c) *personnel involved with the process meet standards of reliability, trustworthiness and loyalty required by their positions and have appropriate training;*
- (d) *the division of responsibilities among authorized officials is designed to prevent the issuance of unauthorized SIDs.*

3. Processing of applications; suspension or withdrawal of SIDs; appeal procedures

Processes and procedures are in place to ensure the necessary security for the processing of applications, the completion of the blank SIDs into personalized SIDs by the authority and unit responsible for issuing them, and the delivery of the SIDs, including:

- (a) *processes for verification and approval ensuring that SIDs, when first applied for and when renewed, are issued only on the basis of:*

- *(i)* *applications completed with all information required by Annex I,*
- *(ii)* *proof of identity of the applicant in accordance with the law and practice of the issuing State,*
- *(iii)* *proof of nationality or permanent residence,*
- *(iv)* *proof that the applicant is a seafarer within the meaning of Article 1,*
- *(v)* *assurance that applicants, especially those with more than one nationality or having the status of permanent residents, are not issued with more than one SID,*
- *(vi)* *verification that the applicant does not constitute a risk to security, with proper respect for the fundamental rights and freedoms set out in international instruments.*

(b) *the processes ensure that:*

- *(i)* *the particulars of each item contained in Annex II are entered in the database simultaneously with issuance of the SID,*
- *(ii)* *the data, photograph, signature and biometric gathered from the applicant correspond to the applicant, and*
- *(iii)* *the data, photograph, signature and biometric gathered from the applicant are linked to the application throughout the processing, issuance and delivery of the SID.*

(c) *prompt action is taken to update the database when an issued SID is suspended or withdrawn;*

(d) *an extension and/or renewal system has been established to provide for circumstances where a seafarer is in need of extension or renewal of his or her SID and in circumstances where the SID is lost;*

(e) *the circumstances in which SIDs may be suspended or withdrawn are established in consultation with shipowners' and seafarers' organizations;*

(f) *effective and transparent appeal procedures are in place.*

4. Operation, security and maintenance of the database

Processes and procedures are in place to ensure the necessary security for the operation and maintenance of the database, including the following:

(a) *the database is secure from tampering and from unauthorized access;*

(b) *data are current, protected against loss of information and available for query at all times through the focal point;*

(c) *databases are not appended, copied, linked or written to other databases; information from the database is not used for purposes other than authenticating the seafarers' identity;*

(d) *the individual's rights are respected, including:*

- *(i)* *the right to privacy in the collection, storage, handling and communication of personal data; and*
- *(ii)* *the right of access to data concerning him or her and to have any inaccuracies corrected in a timely manner.*

5. Quality control of procedures and periodic evaluations

(a) *Processes and procedures are in place to ensure the necessary security through the quality control of procedures and periodic evaluations, including the monitoring of processes, to ensure that required performance standards are met, for:*

- *(i)* *production and delivery of blank SIDs;*
- *(ii)* *custody, handling and accountability for blank, voided and personalized SIDs;*

- *(iii)* *processing of applications, completion of blank SIDs into personalized SIDs by the authority and unit responsible for issuance and delivery; and*
- *(iv)* *operation, security and maintenance of the database.*

(b) *Periodic reviews are carried out to ensure the reliability of the issuance system and of the procedures and their conformity with the requirements of this Convention.*

(c) *Procedures are in place to protect the confidentiality of information contained in reports on periodic evaluations provided by other ratifying Members.*

Part B. Recommended procedures and practices

1. Production and delivery of blank SIDs

1.1. In the interest of security and uniformity of SIDs, the competent authority should select an effective source for the production of blank SIDs to be issued by the Member.

1.2. If the blanks are to be produced on the premises of the authority responsible for the issuance of SIDs ("the issuing authority"), section 2.2 below applies.

1.3. If an outside enterprise is selected, the competent authority should:

1.3.1. check that the enterprise is of undisputed integrity, financial stability and reliability;

1.3.2. require the enterprise to designate all the employees who will be engaged in the production of blank SIDs;

1.3.3. require the enterprise to furnish the authority with proof that demonstrates that there are adequate systems in place to ensure the reliability, trustworthiness and loyalty of designated employees and to satisfy the authority that it provides each such employee with adequate means of subsistence and adequate job security;

1.3.4. conclude a written agreement with the enterprise which, without prejudice to the authority's own responsibility for SIDs, should, in particular, establish the specifications and directions referred to under section 1.5 below and require the enterprise:

1.3.4.1. to ensure that only the designated employees, who must have assumed strict obligations of confidentiality, are engaged in the production of the blank SIDs;

1.3.4.2. to take all necessary security measures for the transport of the blank SIDs from its premises to the premises of the issuing authority. Issuing agents cannot be absolved from the liability on the grounds that they are not negligent in this regard;

1.3.4.3. to accompany each consignment with a precise statement of its contents; this statement should, in particular, specify the reference numbers of the SIDs in each package.

1.3.5. ensure that the agreement includes a provision to allow for completion if the original contractor is unable to continue;

1.3.6. satisfy itself, before signing the agreement, that the enterprise has the means of properly performing all the above obligations.

1.4. If the blank SIDs are to be supplied by an authority or enterprise outside the Member's territory, the competent authority of the Member may mandate an appropriate authority in the foreign country to ensure that the requirements recommended in this section are met.

1.5. The competent authority should inter alia:

1.5.1. establish detailed specifications for all materials to be used in the production of the blank SIDs; these materials should conform to the general specifications set out in Annex I to this Convention;

1.5.2. establish precise specifications relating to the form and content of the blank SIDs as set out in Annex I;

1.5.3. ensure that the specifications enable uniformity in the printing of blank SIDs if different printers are subsequently used;

1.5.4. provide clear directions for the generation of a unique document number to be printed on each blank SID in a sequential manner in accordance with Annex I; and

1.5.5. establish precise specifications governing the custody of all materials during the production process.

2. *Custody, handling and accountability for blank and completed SIDs*

2.1. All operations relating to the issuance process (including the custody of blank, voided and completed SIDs, the implements and materials for completing them, the processing of applications, the issuance of SIDs, the maintenance and the security of databases) should be carried out under the direct control of the issuing authority.

2.2. The issuing authority should prepare an appraisal of all officials involved in the issuance process establishing, in the case of each of them, a record of reliability, trustworthiness and loyalty.

2.3. The issuing authority should ensure that no officials involved in the issuance process are members of the same immediate family.

2.4. The individual responsibilities of the officials involved in the issuance process should be adequately defined by the issuing authority.

2.5. No single official should be responsible for carrying out all the operations required in the processing of an application for a SID and the preparation of the corresponding SID. The official who assigns applications to an official responsible for issuing SIDs should not be involved in the issuance process. There should be a rotation in the officials assigned to the different duties related to the processing of applications and the issuance of SIDs.

2.6. The issuing authority should draw up internal rules ensuring:

2.6.1. that the blank SIDs are kept secured and released only to the extent necessary to meet expected day-to-day operations and only to the officials responsible for completing them into personalized SIDs or to any specially authorized official, and that surplus blank SIDs are returned at the end of each day; measures to secure SIDs should be understood as including the use of devices for the prevention of unauthorized access and detection of intruders;

2.6.2. that any blank SIDs used as specimens are defaced and marked as such;

2.6.3. that each day a record, to be stored in a safe place, is maintained of the whereabouts of each blank SID and of each personalized SID that has not yet been issued, also identifying those that are secured and those that are in the possession of a specified official or officials; the record should be maintained by an official who is not involved in the handling of the blank SIDs or SIDs that have not yet been issued;

2.6.4. that no person should have access to the blank SIDs and to the implements and materials for completing them other than the officials responsible for completing the blank SIDs or any specially authorized official;

2.6.5. that each personalized SID is kept secured and released only to the official responsible for issuing the SID or to any specially authorized official;

2.6.5.1. the specially authorized officials should be limited to:

(a) persons acting under the written authorization of the executive head of the authority or of any person officially representing the executive head, and

(b) the controller referred to in section 5 below and persons appointed to carry out an audit or other control;

2.6.6. that officials are strictly prohibited from any involvement in the issuance process for a SID applied for by a member of their family or a close friend;

2.6.7. that any theft or attempted theft of SIDs or of implements or materials for personalizing them should be promptly reported to the police authorities for investigation.

2.7. Errors in the issuance process should invalidate the SID concerned, which may not be corrected and issued.

3. *Processing of applications; suspension or withdrawal of SIDs; appeal procedures*

3.1. The issuing authority should ensure that all officials with responsibility concerning the review of applications for SIDs have received relevant training in fraud detection and in the use of computer technology.

3.2. The issuing authority should draw up rules ensuring that SIDs are issued only on the basis of: an application completed and signed by the seafarer concerned; proof of identity; proof of nationality or permanent residence; and proof that the applicant is a seafarer.

3.3. The application should contain all the information specified as mandatory in Annex I to this Convention. The application form should require applicants to note that they will be liable to prosecution and penal sanctions if they make any statement that they know to be false.

3.4. When a SID is first applied for, and whenever subsequently considered necessary on the occasion of a renewal:

3.4.1. the application, completed except for the signature, should be presented by the applicant in person, to an official designated by the issuing authority;

3.4.2. a digital or original photograph and the biometric of the applicant should be taken under the control of the designated official;

3.4.3. the application should be signed in the presence of the designated official;

3.4.4. the application should then be transmitted by the designated official directly to the issuing authority for processing.

3.5. Adequate measures should be adopted by the issuing authority to ensure the security and the confidentiality of the digital or original photograph and the biometric.

3.6. The proof of identity provided by the applicant should be in accordance with the laws and practice of the issuing State. It may consist of a recent photograph of the applicant, certified as being a true likeness of him or her by the shipowner or shipmaster or other employer of the applicant or the director of the applicant's training establishment.

3.7. The proof of nationality or permanent residence will normally consist of the applicant's passport or certificate of admission as a permanent resident.

3.8. Applicants should be asked to declare all other nationalities that they may possess and affirm that they have not been issued with and have not applied for a SID from any other Member.

3.9. The applicant should not be issued with a SID for so long as he or she possesses another SID.

3.9.1. An early renewal system should apply in circumstances where a seafarer is aware in advance that the period of service is such that he or she will be unable to make his or her application at the date of expiry or renewal;

3.9.2. An extension system should apply in circumstances where an extension of a SID is required due to an unforeseen extension of the period of service;

3.9.3. A replacement system should apply in circumstances where a SID is lost. A suitable temporary document can be issued.

3.10. The proof that the applicant is a seafarer, within the meaning of Article 1 of this Convention should at least consist of:

3.10.1. a previous SID, or a seafarers' discharge book; or

3.10.2. a certificate of competency, qualification or other relevant training; or

3.10.3. equally cogent evidence.

3.11. Supplementary proof should be sought where deemed appropriate.

3.12. All applications should be subject to at least the following verifications by a competent official of the issuing authority of SIDs:

3.12.1. verification that the application is complete and shows no inconsistency raising doubts as to the truth of the statements made;

3.12.2. verification that the details given and the signature correspond to those on the applicant's passport or other reliable document;

3.12.3. verification, with the passport authority or other competent authority, of the genuineness of the passport or other document produced; where there is reason to doubt the genuineness of the passport, the original should be sent to the authority concerned; otherwise, a copy of the relevant pages may be sent;

3.12.4. comparison of the photograph provided, where appropriate, with the digital photograph referred to in section 3.4.2 above;

3.12.5. verification of the apparent genuineness of the certification referred to in section 3.6 above;

3.12.6. verification that the proof referred to in section 3.10 substantiates that the applicant is indeed a seafarer;

3.12.7. verification, in the database referred to in Article 4 of the Convention, to ensure that a person corresponding to the applicant has not already been issued with a SID; if the applicant has or may have more than one nationality or any permanent residence outside the country of nationality, the necessary inquiries should also be made with the competent authorities of the other country or countries concerned;

3.12.8. verification, in any relevant national or international database that may be accessible to the issuing authority, to ensure that a person corresponding to the applicant does not constitute a possible security risk.

3.13. The official referred to in section 3.12 above should prepare brief notes for the record indicating the results of each of the above verifications, and drawing attention to the facts that justify the conclusion that the applicant is a seafarer.

3.14. Once fully checked, the application, accompanied by the supporting documents and the notes for the record, should be forwarded to the official responsible for completion of the SID to be issued to the applicant.

3.15. The completed SID, accompanied by the related file in the issuing authority, should then be forwarded to a senior official of that authority for approval.

3.16. The senior official should give such approval only if satisfied, after review of at least the notes for the record, that the procedures have been properly followed and that the issuance of the SID to the applicant is justified.

3.17. This approval should be given in writing and be accompanied by explanations concerning any features of the application that need special consideration.

3.18. The SID (together with the passport or similar document provided) should be handed to the applicant directly against receipt, or sent to the applicant or, if the latter has so requested, to his or her shipmaster or employer, in both cases by reliable postal communication requiring advice of receipt.

3.19. When the SID is issued to the applicant, the particulars specified in Annex II to the Convention should be entered in the database referred to in Article 4 of the Convention.

3.20. The rules of the issuing authority should specify a maximum period for receipt after dispatch. If advice of receipt is not received within that period and after due notification of the seafarer, an appropriate annotation should be made in the database and the SID should be officially reported as lost and the seafarer informed.

3.21. All annotations to be made, such as, in particular, the brief notes for the record (see section 3.13 above) and the explanations referred to in section 3.17 should be kept in a safe place during the period of validity of the SID and for three years afterwards. Those annotations and explanations required by section 3.17 should be recorded in a separate internal database, and rendered accessible: (a) to persons responsible for monitoring operations; (b) to officials involved in the review of applications for SIDs; and (c) for training purposes.

3.22. When information is received suggesting that a SID was wrongly issued or that the conditions for its issue are no longer applicable, the matter should be promptly notified to the issuing authority with a view to its rapid withdrawal.

3.23. When a SID is suspended or withdrawn the issuing authority should immediately update its database to indicate that this SID is not currently recognized.

3.24. If an application for a SID is refused or a decision is taken to suspend or withdraw a SID, the applicant should be officially informed of his or her right of appeal and fully informed of the reasons for the decision.

3.25. The procedures for appeal should be as rapid as possible and consistent with the need for fair and complete consideration.

4. Operation, security and maintenance of the database

4.1. The issuing authority should make the necessary arrangements and rules to implement Article 4 of this Convention, ensuring in particular:

4.1.1. the availability of a focal point or electronic access over 24 hours a day, seven days a week, as required under paragraphs 4, 5 and 6 of Article 4 of the Convention;

4.1.2. the security of the database;

4.1.3. the respect for individual rights in the storage, handling and communication of data;

4.1.4. the respect for the seafarer's right to verify the accuracy of data relating to him or her and to have corrected, in a timely manner, any inaccuracies found.

4.2. The issuing authority should draw up adequate procedures for protecting the database, including:

4.2.1. a requirement for the regular creation of back-up copies of the database, to be stored on media held in a safe location away from the premises of the issuing authority;

4.2.2. the restriction to specially authorized officials of permission to access or make changes to an entry in the database once the entry has been confirmed by the official making it.

5. *Quality control of procedures and periodic evaluations*

5.1. The issuing authority should appoint a senior official of recognized integrity, loyalty and reliability, who is not involved in the custody or handling of SIDs, to act as controller:

5.1.1. to monitor on a continuous basis the implementation of these minimum requirements;

5.1.2. to draw immediate attention to any shortcomings in the implementation;

5.1.3. to provide the executive head and the concerned officials with advice on improvements to the procedures for the issuance of SIDs; and

5.1.4. to submit a quality-control report to management on the above. The controller should, if possible, be familiar with all the operations to be monitored.

5.2. The controller should report directly to the executive head of the issuing authority.

5.3. All officials of the issuing authority, including the executive head, should be placed under a duty to provide the controller with all documentation or information that the controller considers relevant to the performance of his or her tasks.

5.4. The issuing authority should make appropriate arrangements to ensure that officials can speak freely to the controller without fear of victimization.

5.5. The terms of reference of the controller should require that particular attention be given to the following tasks:

5.5.1. verifying that the resources, premises, equipment and staff are sufficient for the efficient performance of the functions of the issuing authority;

5.5.2. ensuring that the arrangements for the safe custody of the blank and completed SIDs are adequate;

5.5.3. ensuring that adequate rules, arrangements or procedures are in place in accordance with sections 2.6, 3.2, 4 and 5.4 above.

5.5.4. ensuring that those rules and procedures, as well as arrangements, are well known and understood by the officials concerned;

5.5.5. detailed monitoring on a random basis of each action carried out, including the related annotations and other records, in processing particular cases, from the receipt of the application for a SID to the end of the procedure for its issuance;

5.5.6. verification of the efficacy of the security measures used for the custody of blank SIDs, implements and materials;

5.5.7. verification, if necessary with the aid of a trusted expert, of the security and veracity of the information stored electronically and that the requirement for 24 hours a day, seven days a week access is maintained;

5.5.8. investigating any reliable report of a possible wrongful issuance of a SID or of a possible falsification or fraudulent obtention of a SID, in order to identify any internal malpractice or weakness in systems that could have resulted in or assisted the wrongful issuance or falsification or fraud;

5.5.9. investigating complaints alleging inadequate access to the details in the database given the requirements of paragraphs 2, 3 and 5 of Article 4 of the Convention, or inaccuracies in those details;

5.5.10. ensuring that reports identifying improvements to the issuance procedures and areas of weakness have been acted upon in a timely and effective manner by the executive head of the issuing authority;

5.5.11. maintaining records of quality-control checks that have been carried out;

5.5.12. ensuring that management reviews of quality-control checks have been performed and that records of such reviews are maintained.

5.6. The executive head of the issuing authority should ensure a periodic evaluation of the reliability of the issuance system and procedures, and of their conformity with the requirements of this Convention. Such evaluation should take into account the following:

5.6.1. findings of any audits of the issuance system and procedures;

5.6.2. reports and findings of investigations and of other indications relevant to the effectiveness of corrective action taken as a result of reported weaknesses or breaches of security;

5.6.3. records of SIDs issued, lost, voided or spoiled;

5.6.4. records relating to the functioning of quality control;

5.6.5. records of problems with respect to the reliability or security of the electronic database, including inquiries made to the database;

5.6.6. effects of changes to the issuance system and procedures resulting from technological improvements or innovations in the SID issuance procedures;

5.6.7. conclusions of management reviews;

5.6.8. audit of procedures to ensure that they are applied in a manner consistent with respect for fundamental principles and rights at work embodied in relevant ILO instruments.

5.7. Procedures and processes should be put in place to prevent unauthorized disclosure of reports provided by other Members.

5.8. All audit procedures and processes should ensure that the production techniques and security practices, including the stock control procedures, are sufficient to meet the requirements of this Annex.

PART C

FISHING

WORK IN FISHING CONVENTION, 2007 (No. 188)

Convention concerning work in the fishing sector

Adopted: 14 June 2007

The General Conference of the International Labour Organization,

Having been convened at Geneva by the Governing Body of the International Labour Office, and having met in its ninety-sixth Session on 30 May 2007, and

Recognizing that globalization has a profound impact on the fishing sector, and

Noting the ILO Declaration on Fundamental Principles and Rights at Work, 1998, and

Taking into consideration the fundamental rights to be found in the following international labour Conventions: the Forced Labour Convention, 1930 (No. 29), the Freedom of Association and Protection of the Right to Organise Convention, 1948 (No. 87), the Right to Organise and Collective Bargaining Convention, 1949 (No. 98), the Equal Remuneration Convention, 1951 (No. 100), the Abolition of Forced Labour Convention, 1957 (No. 105), the Discrimination (Employment and Occupation) Convention, 1958 (No. 111), the Minimum Age Convention, 1973 (No. 138), and the Worst Forms of Child Labour Convention, 1999 (No. 182), and

Noting the relevant instruments of the International Labour Organization, in particular the Occupational Safety and Health Convention (No. 155) and Recommendation (No. 164), 1981, and the Occupational Health Services Convention (No. 161) and Recommendation (No. 171), 1985, and

Noting, in addition, the Social Security (Minimum Standards) Convention, 1952 (No. 102), and considering that the provisions of Article 77 of that Convention should not be an obstacle to protection extended by Members to fishers under social security schemes, and

Recognizing that the International Labour Organization considers fishing as a hazardous occupation when compared to other occupations, and

Noting also Article 1, paragraph 3, of the Seafarers' Identity Documents Convention (Revised), 2003 (No. 185), and

Mindful of the core mandate of the Organization, which is to promote decent conditions of work, and

Mindful of the need to protect and promote the rights of fishers in this regard, and

Recalling the United Nations Convention on the Law of the Sea, 1982, and

Taking into account the need to revise the following international Conventions adopted by the International Labour Conference specifically concerning the fishing sector, namely the Minimum Age (Fishermen) Convention, 1959 (No. 112), the Medical Examination (Fishermen) Convention, 1959 (No. 113), the Fishermen's Articles of Agreement Convention, 1959 (No. 114), and the Accommodation of Crews (Fishermen) Convention, 1966 (No. 126), to bring them up to date and to reach a greater number of the world's fishers, particularly those working on board smaller vessels, and

Noting that the objective of this Convention is to ensure that fishers have decent conditions of work on board fishing vessels with regard to minimum requirements for work on board; conditions of service; accommodation and food; occupational safety and health protection; medical care and social security, and

Having decided upon the adoption of certain proposals with regard to work in the fishing sector, which is the fourth item on the agenda of the session, and

Having determined that these proposals shall take the form of an international Convention;

adopts this fourteenth day of June of the year two thousand and seven the following Convention, which may be cited as the Work in Fishing Convention, 2007.

PART I. DEFINITIONS AND SCOPE

DEFINITIONS

Article 1

1. For the purposes of the Convention:

(a) "commercial fishing" means all fishing operations, including fishing operations on rivers, lakes or canals, with the exception of subsistence fishing and recreational fishing;

(b) "competent authority" means the minister, government department or other authority having power to issue and enforce regulations, orders or other instructions having the force of law in respect of the subject matter of the provision concerned;

(c) "consultation" means consultation by the competent authority with the representative organizations of employers and workers concerned, and in particular the representative organizations of fishing vessel owners and fishers, where they exist;

(d) "fishing vessel owner" means the owner of the fishing vessel or any other organization or person, such as the manager, agent or bareboat charterer, who has assumed the responsibility for the operation of the vessel from the owner and who, on assuming such responsibility, has agreed to take over the duties and responsibilities imposed on fishing vessel owners in accordance with the Convention, regardless of whether any other organization or person fulfils certain of the duties or responsibilities on behalf of the fishing vessel owner;

(e) "fisher" means every person employed or engaged in any capacity or carrying out an occupation on board any fishing vessel, including persons working on board who are paid on the basis of a share of the catch but excluding pilots, naval personnel, other persons in the permanent service of a government, shore-based persons carrying out work aboard a fishing vessel and fisheries observers;

(f) "fisher's work agreement" means a contract of employment, articles of agreement or other similar arrangements, or any other contract governing a fisher's living and working conditions on board a vessel;

(g) "fishing vessel" or "vessel" means any ship or boat, of any nature whatsoever, irrespective of the form of ownership, used or intended to be used for the purpose of commercial fishing;

(h) "gross tonnage" means the gross tonnage calculated in accordance with the tonnage measurement regulations contained in Annex I to the International Convention on Tonnage Measurement of Ships, 1969, or any instrument amending or replacing it;

(i) "length" (L) shall be taken as 96 per cent of the total length on a waterline at 85 per cent of the least moulded depth measured from the keel line, or as the length from the foreside of the stem to the axis of the rudder stock on that waterline, if that be greater. In vessels designed with rake of keel, the waterline on which this length is measured shall be parallel to the designed waterline;

(j) "length overall" (LOA) shall be taken as the distance in a straight line parallel to the designed waterline between the foremost point of the bow and the aftermost point of the stern;

(k) "recruitment and placement service" means any person, company, institution, agency or other organization, in the public or the private sector, which is engaged in recruiting fishers on behalf of, or placing fishers with, fishing vessel owners;

(l) "skipper" means the fisher having command of a fishing vessel.

SCOPE

Article 2

1. Except as otherwise provided herein, this Convention applies to all fishers and all fishing vessels engaged in commercial fishing operations.

2. In the event of doubt as to whether a vessel is engaged in commercial fishing, the question shall be determined by the competent authority after consultation.

3. Any Member, after consultation, may extend, in whole or in part, to fishers working on smaller vessels the protection provided in this Convention for fishers working on vessels of 24 metres in length and over.

Article 3

1. Where the application of the Convention raises special problems of a substantial nature in the light of the particular conditions of service of the fishers or of the fishing vessels' operations concerned, a Member may, after consultation, exclude from the requirements of this Convention, or from certain of its provisions:

(a) fishing vessels engaged in fishing operations in rivers, lakes or canals;

(b) limited categories of fishers or fishing vessels.

2. In case of exclusions under the preceding paragraph, and where practicable, the competent authority shall take measures, as appropriate, to extend progressively the requirements under this Convention to the categories of fishers and fishing vessels concerned.

3. Each Member which ratifies this Convention shall:

(a) in its first report on the application of this Convention submitted under article 22 of the Constitution of the International Labour Organisation:

  (i) list any categories of fishers or fishing vessels excluded under paragraph 1;

  (ii) give the reasons for any such exclusions, stating the respective positions of the representative organizations of employers and workers concerned, in particular the representative organizations of fishing vessel owners and fishers, where they exist; and

  (iii) describe any measures taken to provide equivalent protection to the excluded categories; and

(b) in subsequent reports on the application of the Convention, describe any measures taken in accordance with paragraph 2.

Article 4

1. Where it is not immediately possible for a Member to implement all of the measures provided for in this Convention owing to special problems of a substantial nature in the light of insufficiently developed infrastructure or institutions, the Member may, in accordance with a plan drawn up in consultation, progressively implement all or some of the following provisions:

(a) Article 10, paragraph 1;

(b) Article 10, paragraph 3, in so far as it applies to vessels remaining at sea for more than three days;

(c) Article 15;

(d) Article 20;

(e) Article 33; and

(f) Article 38.

2. Paragraph 1 does not apply to fishing vessels which:

(a) are 24 metres in length and over; or

(b) remain at sea for more than seven days; or

(c) normally navigate at a distance exceeding 200 nautical miles from the coastline of the flag State or navigate beyond the outer edge of its continental shelf, whichever distance from the coastline is greater; or

(d) are subject to port State control as provided for in Article 43 of this Convention, except where port State control arises through a situation of force majeure,

nor to fishers working on such vessels.

3. Each Member which avails itself of the possibility afforded in paragraph 1 shall:

(a) in its first report on the application of this Convention submitted under article 22 of the Constitution of the International Labour Organisation:
   (i) indicate the provisions of the Convention to be progressively implemented;
   (ii) explain the reasons and state the respective positions of representative organizations of employers and workers concerned, and in particular the representative organizations of fishing vessel owners and fishers, where they exist; and
   (iii) describe the plan for progressive implementation; and

(b) in subsequent reports on the application of this Convention, describe measures taken with a view to giving effect to all of the provisions of the Convention.

Article 5

1. For the purpose of this Convention, the competent authority, after consultation, may decide to use length overall (LOA) in place of length (L) as the basis for measurement, in accordance with the equivalence set out in Annex I. In addition, for the purpose of the paragraphs specified in Annex III of this Convention, the competent authority, after consultation, may decide to use gross tonnage in place of length (L) or length overall (LOA) as the basis for measurement in accordance with the equivalence set out in Annex III.

2. In the reports submitted under article 22 of the Constitution, the Member shall communicate the reasons for the decision taken under this Article and any comments arising from the consultation.

PART II. GENERAL PRINCIPLES

IMPLEMENTATION

Article 6

1. Each Member shall implement and enforce laws, regulations or other measures that it has adopted to fulfil its commitments under this Convention with respect to fishers and fishing vessels under its jurisdiction. Other measures may include collective agreements, court decisions, arbitration awards, or other means consistent with national law and practice.

2. Nothing in this Convention shall affect any law, award or custom, or any agreement between fishing vessel owners and fishers, which ensures more favourable conditions than those provided for in this Convention.

COMPETENT AUTHORITY AND COORDINATION

Article 7

Each Member shall:

(a) designate the competent authority or authorities; and

(b) establish mechanisms for coordination among relevant authorities for the fishing sector at the national and local levels, as appropriate, and define their functions and responsibilities, taking into account their complementarities and national conditions and practice.

RESPONSIBILITIES OF FISHING VESSEL OWNERS, SKIPPERS AND FISHERS

Article 8

1. The fishing vessel owner has the overall responsibility to ensure that the skipper is provided with the necessary resources and facilities to comply with the obligations of this Convention.

2. The skipper has the responsibility for the safety of the fishers on board and the safe operation of the vessel, including but not limited to the following areas:

(a) providing such supervision as will ensure that, as far as possible, fishers perform their work in the best conditions of safety and health;

(b) managing the fishers in a manner which respects safety and health, including prevention of fatigue;

(c) facilitating on-board occupational safety and health awareness training; and

(d) ensuring compliance with safety of navigation, watchkeeping and associated good seamanship standards.

3. The skipper shall not be constrained by the fishing vessel owner from taking any decision which, in the professional judgement of the skipper, is necessary for the safety of the vessel and its safe navigation and safe operation, or the safety of the fishers on board.

4. Fishers shall comply with the lawful orders of the skipper and applicable safety and health measures.

PART III. MINIMUM REQUIREMENTS FOR WORK ON BOARD FISHING VESSELS

MINIMUM AGE

Article 9

1. The minimum age for work on board a fishing vessel shall be 16 years. However, the competent authority may authorize a minimum age of 15 for persons who are no longer subject to compulsory schooling as provided by national legislation, and who are engaged in vocational training in fishing.

2. The competent authority, in accordance with national laws and practice, may authorize persons of the age of 15 to perform light work during school holi-

days. In such cases, it shall determine, after consultation, the kinds of work permitted and shall prescribe the conditions in which such work shall be undertaken and the periods of rest required.

3. The minimum age for assignment to activities on board fishing vessels, which by their nature or the circumstances in which they are carried out are likely to jeopardize the health, safety or morals of young persons, shall not be less than 18 years.

4. The types of activities to which paragraph 3 of this Article applies shall be determined by national laws or regulations, or by the competent authority, after consultation, taking into account the risks concerned and the applicable international standards.

5. The performance of the activities referred to in paragraph 3 of this Article as from the age of 16 may be authorized by national laws or regulations, or by decision of the competent authority, after consultation, on condition that the health, safety and morals of the young persons concerned are fully protected and that the young persons concerned have received adequate specific instruction or vocational training and have completed basic pre-sea safety training.

6. The engagement of fishers under the age of 18 for work at night shall be prohibited. For the purpose of this Article, "night" shall be defined in accordance with national law and practice. It shall cover a period of at least nine hours starting no later than midnight and ending no earlier than 5 a.m. An exception to strict compliance with the night work restriction may be made by the competent authority when:

(a) the effective training of the fishers concerned, in accordance with established programmes and schedules, would be impaired; or

(b) the specific nature of the duty or a recognized training programme requires that fishers covered by the exception perform duties at night and the authority determines, after consultation, that the work will not have a detrimental impact on their health or well-being.

7. Nothing in this Article shall affect any obligations assumed by the Member arising from the ratification of any other international labour Convention.

MEDICAL EXAMINATION

Article 10

1. No fishers shall work on board a fishing vessel without a valid medical certificate attesting to fitness to perform their duties.

2. The competent authority, after consultation, may grant exemptions from the application of paragraph 1 of this Article, taking into account the safety and health of fishers, size of the vessel, availability of medical assistance and evacuation, duration of the voyage, area of operation, and type of fishing operation.

3. The exemptions in paragraph 2 of this Article shall not apply to a fisher working on a fishing vessel of 24 metres in length and over or which normally remains at sea for more than three days. In urgent cases, the competent authority may

permit a fisher to work on such a vessel for a period of a limited and specified duration until a medical certificate can be obtained, provided that the fisher is in possession of an expired medical certificate of a recent date.

Article 11

Each Member shall adopt laws, regulations or other measures providing for:

(a) the nature of medical examinations;

(b) the form and content of medical certificates;

(c) the issue of a medical certificate by a duly qualified medical practitioner or, in the case of a certificate solely concerning eyesight, by a person recognized by the competent authority as qualified to issue such a certificate; these persons shall enjoy full independence in exercising their professional judgement;

(d) the frequency of medical examinations and the period of validity of medical certificates;

(e) the right to a further examination by a second independent medical practitioner in the event that a person has been refused a certificate or has had limitations imposed on the work he or she may perform; and

(f) other relevant requirements.

Article 12

In addition to the requirements set out in Article 10 and Article 11, on a fishing vessel of 24 metres in length and over, or on a vessel which normally remains at sea for more than three days:

1. The medical certificate of a fisher shall state, at a minimum, that:

(a) the hearing and sight of the fisher concerned are satisfactory for the fisher's duties on the vessel; and

(b) the fisher is not suffering from any medical condition likely to be aggravated by service at sea or to render the fisher unfit for such service or to endanger the safety or health of other persons on board.

2. The medical certificate shall be valid for a maximum period of two years unless the fisher is under the age of 18, in which case the maximum period of validity shall be one year.

3. If the period of validity of a certificate expires in the course of a voyage, the certificate shall remain in force until the end of that voyage.

PART IV. CONDITIONS OF SERVICE

MANNING AND HOURS OF REST

Article 13

Each Member shall adopt laws, regulations or other measures requiring that owners of fishing vessels flying its flag ensure that:

(a) their vessels are sufficiently and safely manned for the safe navigation and operation of the vessel and under the control of a competent skipper; and

(b) fishers are given regular periods of rest of sufficient length to ensure safety and health.

Article 14

1. In addition to the requirements set out in Article 13, the competent authority shall:

(a) for vessels of 24 metres in length and over, establish a minimum level of manning for the safe navigation of the vessel, specifying the number and the qualifications of the fishers required;

(b) for fishing vessels regardless of size remaining at sea for more than three days, after consultation and for the purpose of limiting fatigue, establish the minimum hours of rest to be provided to fishers. Minimum hours of rest shall not be less than:

   (i) ten hours in any 24-hour period; and

   (ii) 77 hours in any seven-day period.

2. The competent authority may permit, for limited and specified reasons, temporary exceptions to the limits established in paragraph 1(b) of this Article. However, in such circumstances, it shall require that fishers shall receive compensatory periods of rest as soon as practicable.

3. The competent authority, after consultation, may establish alternative requirements to those in paragraphs 1 and 2 of this Article. However, such alternative requirements shall be substantially equivalent and shall not jeopardize the safety and health of the fishers.

4. Nothing in this Article shall be deemed to impair the right of the skipper of a vessel to require a fisher to perform any hours of work necessary for the immediate safety of the vessel, the persons on board or the catch, or for the purpose of giving assistance to other boats or ships or persons in distress at sea. Accordingly, the skipper may suspend the schedule of hours of rest and require a fisher to perform any hours of work necessary until the normal situation has been restored. As soon as practicable after the normal situation has been restored, the skipper shall ensure that any fishers who have performed work in a scheduled rest period are provided with an adequate period of rest.

CREW LIST

Article 15

Every fishing vessel shall carry a crew list, a copy of which shall be provided to authorized persons ashore prior to departure of the vessel, or communicated ashore immediately after departure of the vessel. The competent authority shall determine to whom and when such information shall be provided and for what purpose or purposes.

FISHER'S WORK AGREEMENT

Article 16

Each Member shall adopt laws, regulations or other measures:

(a) requiring that fishers working on vessels flying its flag have the protection of a fisher's work agreement that is comprehensible to them and is consistent with the provisions of this Convention; and

(b) specifying the minimum particulars to be included in fishers' work agreements in accordance with the provisions contained in Annex II.

Article 17

Each Member shall adopt laws, regulations or other measures regarding:

(a) procedures for ensuring that a fisher has an opportunity to review and seek advice on the terms of the fisher's work agreement before it is concluded;

(b) where applicable, the maintenance of records concerning the fisher's work under such an agreement; and

(c) the means of settling disputes in connection with a fisher's work agreement.

Article 18

The fisher's work agreement, a copy of which shall be provided to the fisher, shall be carried on board and be available to the fisher and, in accordance with national law and practice, to other concerned parties on request.

Article 19

Articles 16 to 18 and Annex II do not apply to a fishing vessel owner who is also single-handedly operating the vessel.

Article 20

It shall be the responsibility of the fishing vessel owner to ensure that each fisher has a written fisher's work agreement signed by both the fisher and the fishing vessel owner or by an authorized representative of the fishing vessel owner (or, where fishers are not employed or engaged by the fishing vessel owner, the fishing vessel owner shall have evidence of contractual or similar arrangements) providing decent work and living conditions on board the vessel as required by this Convention.

REPATRIATION

Article 21

1. Members shall ensure that fishers on a fishing vessel that flies their flag and that enters a foreign port are entitled to repatriation in the event that the fisher's

work agreement has expired or has been terminated for justified reasons by the fisher or by the fishing vessel owner, or the fisher is no longer able to carry out the duties required under the work agreement or cannot be expected to carry them out in the specific circumstances. This also applies to fishers from that vessel who are transferred for the same reasons from the vessel to the foreign port.

2. The cost of the repatriation referred to in paragraph 1 of this Article shall be borne by the fishing vessel owner, except where the fisher has been found, in accordance with national laws, regulations or other measures, to be in serious default of his or her work agreement obligations.

3. Members shall prescribe, by means of laws, regulations or other measures, the precise circumstances entitling a fisher covered by paragraph 1 of this Article to repatriation, the maximum duration of service periods on board following which a fisher is entitled to repatriation, and the destinations to which fishers may be repatriated.

4. If a fishing vessel owner fails to provide for the repatriation referred to in this Article, the Member whose flag the vessel flies shall arrange for the repatriation of the fisher concerned and shall be entitled to recover the cost from the fishing vessel owner.

5. National laws and regulations shall not prejudice any right of the fishing vessel owner to recover the cost of repatriation under third party contractual agreements.

RECRUITMENT AND PLACEMENT

Article 22

Recruitment and placement of fishers

1. Each Member that operates a public service providing recruitment and placement for fishers shall ensure that the service forms part of, or is coordinated with, a public employment service for all workers and employers.

2. Any private service providing recruitment and placement for fishers which operates in the territory of a Member shall do so in conformity with a standardized system of licensing or certification or other form of regulation, which shall be established, maintained or modified only after consultation.

3. Each Member shall, by means of laws, regulations or other measures:

(a) prohibit recruitment and placement services from using means, mechanisms or lists intended to prevent or deter fishers from engaging for work;

(b) require that no fees or other charges for recruitment or placement of fishers be borne directly or indirectly, in whole or in part, by the fisher; and

(c) determine the conditions under which any licence, certificate or similar authorization of a private recruitment or placement service may be suspended or withdrawn in case of violation of relevant laws or regulations; and specify the conditions under which private recruitment and placement services can operate.

Private employment agencies

4. A Member which has ratified the Private Employment Agencies Convention, 1997 (No. 181), may allocate certain responsibilities under this Convention to private employment agencies that provide the services referred to in paragraph 1(b) of Article 1 of that Convention. The respective responsibilities of any such private employment agencies and of the fishing vessel owners, who shall be the "user enterprise" for the purpose of that Convention, shall be determined and allocated, as provided for in Article 12 of that Convention. Such a Member shall adopt laws, regulations or other measures to ensure that no allocation of the respective responsibilities or obligations to the private emloyment agencies providing the service and to the "user enterprise" pursuant to this Convention shall preclude the fisher from asserting a right to a lien arising against the fishing vessel.

5. Notwithstanding the provisions of paragraph 4, the fishing vessel owner shall be liable in the event that the private employment agency defaults on its obligations to a fisher for whom, in the context of the Private Employment Agencies Convention, 1997 (No. 181), the fishing vessel owner is the "user enterprise".

6. Nothing in this Convention shall be deemed to impose on a Member the obligation to allow the operation in its fishing sector of private employment agencies as referred to in paragraph 4 of this Article.

PAYMENT OF FISHERS

Article 23

Each Member, after consultation, shall adopt laws, regulations or other measures providing that fishers who are paid a wage are ensured a monthly or other regular payment.

Article 24

Each Member shall require that all fishers working on board fishing vessels shall be given a means to transmit all or part of their payments received, including advances, to their families at no cost.

PART V. ACCOMMODATION AND FOOD

Article 25

Each Member shall adopt laws, regulations or other measures for fishing vessels that fly its flag with respect to accommodation, food and potable water on board.

Article 26

Each Member shall adopt laws, regulations or other measures requiring that accommodation on board fishing vessels that fly its flag shall be of sufficient size and quality and appropriately equipped for the service of the vessel and the length of time fishers live on board. In particular, such measures shall address, as appropriate, the following issues:

(a) approval of plans for the construction or modification of fishing vessels in respect of accommodation;

(b) maintenance of accommodation and galley spaces with due regard to hygiene and overall safe, healthy and comfortable conditions;

(c) ventilation, heating, cooling and lighting;

(d) mitigation of excessive noise and vibration;

(e) location, size, construction materials, furnishing and equipping of sleeping rooms, mess rooms and other accommodation spaces;

(f) sanitary facilities, including toilets and washing facilities, and supply of sufficient hot and cold water; and

(g) procedures for responding to complaints concerning accommodation that does not meet the requirements of this Convention.

Article 27

Each Member shall adopt laws, regulations or other measures requiring that:

(a) the food carried and served on board be of a sufficient nutritional value, quality and quantity;

(b) potable water be of sufficient quality and quantity; and

(c) the food and water shall be provided by the fishing vessel owner at no cost to the fisher. However, in accordance with national laws and regulations, the cost can be recovered as an operational cost if the collective agreement governing a share system or a fisher's work agreement so provides.

Article 28

1. The laws, regulations or other measures to be adopted by the Member in accordance with Articles 25 to 27 shall give full effect to Annex III concerning fishing vessel accommodation. Annex III may be amended in the manner provided for in Article 45.

2. A Member which is not in a position to implement the provisions of Annex III may, after consultation, adopt provisions in its laws and regulations or other measures which are substantially equivalent to the provisions set out in Annex III, with the exception of provisions related to Article 27.

PART VI. MEDICAL CARE, HEALTH PROTECTION AND SOCIAL SECURITY

MEDICAL CARE

Article 29

Each Member shall adopt laws, regulations or other measures requiring that:

(a) fishing vessels carry appropriate medical equipment and medical supplies for the service of the vessel, taking into account the number of fishers on board, the area of operation and the length of the voyage;

(b) fishing vessels have at least one fisher on board who is qualified or trained in first aid and other forms of medical care and who has the necessary knowledge to use the medical equipment and supplies for the vessel concerned, taking into account the number of fishers on board, the area of operation and the length of the voyage;

(c) medical equipment and supplies carried on board be accompanied by instructions or other information in a language and format understood by the fisher or fishers referred to in subparagraph (b);

(d) fishing vessels be equipped for radio or satellite communication with persons or services ashore that can provide medical advice, taking into account the area of operation and the length of the voyage; and

(e) fishers have the right to medical treatment ashore and the right to be taken ashore in a timely manner for treatment in the event of serious injury or illness.

Article 30

For fishing vessels of 24 metres in length and over, taking into account the number of fishers on board, the area of operation and the duration of the voyage, each Member shall adopt laws, regulations or other measures requiring that:

(a) the competent authority prescribe the medical equipment and medical supplies to be carried on board;

(b) the medical equipment and medical supplies carried on board be properly maintained and inspected at regular intervals established by the competent authority by responsible persons designated or approved by the competent authority;

(c) the vessels carry a medical guide adopted or approved by the competent authority, or the latest edition of the *International Medical Guide for Ships*;

(d) the vessels have access to a prearranged system of medical advice to vessels at sea by radio or satellite communication, including specialist advice, which shall be available at all times;

(e) the vessels carry on board a list of radio or satellite stations through which medical advice can be obtained; and

(f) to the extent consistent with the Member's national law and practice, medical care while the fisher is on board or landed in a foreign port be provided free of charge to the fisher.

OCCUPATIONAL SAFETY AND HEALTH AND ACCIDENT PREVENTION

Article 31

Each Member shall adopt laws, regulations or other measures concerning:

(a) the prevention of occupational accidents, occupational diseases and work-related risks on board fishing vessels, including risk evaluation and management, training and on-board instruction of fishers;

(b) training for fishers in the handling of types of fishing gear they will use and in the knowledge of the fishing operations in which they will be engaged;

(c) the obligations of fishing vessel owners, fishers and others concerned, due account being taken of the safety and health of fishers under the age of 18;

(d) the reporting and investigation of accidents on board fishing vessels flying its flag; and

(e) the setting up of joint committees on occupational safety and health or, after consultation, of other appropriate bodies.

Article 32

1. The requirements of this Article shall apply to fishing vessels of 24 metres in length and over normally remaining at sea for more than three days and, after consultation, to other vessels, taking into account the number of fishers on board, the area of operation, and the duration of the voyage.

2. The competent authority shall:

(a) after consultation, require that the fishing vessel owner, in accordance with national laws, regulations, collective bargaining agreements and practice, establish on-board procedures for the prevention of occupational accidents, injuries and diseases, taking into account the specific hazards and risks on the fishing vessel concerned; and

(b) require that fishing vessel owners, skippers, fishers and other relevant persons be provided with sufficient and suitable guidance, training material, or other appropriate information on how to evaluate and manage risks to safety and health on board fishing vessels.

3. Fishing vessel owners shall:

(a) ensure that every fisher on board is provided with appropriate personal protective clothing and equipment;

(b) ensure that every fisher on board has received basic safety training approved by the competent authority; the competent authority may grant written exemptions from this requirement for fishers who have demonstrated equivalent knowledge and experience; and

(c) ensure that fishers are sufficiently and reasonably familiarized with equipment and its methods of operation, including relevant safety measures, prior to using the equipment or participating in the operations concerned.

Article 33

Risk evaluation in relation to fishing shall be conducted, as appropriate, with the participation of fishers or their representatives.

SOCIAL SECURITY

Article 34

Each Member shall ensure that fishers ordinarily resident in its territory, and their dependants to the extent provided in national law, are entitled to benefit from social security protection under conditions no less favourable than those applicable to other workers, including employed and self-employed persons, ordinarily resident in its territory.

Article 35

Each Member shall undertake to take steps, according to national circumstances, to achieve progressively comprehensive social security protection for all fishers who are ordinarily resident in its territory.

Article 36

Members shall cooperate through bilateral or multilateral agreements or other arrangements, in accordance with national laws, regulations or practice:

(a) to achieve progressively comprehensive social security protection for fishers, taking into account the principle of equality of treatment irrespective of nationality; and

(b) to ensure the maintenance of social security rights which have been acquired or are in the course of acquisition by all fishers regardless of residence.

Article 37

Notwithstanding the attribution of responsibilities in Articles 34, 35 and 36, Members may determine, through bilateral and multilateral agreements and through provisions adopted in the framework of regional economic integration organizations, other rules concerning the social security legislation to which fishers are subject.

PROTECTION IN THE CASE OF WORK-RELATED SICKNESS, INJURY OR DEATH

Article 38

1. Each Member shall take measures to provide fishers with protection, in accordance with national laws, regulations or practice, for work-related sickness, injury or death.

2. In the event of injury due to occupational accident or disease, the fisher shall have access to:

(a) appropriate medical care; and

(b) the corresponding compensation in accordance with national laws and regulations.

3. Taking into account the characteristics within the fishing sector, the protection referred to in paragraph 1 of this Article may be ensured through:

(a) a system for fishing vessel owners' liability; or

(b) compulsory insurance, workers' compensation or other schemes.

Article 39

1. In the absence of national provisions for fishers, each Member shall adopt laws, regulations or other measures to ensure that fishing vessel owners are

responsible for the provision to fishers on vessels flying its flag, of health protection and medical care while employed or engaged or working on a vessel at sea or in a foreign port. Such laws, regulations or other measures shall ensure that fishing vessel owners are responsible for defraying the expenses of medical care, including related material assistance and support, during medical treatment in a foreign country, until the fisher has been repatriated.

2. National laws or regulations may permit the exclusion of the liability of the fishing vessel owner if the injury occurred otherwise than in the service of the vessel or the sickness or infirmity was concealed during engagement, or the injury or sickness was due to wilful misconduct of the fisher.

PART VII. COMPLIANCE AND ENFORCEMENT

Article 40

Each Member shall effectively exercise its jurisdiction and control over vessels that fly its flag by establishing a system for ensuring compliance with the requirements of this Convention including, as appropriate, inspections, reporting, monitoring, complaint procedures, appropriate penalties and corrective measures, in accordance with national laws or regulations.

Article 41

1. Members shall require that fishing vessels remaining at sea for more than three days, which:

(a) are 24 metres in length and over; or

(b) normally navigate at a distance exceeding 200 nautical miles from the coastline of the flag State or navigate beyond the outer edge of its continental shelf, whichever distance from the coastline is greater,

carry a valid document issued by the competent authority stating that the vessel has been inspected by the competent authority or on its behalf, for compliance with the provisions of this Convention concerning living and working conditions.

2. The period of validity of such document may coincide with the period of validity of a national or an international fishing vessel safety certificate, but in no case shall such period of validity exceed five years.

Article 42

1. The competent authority shall appoint a sufficient number of qualified inspectors to fulfil its responsibilities under Article 41.

2. In establishing an effective system for the inspection of living and working conditions on board fishing vessels, a Member, where appropriate, may authorize public institutions or other organizations that it recognizes as competent and independent to carry out inspections and issue documents. In all cases, the Member shall remain fully responsible for the inspection and issuance of the related documents concerning the living and working conditions of the fishers on fishing vessels that fly its flag.

Article 43

1. A Member which receives a complaint or obtains evidence that a fishing vessel that flies its flag does not conform to the requirements of this Convention shall take the steps necessary to investigate the matter and ensure that action is taken to remedy any deficiencies found.

2. If a Member, in whose port a fishing vessel calls in the normal course of its business or for operational reasons, receives a complaint or obtains evidence that such vessel does not conform to the requirements of this Convention, it may prepare a report addressed to the government of the flag State of the vessel, with a copy to the Director-General of the International Labour Office, and may take measures necessary to rectify any conditions on board which are clearly hazardous to safety or health.

3. In taking the measures referred to in paragraph 2 of this Article, the Member shall notify forthwith the nearest representative of the flag State and, if possible, shall have such representative present. The Member shall not unreasonably detain or delay the vessel.

4. For the purpose of this Article, the complaint may be submitted by a fisher, a professional body, an association, a trade union or, generally, any person with an interest in the safety of the vessel, including an interest in safety or health hazards to the fishers on board.

5. This Article does not apply to complaints which a Member considers to be manifestly unfounded.

Article 44

Each Member shall apply this Convention in such a way as to ensure that the fishing vessels flying the flag of any State that has not ratified this Convention do not receive more favourable treatment than fishing vessels that fly the flag of any Member that has ratified it.

PART VIII. AMENDMENT OF ANNEXES I, II AND III

Article 45

1. Subject to the relevant provisions of this Convention, the International Labour Conference may amend Annexes I, II and III. The Governing Body of the International Labour Office may place an item on the agenda of the Conference regarding proposals for such amendments established by a tripartite meeting of experts. The decision to adopt the proposals shall require a majority of two-thirds of the votes cast by the delegates present at the Conference, including at least half the Members that have ratified this Convention.

2. Any amendment adopted in accordance with paragraph 1 of this Article shall enter into force six months after the date of its adoption for any Member that has ratified this Convention, unless such Member has given written notice to the Director-General of the International Labour Office that it shall not enter into force for that Member, or shall only enter into force at a later date upon subsequent written notification.

Part IX. Final provisions

Article 46

This Convention revises the Minimum Age (Fishermen) Convention, 1959 (No. 112), the Medical Examination (Fishermen) Convention, 1959 (No. 113), the Fishermen's Articles of Agreement Convention, 1959 (No. 114), and the Accommodation of Crews (Fishermen) Convention, 1966 (No. 126).

Article 47

The formal ratifications of this Convention shall be communicated to the Director-General of the International Labour Office for registration.

Article 48

1. This Convention shall be binding only upon those Members of the International Labour Organization whose ratifications have been registered with the Director-General of the International Labour Office.

2. It shall come into force 12 months after the date on which the ratifications of ten Members, eight of which are coastal States, have been registered with the Director-General.

3. Thereafter, this Convention shall come into force for any Member 12 months after the date on which its ratification is registered.

Article 49

1. A Member which has ratified this Convention may denounce it after the expiration of ten years from the date on which the Convention first comes into force, by an act communicated to the Director-General of the International Labour Office for registration. Such denunciation shall not take effect until one year after the date on which it is registered.

2. Each Member which has ratified this Convention and which does not, within the year following the expiration of the period of ten years mentioned in the preceding paragraph, exercise the right of denunciation provided for in this Article, will be bound for another period of ten years and, thereafter, may denounce this Convention within the first year of each new period of ten years under the terms provided for in this Article.

Article 50

1. The Director-General of the International Labour Office shall notify all Members of the International Labour Organization of the registration of all ratifications, declarations and denunciations that have been communicated by the Members of the Organization.

2. When notifying the Members of the Organization of the registration of the last of the ratifications required to bring the Convention into force, the Director-General shall draw the attention of the Members of the Organization to the date upon which the Convention will come into force.

Article 51

The Director-General of the International Labour Office shall communicate to the Secretary-General of the United Nations for registration in accordance with Article 102 of the Charter of the United Nations full particulars of all ratifications, declarations and denunciations registered by the Director-General.

Article 52

At such times as it may consider necessary, the Governing Body of the International Labour Office shall present to the General Conference a report on the working of this Convention and shall examine the desirability of placing on the agenda of the Conference the question of its revision in whole or in part, taking into account also the provisions of Article 45.

Article 53

1. Should the Conference adopt a new Convention revising this Convention, then, unless the new Convention otherwise provides:

(a) the ratification by a Member of the new revising Convention shall *ipso jure* involve the immediate denunciation of this Convention, notwithstanding the provisions of Article 49 above, if and when the new revising Convention shall have come into force;

(b) as from the date when the new revising Convention comes into force this Convention shall cease to be open to ratification by the Members.

2. This Convention shall in any case remain in force in its actual form and content for those Members which have ratified it but have not ratified the revising Convention.

Article 54

The English and French versions of the text of this Convention are equally authoritative.

Annex I

EQUIVALENCE IN MEASUREMENT

For the purpose of this Convention, where the competent authority, after consultation, decides to use length overall (LOA) rather than length (L) as the basis of measurement:

(a) a length overall (LOA) of 16.5 metres shall be considered equivalent to a length (L) of 15 metres;

(b) a length overall (LOA) of 26.5 metres shall be considered equivalent to a length (L) of 24 metres;

(c) a length overall (LOA) of 50 metres shall be considered equivalent to a length (L) of 45 metres.

Annex II

FISHER'S WORK AGREEMENT

The fisher's work agreement shall contain the following particulars, except in so far as the inclusion of one or more of them is rendered unnecessary by the fact that the matter is regulated in another manner by national laws or regulations, or a collective bargaining agreement where applicable:

(a) the fisher's family name and other names, date of birth or age, and birthplace;

(b) the place at which and date on which the agreement was concluded;

(c) the name of the fishing vessel or vessels and the registration number of the vessel or vessels on board which the fisher undertakes to work;

(d) the name of the employer, or fishing vessel owner, or other party to the agreement with the fisher;

(e) the voyage or voyages to be undertaken, if this can be determined at the time of making the agreement;

(f) the capacity in which the fisher is to be employed or engaged;

(g) if possible, the place at which and date on which the fisher is required to report on board for service;

(h) the provisions to be supplied to the fisher, unless some alternative system is provided for by national law or regulation;

(i) the amount of wages, or the amount of the share and the method of calculating such share if remuneration is to be on a share basis, or the amount of the wage and share and the method of calculating the latter if remuneration is to be on a combined basis, and any agreed minimum wage;

(j) the termination of the agreement and the conditions thereof, namely:

  (i) if the agreement has been made for a definite period, the date fixed for its expiry;

  (ii) if the agreement has been made for a voyage, the port of destination and the time which has to expire after arrival before the fisher shall be discharged;

  (iii) if the agreement has been made for an indefinite period, the conditions which shall entitle either party to rescind it, as well as the required period of notice for rescission, provided that such period shall not be less for the employer, or fishing vessel owner or other party to the agreement with the fisher;

(k) the protection that will cover the fisher in the event of sickness, injury or death in connection with service;

(l) the amount of paid annual leave or the formula used for calculating leave, where applicable;

(m) the health and social security coverage and benefits to be provided to the fisher by the employer, fishing vessel owner, or other party or parties to the fisher's work agreement, as applicable;

(n) the fisher's entitlement to repatriation;

(o) a reference to the collective bargaining agreement, where applicable;

(p) the minimum periods of rest, in accordance with national laws, regulations or other measures; and

(q) any other particulars which national law or regulation may require.

Annex III

Fishing vessel accommodation

General provisions

1. For the purposes of this Annex:

(a) "new fishing vessel" means a vessel for which:

(i) the building or major conversion contract has been placed on or after the date of the entry into force of the Convention for the Member concerned; or

(ii) the building or major conversion contract has been placed before the date of the entry into force of the Convention for the Member concerned, and which is delivered three years or more after that date; or

(iii) in the absence of a building contract, on or after the date of the entry into force of the Convention for the Member concerned:

- the keel is laid, or
- construction identifiable with a specific vessel begins, or
- assembly has commenced comprising at least 50 tonnes or 1 per cent of the estimated mass of all structural material, whichever is less;

(b) "existing vessel" means a vessel that is not a new fishing vessel.

2. The following shall apply to all new, decked fishing vessels, subject to any exclusions provided for in accordance with Article 3 of the Convention. The competent authority may, after consultation, also apply the requirements of this Annex to existing vessels, when and in so far as it determines that this is reasonable and practicable.

3. The competent authority, after consultation, may permit variations to the provisions of this Annex for fishing vessels normally remaining at sea for less than 24 hours where the fishers do not live on board the vessel in port. In the case of such vessels, the competent authority shall ensure that the fishers concerned have adequate facilities for resting, eating and sanitation purposes.

4. Any variations made by a Member under paragraph 3 of this Annex shall be reported to the International Labour Office under article 22 of the Constitution of the International Labour Organisation.

5. The requirements for vessels of 24 metres in length and over may be applied to vessels between 15 and 24 metres in length where the competent authority determines, after consultation, that this is reasonable and practicable.

6. Fishers working on board feeder vessels which do not have appropriate accommodation and sanitary facilities shall be provided with such accommodation and facilities on board the mother vessel.

7. Members may extend the requirements of this Annex regarding noise and vibration, ventilation, heating and air conditioning, and lighting to enclosed working spaces and spaces used for storage if, after consultation, such application is considered appropriate and will not have a negative influence on the function of the process or working conditions or the quality of the catches.

8. The use of gross tonnage as referred to in Article 5 of the Convention is limited to the following specified paragraphs of this Annex: 14, 37, 38, 41, 43, 46, 49, 53, 55, 61, 64, 65 and 67. For these purposes, where the competent authority, after consultation, decides to use gross tonnage (gt) as the basis of measurement:

(a) a gross tonnage of 75 gt shall be considered equivalent to a length (L) of 15 metres or a length overall (LOA) of 16.5 metres;

(b) a gross tonnage of 300 gt shall be considered equivalent to a length (L) of 24 metres or a length overall (LOA) of 26.5 metres;

(c) a gross tonnage of 950 gt shall be considered equivalent to a length (L) of 45 metres or a length overall (LOA) of 50 metres.

Planning and control

9. The competent authority shall satisfy itself that, on every occasion when a vessel is newly constructed or the crew accommodation of a vessel has been reconstructed, such vessel complies with the requirements of this Annex. The competent authority shall, to the extent practicable, require compliance with this Annex when the crew accommodation of a vessel is substantially altered and, for a vessel that changes the flag it flies to the flag of the Member, require compliance with those requirements of this Annex that are applicable in accordance with paragraph 2 of this Annex.

10. For the occasions noted in paragraph 9 of this Annex, for vessels of 24 metres in length and over, detailed plans and information concerning accommodation shall be required to be submitted for approval to the competent authority, or an entity authorized by it.

11. For vessels of 24 metres in length and over, on every occasion when the crew accommodation of the fishing vessel has been reconstructed or substantially altered, the competent authority shall inspect the accommodation for compliance with the requirements of the Convention, and when the vessel changes the flag it flies to the flag of the Member, for compliance with those requirements of this Annex that are applicable in accordance with paragraph 2 of this Annex. The competent authority may carry out additional inspections of crew accommodation at its discretion.

12. When a vessel changes flag, any alternative requirements which the competent authority of the Member whose flag the ship was formerly flying may have adopted in accordance with paragraphs 15, 39, 47 or 62 of this Annex cease to apply to the vessel.

Design and construction

Headroom

13. There shall be adequate headroom in all accommodation spaces. For spaces where fishers are expected to stand for prolonged periods, the minimum headroom shall be prescribed by the competent authority.

14. For vessels of 24 metres in length and over, the minimum permitted headroom in all accommodation where full and free movement is necessary shall not be less than 200 centimetres.

15. Notwithstanding the provisions of paragraph 14, the competent authority may, after consultation, decide that the minimum permitted headroom shall not be less than 190 centimetres in any space - or part of any space - in such accommodation, where it is satisfied that this is reasonable and will not result in discomfort to the fishers.

Openings into and between accommodation spaces

16. There shall be no direct openings into sleeping rooms from fish rooms and machinery spaces, except for the purpose of emergency escape. Where reasonable and practicable, direct openings from galleys, storerooms, drying rooms or communal sanitary areas shall be avoided unless expressly provided otherwise.

17. For vessels of 24 metres in length and over, there shall be no direct openings, except for the purpose of emergency escape, into sleeping rooms from fish rooms and

machinery spaces or from galleys, storerooms, drying rooms or communal sanitary areas; that part of the bulkhead separating such places from sleeping rooms and external bulkheads shall be efficiently constructed of steel or another approved material and shall be watertight and gas-tight. This provision does not exclude the possibility of sanitary areas being shared between two cabins.

Insulation

18. Accommodation spaces shall be adequately insulated; the materials used to construct internal bulkheads, panelling and sheeting, and floors and joinings shall be suitable for the purpose and shall be conducive to ensuring a healthy environment. Sufficient drainage shall be provided in all accommodation spaces.

Other

19. All practicable measures shall be taken to protect fishing vessels' crew accommodation against flies and other insects, particularly when vessels are operating in mosquito-infested areas.

20. Emergency escapes from all crew accommodation spaces shall be provided as necessary.

Noise and vibration

21. The competent authority shall take measures to limit excessive noise and vibration in accommodation spaces and, as far as practicable, in accordance with relevant international standards.

22. For vessels of 24 metres in length and over, the competent authority shall adopt standards for noise and vibration in accommodation spaces which shall ensure adequate protection to fishers from the effects of such noise and vibration, including the effects of noise- and vibration-induced fatigue.

Ventilation

23. Accommodation spaces shall be ventilated, taking into account climatic conditions. The system of ventilation shall supply air in a satisfactory condition whenever fishers are on board.

24. Ventilation arrangements or other measures shall be such as to protect non-smokers from tobacco smoke.

25. Vessels of 24 metres in length and over shall be equipped with a system of ventilation for accommodation, which shall be controlled so as to maintain the air in a satisfactory condition and to ensure sufficiency of air movement in all weather conditions and climates. Ventilation systems shall be in operation at all times when fishers are on board.

Heating and air conditioning

26. Accommodation spaces shall be adequately heated, taking into account climatic conditions.

27. For vessels of 24 metres in length and over, adequate heat shall be provided, through an appropriate heating system, except in fishing vessels operating exclusively in tropical climates. The system of heating shall provide heat in all conditions, as necessary, and shall be in operation when fishers are living or working on board, and when conditions so require.

28. For vessels of 24 metres in length and over, with the exception of those regularly engaged in areas where temperate climatic conditions do not require it, air conditioning shall be provided in accommodation spaces, the bridge, the radio room and any centralized machinery control room.

Lighting

29. All accommodation spaces shall be provided with adequate light.

30. Wherever practicable, accommodation spaces shall be lit with natural light in addition to artificial light. Where sleeping spaces have natural light, a means of blocking the light shall be provided.

31. Adequate reading light shall be provided for every berth in addition to the normal lighting of the sleeping room.

32. Emergency lighting shall be provided in sleeping rooms.

33. Where a vessel is not fitted with emergency lighting in mess rooms, passageways, and any other spaces that are or may be used for emergency escape, permanent night lighting shall be provided in such spaces.

34. For vessels of 24 metres in length and over, lighting in accommodation spaces shall meet a standard established by the competent authority. In any part of the accommodation space available for free movement, the minimum standard for such lighting shall be such as to permit a person with normal vision to read an ordinary printed newspaper on a clear day.

Sleeping rooms

General

35. Where the design, dimensions or purpose of the vessel allow, the sleeping accommodation shall be located so as to minimize the effects of motion and acceleration but shall in no case be located forward of the collision bulkhead.

Floor area

36. The number of persons per sleeping room and the floor area per person, excluding space occupied by berths and lockers, shall be such as to provide adequate space and comfort for the fishers on board, taking into account the service of the vessel.

37. For vessels of 24 metres in length and over but which are less than 45 metres in length, the floor area per person of sleeping rooms, excluding space occupied by berths and lockers, shall not be less than 1.5 square metres.

38. For vessels of 45 metres in length and over, the floor area per person of sleeping rooms, excluding space occupied by berths and lockers, shall not be less than 2 square metres.

39. Notwithstanding the provisions of paragraphs 37 and 38, the competent authority may, after consultation, decide that the minimum permitted floor area per person of sleeping rooms, excluding space occupied by berths and lockers, shall not be less than 1.0 and 1.5 square metres respectively, where the competent authority is satisfied that this is reasonable and will not result in discomfort to the fishers.

Persons per sleeping room

40. To the extent not expressly provided otherwise, the number of persons allowed to occupy each sleeping room shall not be more than six.

41. For vessels of 24 metres in length and over, the number of persons allowed to occupy each sleeping room shall not be more than four. The competent authority may permit exceptions to this requirement in particular cases if the size, type or intended service of the vessel makes the requirement unreasonable or impracticable.

42. To the extent not expressly provided otherwise, a separate sleeping room or sleeping rooms shall be provided for officers, wherever practicable.

43. For vessels of 24 metres in length and over, sleeping rooms for officers shall be for one person wherever possible and in no case shall the sleeping room contain more than two berths. The competent authority may permit exceptions to the requirements of this paragraph in particular cases if the size, type or intended service of the vessel makes the requirements unreasonable or impracticable.

Other

44. The maximum number of persons to be accommodated in any sleeping room shall be legibly and indelibly marked in a place in the room where it can be conveniently seen.

45. Individual berths of appropriate dimensions shall be provided. Mattresses shall be of a suitable material.

46. For vessels of 24 metres in length and over, the minimum inside dimensions of the berths shall not be less than 198 by 80 centimetres.

47. Notwithstanding the provisions of paragraph 46, the competent authority may, after consultation, decide that the minimum inside dimensions of the berths shall not be less than 190 by 70 centimetres, where it is satisfied that this is reasonable and will not result in discomfort to the fishers.

48. Sleeping rooms shall be so planned and equipped as to ensure reasonable comfort for the occupants and to facilitate tidiness. Equipment provided shall include berths, individual lockers sufficient for clothing and other personal effects, and a suitable writing surface.

49. For vessels of 24 metres in length and over, a desk suitable for writing, with a chair, shall be provided.

50. Sleeping accommodation shall be situated or equipped, as practicable, so as to provide appropriate levels of privacy for men and for women.

Mess rooms

51. Mess rooms shall be as close as possible to the galley, but in no case shall be located forward of the collision bulkhead.

52. Vessels shall be provided with mess-room accommodation suitable for their service. To the extent not expressly provided otherwise, mess-room accommodation shall be separate from sleeping quarters, where practicable.

53. For vessels of 24 metres in length and over, mess-room accommodation shall be separate from sleeping quarters.

54. The dimensions and equipment of each mess room shall be sufficient for the number of persons likely to use it at any one time.

55. For vessels of 24 metres in length and over, a refrigerator of sufficient capacity and facilities for making hot and cold drinks shall be available and accessible to fishers at all times.

Tubs or showers, toilets and washbasins

56. Sanitary facilities, which include toilets, washbasins, and tubs or showers, shall be provided for all persons on board, as appropriate for the service of the vessel. These facilities shall meet at least minimum standards of health and hygiene and reasonable standards of quality.

57. The sanitary accommodation shall be such as to eliminate contamination of other spaces as far as practicable. The sanitary facilities shall allow for reasonable privacy.

58. Cold fresh water and hot fresh water shall be available to all fishers and other persons on board, in sufficient quantities to allow for proper hygiene. The competent authority may establish, after consultation, the minimum amount of water to be provided.

59. Where sanitary facilities are provided, they shall be fitted with ventilation to the open air, independent of any other part of the accommodation.

60. All surfaces in sanitary accommodation shall be such as to facilitate easy and effective cleaning. Floors shall have a non-slip deck covering.

61. On vessels of 24 metres in length and over, for all fishers who do not occupy rooms to which sanitary facilities are attached, there shall be provided at least one tub or shower or both, one toilet, and one washbasin for every four persons or fewer.

62. Notwithstanding the provisions of paragraph 61, the competent authority may, after consultation, decide that there shall be provided at least one tub or shower or both and one washbasin for every six persons or fewer, and at least one toilet for every eight persons or fewer, where the competent authority is satisfied that this is reasonable and will not result in discomfort to the fishers.

Laundry facilities

63. Amenities for washing and drying clothes shall be provided as necessary, taking into account the service of the vessel, to the extent not expressly provided otherwise.

64. For vessels of 24 metres in length and over, adequate facilities for washing, drying and ironing clothes shall be provided.

65. For vessels of 45 metres in length and over, adequate facilities for washing, drying and ironing clothes shall be provided in a compartment separate from sleeping rooms, mess rooms and toilets, and shall be adequately ventilated, heated and equipped with lines or other means for drying clothes.

Facilities for sick and injured fishers

66. Whenever necessary, a cabin shall be made available for a fisher who suffers illness or injury.

67. For vessels of 45 metres in length and over, there shall be a separate sick bay. The space shall be properly equipped and shall be maintained in a hygienic state.

Other facilities

68. A place for hanging foul-weather gear and other personal protective equipment shall be provided outside of, but convenient to, sleeping rooms.

Bedding, mess utensils and miscellaneous provisions

69. Appropriate eating utensils, and bedding and other linen shall be provided to all fishers on board. However, the cost of the linen can be recovered as an operational cost if the collective agreement or the fisher's work agreement so provides.

Recreational facilities

70. For vessels of 24 metres in length and over, appropriate recreational facilities, amenities and services shall be provided for all fishers on board. Where appropriate, mess rooms may be used for recreational activities.

Communication facilities

71. All fishers on board shall be given reasonable access to communication facilities, to the extent practicable, at a reasonable cost and not exceeding the full cost to the fishing vessel owner.

Galley and food storage facilities

72. Cooking equipment shall be provided on board. To the extent not expressly provided otherwise, this equipment shall be fitted, where practicable, in a separate galley.

73. The galley, or cooking area where a separate galley is not provided, shall be of adequate size for the purpose, well lit and ventilated, and properly equipped and maintained.

74. For vessels of 24 metres in length and over, there shall be a separate galley.

75. The containers of butane or propane gas used for cooking purposes in a galley shall be kept on the open deck and in a shelter which is designed to protect them from external heat sources and external impact.

76. A suitable place for provisions of adequate capacity shall be provided which can be kept dry, cool and well ventilated in order to avoid deterioration of the stores and, to the extent not expressly provided otherwise, refrigerators or other low-temperature storage shall be used, where possible.

77. For vessels of 24 metres in length and over, a provisions storeroom and refrigerator and other low-temperature storage shall be used.

Food and potable water

78. Food and potable water shall be sufficient, having regard to the number of fishers, and the duration and nature of the voyage. In addition, they shall be suitable in respect of nutritional value, quality, quantity and variety, having regard as well to the fishers' religious requirements and cultural practices in relation to food.

79. The competent authority may establish requirements for the minimum standards and quantity of food and water to be carried on board.

Clean and habitable conditions

80. Accommodation shall be maintained in a clean and habitable condition and shall be kept free of goods and stores which are not the personal property of the occupants or for their safety or rescue.

81. Galley and food storage facilities shall be maintained in a hygienic condition.

82. Waste shall be kept in closed, well-sealed containers and removed from food-handling areas whenever necessary.

Inspections by the skipper or under the authority of the skipper

83. For vessels of 24 metres in length and over, the competent authority shall require frequent inspections to be carried out, by or under the authority of the skipper, to ensure that:

(a) accommodation is clean, decently habitable and safe, and is maintained in a good state of repair;

(b) food and water supplies are sufficient; and

(c) galley and food storage spaces and equipment are hygienic and in a proper state of repair.

The results of such inspections, and the actions taken to address any deficiencies found, shall be recorded and available for review.

Variations

84. The competent authority, after consultation, may permit derogations from the provisions in this Annex to take into account, without discrimination, the interests of fishers having differing and distinctive religious and social practices, on condition that such derogations do not result in overall conditions less favourable than those which would result from the application of this Annex.

WORK IN FISHING RECOMMENDATION, 2007 (No. 199)

Recommendation concerning work in the fishing sector

Adopted: 14 June 2007

The General Conference of the International Labour Organization,

Having been convened at Geneva by the Governing Body of the International Labour Office, and having met in its ninety-sixth Session on 30 May 2007, and

Noting the Vocational Training (Fishermen) Recommendation, 1966 (No. 126), and

Taking into account the need to supersede the Work in Fishing Recommendation, 2005 (No. 196), which revised the Hours of Work (Fishing) Recommendation, 1920 (No. 7), and

Having decided upon the adoption of certain proposals with regard to work in the fishing sector, which is the fourth item on the agenda of the session, and

Having determined that these proposals shall take the form of a Recommendation supplementing the Work in Fishing Convention, 2007 (hereinafter referred to as "the Convention") and superseding the Work in Fishing Recommendation, 2005 (No. 196);

adopts this fourteenth day of June of the year two thousand and seven the following Recommendation, which may be cited as the Work in Fishing Recommendation, 2007.

PART I. CONDITIONS FOR WORK ON BOARD FISHING VESSELS

Protection of young persons

1. Members should establish the requirements for the pre-sea training of persons between the ages of 16 and 18 working on board fishing vessels, taking into account international instruments concerning training for work on board fishing vessels, including occupational safety and health issues such as night work, hazardous tasks, work with dangerous machinery, manual handling and transport of heavy loads, work in high latitudes, work for excessive periods of time and other relevant issues identified after an assessment of the risks concerned.

2. The training of persons between the ages of 16 and 18 might be provided through participation in an apprenticeship or approved training programme, which should operate under established rules and be monitored by the competent authority, and should not interfere with the person's general education.

3. Members should take measures to ensure that the safety, lifesaving and survival equipment carried on board fishing vessels carrying persons under the age of 18 is appropriate for the size of such persons.

4. The working hours of fishers under the age of 18 should not exceed eight hours per day and 40 hours per week, and they should not work overtime except where unavoidable for safety reasons.

5. Fishers under the age of 18 should be assured sufficient time for all meals and a break of at least one hour for the main meal of the day.

Medical examination

6. When prescribing the nature of the examination, Members should pay due regard to the age of the person to be examined and the nature of the duties to be performed.

7. The medical certificate should be signed by a medical practitioner approved by the competent authority.

8. Arrangements should be made to enable a person who, after examination, is determined to be unfit for work on board fishing vessels or certain types of fishing vessels, or for certain types of work on board, to apply for a further examination by a medical referee or referees who should be independent of any fishing vessel owner or of any organization of fishing vessel owners or fishers.

9. The competent authority should take into account international guidance on medical examination and certification of persons working at sea, such as the (ILO/WHO) *Guidelines for Conducting Pre-Sea and Periodic Medical Fitness Examinations for Seafarers.*

10. For fishers exempted from the application of the provisions concerning medical examination in the Convention, the competent authority should take adequate measures to provide health surveillance for the purpose of occupational safety and health.

Competency and training

11. Members should:

(a) take into account generally accepted international standards concerning training and competencies of fishers in determining the competencies required for skippers, mates, engineers and other persons working on board fishing vessels;

(b) address the following issues, with regard to the vocational training of fishers: national planning and administration, including coordination; financing and training standards; training programmes, including pre-vocational training and also short courses for working fishers; methods of training; and international cooperation; and

(c) ensure that there is no discrimination with regard to access to training.

Part II. Conditions of service

Record of service

12. At the end of each contract, a record of service in regard to that contract should be made available to the fisher concerned, or entered in the fisher's service book.

Special measures

13. For fishers excluded from the scope of the Convention, the competent authority should take measures to provide them with adequate protection with respect to their conditions of work and means of dispute settlement.

Payment of fishers

14. Fishers should have the right to advances against earnings under prescribed conditions.

15. For vessels of 24 metres in length and over, all fishers should be entitled to minimum payment in accordance with national laws, regulations or collective agreements.

Part III. Accommodation

16. When establishing requirements or guidance, the competent authority should take into account relevant international guidance on accommodation, food, and health and hygiene relating to persons working or living on board vessels, including the most recent editions of the (FAO/ILO/IMO) *Code of Safety for Fishermen and Fishing Vessels* and the (FAO/ILO/IMO) *Voluntary Guidelines for the Design, Construction and Equipment of Small Fishing Vessels.*

17. The competent authority should work with relevant organizations and agencies to develop and disseminate educational material and on-board information and guidance concerning safe and healthy accommodation and food on board fishing vessels.

18. Inspections of crew accommodation required by the competent authority should be carried out together with initial or periodic surveys or inspections for other purposes.

Design and construction

19. Adequate insulation should be provided for exposed decks over crew accommodation spaces, external bulkheads of sleeping rooms and mess rooms, machinery casings and boundary bulkheads of galleys and other spaces in which heat is produced, and, as necessary, to prevent condensation or overheating in sleeping rooms, mess rooms, recreation rooms and passageways.

20. Protection should be provided from the heat effects of any steam or hot water service pipes. Main steam and exhaust pipes should not pass through crew

accommodation or through passageways leading to crew accommodation. Where this cannot be avoided, pipes should be adequately insulated and encased.

21. Materials and furnishings used in accommodation spaces should be impervious to dampness, easy to keep clean and not likely to harbour vermin.

Noise and vibration

22. Noise levels for working and living spaces, which are established by the competent authority, should be in conformity with the guidelines of the International Labour Organization on exposure levels to ambient factors in the workplace and, where applicable, the specific protection recommended by the International Maritime Organization, together with any subsequent amending and supplementary instruments for acceptable noise levels on board ships.

23. The competent authority, in conjunction with the competent international bodies and with representatives of organizations of fishing vessel owners and fishers and taking into account, as appropriate, relevant international standards, should review on an ongoing basis the problem of vibration on board fishing vessels with the objective of improving the protection of fishers, as far as practicable, from the adverse effects of vibration.

(1) Such review should cover the effect of exposure to excessive vibration on the health and comfort of fishers and the measures to be prescribed or recommended to reduce vibration on fishing vessels to protect fishers.

(2) Measures to reduce vibration, or its effects, to be considered should include:

(a) instruction of fishers in the dangers to their health of prolonged exposure to vibration;

(b) provision of approved personal protective equipment to fishers where necessary; and

(c) assessment of risks and reduction of exposure in sleeping rooms, mess rooms, recreational accommodation and catering facilities and other fishers' accommodation by adopting measures in accordance with the guidance provided by the (ILO) *Code of practice on ambient factors in the workplace* and any subsequent revisions, taking into account the difference between exposure in the workplace and in the living space.

Heating

24. The heating system should be capable of maintaining the temperature in crew accommodation at a satisfactory level, as established by the competent authority, under normal conditions of weather and climate likely to be met with on service, and should be designed so as not to endanger the safety or health of the fishers or the safety of the vessel.

Lighting

25. Methods of lighting should not endanger the safety or health of the fishers or the safety of the vessel.

Sleeping rooms

26. Each berth should be fitted with a comfortable mattress with a cushioned bottom or a combined mattress, including a spring bottom, or a spring mattress. The cushioning material used should be made of approved material. Berths should not be placed side by side in such a way that access to one berth can be obtained only over another. The lower berth in a double tier should not be less than 0.3 metres above the floor, and the upper berth should be fitted with a dustproof bottom and placed approximately midway between the bottom of the lower berth and the lower side of the deck head beams. Berths should not be arranged in tiers of more than two. In the case of berths placed along the vessel's side, there should be only a single tier when a sidelight is situated above a berth.

27. Sleeping rooms should be fitted with curtains for the sidelights, as well as a mirror, small cabinets for toilet requisites, a book rack and a sufficient number of coat hooks.

28. As far as practicable, berthing of crew members should be so arranged that watches are separated and that no day worker shares a room with a watchkeeper.

29. On vessels of 24 metres in length and over, separate sleeping rooms for men and for women should be provided.

Sanitary accommodation

30. Sanitary accommodation spaces should have:

(a) floors of approved durable material which can be easily cleaned, and which are impervious to dampness and properly drained;

(b) bulkheads of steel or other approved material which should be watertight up to at least 0.23 metres above the level of the deck;

(c) sufficient lighting, heating and ventilation; and

(d) soil pipes and waste pipes of adequate dimensions which are constructed so as to minimize the risk of obstruction and to facilitate cleaning; such pipes should not pass through fresh water or drinking-water tanks, nor should they, if practicable, pass overhead in mess rooms or sleeping accommodation.

31. Toilets should be of an approved type and provided with an ample flush of water, available at all times and independently controllable. Where practicable, they should be situated convenient to, but separate from, sleeping rooms and washrooms. Where there is more than one toilet in a compartment, the toilets should be sufficiently screened to ensure privacy.

32. Separate sanitary facilities should be provided for men and for women.

Recreational facilities

33. Where recreational facilities are required, furnishings should include, as a minimum, a bookcase and facilities for reading, writing and, where practicable, games. Recreational facilities and services should be reviewed frequently to ensure that they are appropriate in the light of changes in the needs of fishers resulting from

technical, operational and other developments. Consideration should also be given to including the following facilities at no cost to the fishers, where practicable:

(a) a smoking room;

(b) television viewing and the reception of radio broadcasts;

(c) projection of films or video films, the stock of which should be adequate for the duration of the voyage and, where necessary, changed at reasonable intervals;

(d) sports equipment including exercise equipment, table games, and deck games;

(e) a library containing vocational and other books, the stock of which should be adequate for the duration of the voyage and changed at reasonable intervals;

(f) facilities for recreational handicrafts; and

(g) electronic equipment such as radio, television, video recorder, CD/DVD player, personal computer and software, and cassette recorder/player.

Food

34. Fishers employed as cooks should be trained and qualified for their position on board.

Part IV. Medical care, health protection and social security

Medical care on board

35. The competent authority should establish a list of medical supplies and equipment appropriate to the risks concerned that should be carried on fishing vessels; such list should include women's sanitary protection supplies together with discreet, environmentally friendly disposal units.

36. Fishing vessels carrying 100 or more fishers should have a qualified medical doctor on board.

37. Fishers should receive training in basic first aid in accordance with national laws and regulations, taking into account applicable international instruments.

38. A standard medical report form should be specially designed to facilitate the confidential exchange of medical and related information concerning individual fishers between the fishing vessel and the shore in cases of illness or injury.

39. For vessels of 24 metres in length and over, in addition to the provisions of Article 32 of the Convention, the following elements should be taken into account:

(a) when prescribing the medical equipment and supplies to be carried on board, the competent authority should take into account international recommendations in this field, such as those contained in the most recent editions of the (ILO/IMO/WHO) *International Medical Guide for Ships* and the (WHO) *Model List of Essential Medicines*, as well as advances in medical knowledge and approved methods of treatment;

(b) inspections of medical equipment and supplies should take place at intervals of no more than 12 months; the inspector should ensure that expiry dates and conditions of storage of all medicines are checked, the contents of the medicine chest are listed and conform to the medical guide used nationally, and medical supplies are labelled with generic names in addition to any brand names used, and with expiry dates and conditions of storage;

(c) the medical guide should explain how the contents of the medical equipment and supplies are to be used, and should be designed to enable persons other than a medical doctor to care for the sick or injured on board, both with and without medical advice by radio or satellite communication; the guide should be prepared taking into account international recommendations in this field, including those contained in the most recent editions of the (ILO/IMO/WHO) *International Medical Guide for Ships* and the (IMO) *Medical First Aid Guide for Use in Accidents Involving Dangerous Goods*; and

(d) medical advice provided by radio or satellite communication should be available free of charge to all vessels irrespective of the flag they fly.

Occupational safety and health

Research, dissemination of information and consultation

40. In order to contribute to the continuous improvement of safety and health of fishers, Members should have in place policies and programmes for the prevention of accidents on board fishing vessels which should provide for the gathering and dissemination of occupational safety and health materials, research and analysis, taking into consideration technological progress and knowledge in the field of occupational safety and health as well as of relevant international instruments.

41. The competent authority should take measures to ensure regular consultations on safety and health matters with the aim of ensuring that all concerned are kept reasonably informed of national, international and other developments in the field and on their possible application to fishing vessels flying the flag of the Member.

42. When ensuring that fishing vessel owners, skippers, fishers and other relevant persons receive sufficient and suitable guidance, training material, or other appropriate information, the competent authority should take into account relevant international standards, codes, guidance and other information. In so doing, the competent authority should keep abreast of and utilize international research and guidance concerning safety and health in the fishing sector, including relevant research in occupational safety and health in general which may be applicable to work on board fishing vessels.

43. Information concerning particular hazards should be brought to the attention of all fishers and other persons on board through official notices containing instructions or guidance, or other appropriate means.

44. Joint committees on occupational safety and health should be established:

(a) ashore; or

(b) on fishing vessels, where determined by the competent authority, after consultation, to be practicable in light of the number of fishers on board the vessel.

Occupational safety and health management systems

45. When establishing methods and programmes concerning safety and health in the fishing sector, the competent authority should take into account any relevant international guidance concerning occupational safety and health management systems, including the *Guidelines on occupational safety and health management systems, ILO-OSH 2001*.

Risk evaluation

46. (1) Risk evaluation in relation to fishing should be conducted, as appropriate, with the participation of fishers or their representatives and should include:

(a) risk assessment and management;

(b) training, taking into consideration the relevant provisions of Chapter III of the International Convention on Standards of Training, Certification and Watchkeeping for Fishing Vessel Personnel, 1995 (STCW-F Convention) adopted by the IMO; and

(c) on-board instruction of fishers.

(2) To give effect to subparagraph (1)(a), Members, after consultation, should adopt laws, regulations or other measures requiring:

(a) the regular and active involvement of all fishers in improving safety and health by continually identifying hazards, assessing risks and taking action to address risks through safety management;

(b) an occupational safety and health management system that may include an occupational safety and health policy, provisions for fisher participation and provisions concerning organizing, planning, implementing and evaluating the system and taking action to improve the system; and

(c) a system for the purpose of assisting in the implementation of a safety and health policy and programme and providing fishers with a forum to influence safety and health matters; on-board prevention procedures should be designed so as to involve fishers in the identification of hazards and potential hazards and in the implementation of measures to reduce or eliminate such hazards.

(3) When developing the provisions referred to in subparagraph (1)(a), Members should take into account the relevant international instruments on risk assessment and management.

Technical specifications

47. Members should address the following, to the extent practicable and as appropriate to the conditions in the fishing sector:

(a) seaworthiness and stability of fishing vessels;

(b) radio communications;

(c) temperature, ventilation and lighting of working areas;

(d) mitigation of the slipperiness of deck surfaces;

(e) machinery safety, including guarding of machinery;

(f) vessel familiarization for fishers and fisheries observers new to the vessel;

(g) personal protective equipment;

(h) firefighting and lifesaving;

(i) loading and unloading of the vessel;

(j) lifting gear;

(k) anchoring and mooring equipment;

(l) safety and health in living quarters;

(m) noise and vibration in work areas;

(n) ergonomics, including in relation to the layout of workstations and manual lifting and handling;

(o) equipment and procedures for the catching, handling, storage and processing of fish and other marine resources;

(p) vessel design, construction and modification relevant to occupational safety and health;

(q) navigation and vessel handling;

(r) hazardous materials used on board the vessel;

(s) safe means of access to and exit from fishing vessels in port;

(t) special safety and health requirements for young persons;

(u) prevention of fatigue; and

(v) other issues related to safety and health.

48. When developing laws, regulations or other measures concerning technical standards relating to safety and health on board fishing vessels, the competent authority should take into account the most recent edition of the (FAO/ILO/IMO) *Code of Safety for Fishermen and Fishing Vessels, Part A*.

Establishment of a list of occupational diseases

49. Members should establish a list of diseases known to arise out of exposure to dangerous substances or conditions in the fishing sector.

Social security

50. For the purpose of extending social security protection progressively to all fishers, Members should maintain up to date information on the following:

(a) the percentage of fishers covered;

(b) the range of contingencies covered; and

(c) the level of benefits.

51. Every person protected under Article 34 of the Convention should have a right of appeal in the case of a refusal of the benefit or of an adverse determination as to the quality or quantity of the benefit.

52. The protections referred to in Articles 38 and 39 of the Convention should be granted throughout the contingency covered.

Part V. Other provisions

53. The competent authority should develop an inspection policy for authorized officers to take the measures referred to in paragraph 2 of Article 43 of the Convention.

54. Members should cooperate with each other to the maximum extent possible in the adoption of internationally agreed guidelines on the policy referred to in paragraph 53 of this Recommendation.

55. A Member, in its capacity as a coastal State, when granting licences for fishing in its exclusive economic zone, may require that fishing vessels comply with the requirements of the Convention. If such licences are issued by coastal States, these States should take into account certificates or other valid documents stating that the vessel concerned has been inspected by the competent authority or on its behalf and has been found to be in compliance with the provisions of the Convention.

RESOLUTIONS ON FISHING ADOPTED BY THE INTERNATIONAL LABOUR CONFERENCE AT ITS 96TH SESSION (Geneva, June 2007)

III

Resolution concerning promotion of the ratification of the Work in Fishing Convention, 2007[1]

The General Conference of the International Labour Organization,

Having adopted the Work in Fishing Convention, 2007,

Noting that the success of the Convention will depend upon its being widely ratified, with the effective implementation of its requirements,

Mindful that the mandate of the Organization includes the promotion of decent work and living conditions;

Invites the Governing Body of the International Labour Office to request the Director-General to give due priority to conducting tripartite work to develop guidelines for flag State implementation and to develop guidelines to establish national action plans for progressive implementation of relevant provisions of the Convention,

Further invites the Governing Body to request the Director-General to give due consideration in the programme and budget for technical cooperation programmes to promote the ratification of the Convention and to assist members requesting assistance in its implementation in such areas as:

- technical assistance for Members, including capacity building for national administrations as well as representative organizations of fishing vessel owners and fishers, and the drafting of national legislation to meet the requirements of the Convention;
- the development of training materials for inspectors and other staff;
- the training of inspectors;

[1] Adopted on 12 June 2007.

- the development of promotional materials and advocacy tools for the Convention;
- national and regional seminars, as well as workshops on the Convention; and
- promoting the ratification and implementation of the Convention within ILO Decent Work Country Programmes.

IV

Resolution concerning port State control[1]

The General Conference of the International Labour Organization,

Having adopted the Work in Fishing Convention, 2007,

Considering that this Convention aims to establish a new pillar of international legislation for the fishing industry,

Mindful of the mandate of the Organization to promote decent work and living conditions,

Noting that sustainable development consists of three pillars: social, economic and environmental,

Noting Articles 43 and 44 of the adopted Convention, which provide for port State responsibilities and control under the terms of "no more favourable treatment",

Noting that the uniform and harmonized implementation of port State responsibilities in accordance with the relevant provisions of the Convention will contribute to the successful implementation of the Convention,

Considering that, given the global nature of the fishing industry, it is important for port State control officers to receive proper guidelines for the performance of their duties,

Recognizing the work done by the International Maritime Organization (IMO) and the Food and Agriculture Organization of the United Nations (FAO) in this area, and the importance that the international community attaches to cooperation among international agencies;

Invites the Governing Body of the International Labour Office to convene a tripartite meeting of experts on the fishing sector to develop suitable guidance for port State control officers concerning the relevant provisions of the Work in Fishing Convention, 2007, and to request that the Office seek the technical expertise of the IMO and FAO and other relevant international bodies in this regard.

---

[1] Adopted on 12 June 2007.

V

Resolution concerning tonnage measurement and accommodation[1]

The General Conference of the International Labour Organization,

Having adopted the Work in Fishing Convention, 2007,

Noting the difficulties caused by making an equivalence between the measurement of the size of vessels in terms of length and gross tonnage and the impact it has in the fishing industries,

Recognizing the impact the International Convention on Tonnage Measurement of Ships, 1969, has on the safe design of vessels, including their accommodation,

Recognizing also the importance of accommodation for the provision of decent work for fishers,

Recalling the resolution concerning tonnage measurement and the accommodation of crews adopted by the 29th Session of the Joint Maritime Commission, which was noted by the Governing Body of the International Labour Office at its 280th Session,

Aware that the International Maritime Organization (IMO) is considering the effects of the International Convention on Tonnage Measurement of Ships, 1969, on ship safety, accommodation, safety, health and welfare, and port charges;

Invites the Governing Body to request the Director-General to monitor these developments and to evaluate any amendment to or interpretation agreements of the International Convention on Tonnage Measurement of Ships, 1969, which may have an impact on the Work in Fishing Convention, 2007, especially on Annex III;

Invites the Governing Body to request the Director-General to report to it any developments which may have an impact on the Work in Fishing Convention, 2007, especially on Annex III;

Further invites the Governing Body to act on such a report by giving due priority, if required, to convening a tripartite meeting of experts, as provided for in Article 45 of the Work in Fishing Convention, 2007, to address the matter with a view to maintaining the relevance of Annex III of that Convention.

[1] Adopted on 12 June 2007.

VI

Resolution concerning promotion of welfare for the fishers[1]

The General Conference of the International Labour Organization,

Having adopted the Work in Fishing Convention, 2007,

Recognizing that the provision of adequate social protection and social security for all is a universally accepted development goal,

Acknowledging the specific nature of the fishing industry and the fact that fishers require special protection;

Invites the Governing Body of the International Labour Office to request the Director-General, in a cost-effective manner, to consider, as appropriate, the following social issues related to fisheries, as part of its programme and budget:

- promotion of the provision of effective social protection and social security to all fishers within the ongoing work of the Organization so as to secure effective social protection for all;
- the particular employment problems that are faced by women in the fishing industry, including discrimination and the barriers to access to employment in the industry;
- the causes of occupational diseases and injuries in the fishing sector;
- the need to encourage member States to strongly ensure that fishers on fishing vessels in their ports are able to have access to fishers' and seafarers' welfare facilities;
- the need to provide member States and social partners with advice on developing strategies to improve the retention of fishers and the recruitment and retention of new entrants in fisheries;
- the issues relating to migrant fishers; and
- the education of fishers and their families by working together with appropriate bodies for the prevention of HIV/AIDS among fishers and in fishing communities.

[1] Adopted on 12 June 2007.

PART D

THE FUNDAMENTAL CONVENTIONS

FREEDOM OF ASSOCIATION AND THE EFFECTIVE RECOGNITION OF THE RIGHT TO COLLECTIVE BARGAINING

All workers and all employers have the right to freely form and join groups for the support and advancement of their occupational interests. This basic human right goes together with freedom of expression and is the basis of democratic representation and governance. People need to be able to exercise their right to influence work-related matters that directly concern them. In other words, their voice needs to be heard and taken into account.

Freedom of association means that workers and employers can set up, join and run their own organizations without interference from the State or one another. Along with this right is the responsibility of people to respect the law of the land. However, the law of the land, in turn, must respect the principle of freedom of association. These principles cannot be ignored or prohibited for any sector of activity or group of workers.

The right freely to run their own activities means that workers' and employers' organizations can independently determine how they best wish to promote and defend their occupational interests. This covers both long-term strategies and action in specific circumstances, including recourse to strike and lock out. They can affiliate independently with international organizations and cooperate within them in pursuit of their mutual interests.

If the collective bargaining system does not produce an acceptable result and strike action is taken, certain limited categories of workers can be excluded from such action to ensure the basic safety of the population and essential functioning of the State.

Voluntary collective bargaining is a process through which employers or their organizations and trade unions or, in their absence, representatives freely designated by the workers discuss and negotiate their relations, in particular terms and conditions of work. Such bargaining in good faith aims at reaching mutually acceptable collective agreements.

The collective bargaining process also covers the phase before actual negotiations information sharing, consultation, joint assessments – as well as the implementation – of collective agreements. Where agreement is not reached, dispute settlement procedures ranging from conciliation through mediation to arbitration may be used.

To realize the principle of freedom of association and the right to collective bargaining in practice requires, among other things:

- a legal basis which guarantees that these rights are enforced;
- an enabling institutional framework, which can be tripartite or between the employers' and workers' organizations;
- the absence of discrimination against individuals who wish to exercise their rights to have their voice heard, and;
- acceptance by employers' and workers' organizations as partners for solving joint problems and dealing with mutual challenges.

Freedom of Association and Protection of the Right to Organise Convention (No. 87)

Adopted: 9 July 1948
Entered into force: 4 July 1950

The General Conference of the International Labour Organisation,

Having been convened at San Francisco by the Governing Body of the International Labour Office, and having met in its Thirty-first Session on 17 June 1948,

Having decided to adopt, in the form of a Convention, certain proposals concerning freedom of association and protection of the right to organise, which is the seventh item on the agenda of the session,

Considering that the Preamble to the Constitution of the International Labour Organisation declares "recognition of the principle of freedom of association" to be a means of improving conditions of labour and of establishing peace,

Considering that the Declaration of Philadelphia reaffirms that "freedom of expression and of association are essential to sustained progress",

Considering that the International Labour Conference, at its Thirtieth Session, unanimously adopted the principles which should form the basis for international regulation,

Considering that the General Assembly of the United Nations, at its Second Session, endorsed these principles and requested the International Labour Organisation to continue every effort in order that it may be possible to adopt one or several international Conventions,

adopts this ninth day of July of the year one thousand nine hundred and forty-eight the following Convention, which may be cited as the Freedom of Association and Protection of the Right to Organise Convention, 1948:

PART I. FREEDOM OF ASSOCIATION

Article 1

Each Member of the International Labour Organisation for which this Convention is in force undertakes to give effect to the following provisions.

Article 2

Workers and employers, without distinction whatsoever, shall have the right to establish and, subject only to the rules of the organisation concerned, to join organisations of their own choosing without previous authorisation.

Article 3

1. Workers' and employers' organisations shall have the right to draw up their constitutions and rules, to elect their representatives in full freedom, to organise their administration and activities and to formulate their programmes.

2. The public authorities shall refrain from any interference which would restrict this right or impede the lawful exercise thereof.

Article 4

Workers' and employers' organisations shall not be liable to be dissolved or suspended by administrative authority.

Article 5

Workers' and employers' organisations shall have the right to establish and join federations and confederations and any such organisation, federation or confederation shall have the right to affiliate with international organisations of workers and employers.

Article 6

The provisions of Articles 2, 3 and 4 hereof apply to federations and confederations of workers' and employers' organisations.

Article 7

The acquisition of legal personality by workers' and employers' organisations, federations and confederations shall not be made subject to conditions of such a character as to restrict the application of the provisions of Articles 2, 3 and 4 hereof.

Article 8

1. In exercising the rights provided for in this Convention workers and employers and their respective organisations, like other persons or organised collectivities, shall respect the law of the land.

2. The law of the land shall not be such as to impair, nor shall it be so applied as to impair, the guarantees provided for in this Convention.

Article 9

1. The extent to which the guarantees provided for in this Convention shall apply to the armed forces and the police shall be determined by national laws or regulations.

2. In accordance with the principle set forth in paragraph 8 of article 19 of the Constitution of the International Labour Organisation the ratification of this Convention by any Member shall not be deemed to affect any existing law, award, custom or agreement in virtue of which members of the armed forces or the police enjoy any right guaranteed by this Convention.

Article 10

In this Convention the term "organisation" means any organisation of workers or of employers for furthering and defending the interests of workers or of employers.

PART II. PROTECTION OF THE RIGHT TO ORGANISE

Article 11

Each Member of the International Labour Organisation for which this Convention is in force undertakes to take all necessary and appropriate measures to ensure that workers and employers may exercise freely the right to organise.

Part III. Miscellaneous provisions

Article 12

1. In respect of the territories referred to in article 35 of the Constitution of the International Labour Organisation as amended by the Constitution of the International Labour Organisation Instrument of Amendment, 1946, other than the territories referred to in paragraphs 4 and 5 of the said Article as so amended, each Member of the Organisation which ratifies this Convention shall communicate to the Director-General of the International Labour Office with or as soon as possible after its ratification a declaration stating:

(a) the territories in respect of which it undertakes that the provisions of the Convention shall be applied without modification;

(b) the territories in respect of which it undertakes that the provisions of the Convention shall be applied subject to modifications, together with details of the said modifications;

(c) the territories in respect of which the Convention is inapplicable and in such cases the grounds on which it is inapplicable;

(d) the territories in respect of which it reserves its decision.

2. The undertakings referred to in subparagraphs (a) and (b) of paragraph 1 of this Article shall be deemed to be an integral part of the ratification and shall have the force of ratification.

3. Any Member may at any time by a subsequent declaration cancel in whole or in part any reservations made in its original declaration in virtue of subparagraphs (b), (c) or (d) of paragraph 1 of this Article.

4. Any Member may, at any time at which this Convention is subject to denunciation in accordance with the provisions of Article 16, communicate to the Director-General a declaration modifying in any other respect the terms of any former declaration and stating the present position in respect of such territories as it may specify.

Article 13

1. Where the subject matter of this Convention is within the self-governing powers of any non-metropolitan territory, the Member responsible for the international relations of that territory may, in agreement with the Government of the territory, communicate to the Director-General of the International Labour Office a declaration accepting on behalf of the territory the obligations of this Convention.

2. A declaration accepting the obligations of this Convention may be communicated to the Director-General of the International Labour Office:

(a) by two or more Members of the Organisation in respect of any territory which is under their joint authority; or

(b) by any international authority responsible for the administration of any territory, in virtue of the Charter of the United Nations or otherwise, in respect of any such territory.

3. Declarations communicated to the Director-General of the International Labour Office in accordance with the preceding paragraphs of this Article shall

indicate whether the provisions of the Convention will be applied in the territory concerned without modification or subject to modifications; when the declaration indicates that the provisions of the Convention will be applied subject to modifications it shall give details of the said modifications.

4. The Member, Members or international authority concerned may at any time by a subsequent declaration renounce in whole or in part the right to have recourse to any modification indicated in any former declaration.

5. The Member, Members or international authority concerned may, at any time at which this Convention is subject to denunciation in accordance with the provisions of Article 16, communicate to the Director-General of the International Labour Office a declaration modifying in any other respect the terms of any former declaration and stating the present position in respect of the application of the Convention.

PART IV. FINAL PROVISIONS

Article 14

The formal ratifications of this Convention shall be communicated to the Director-General of the International Labour Office for registration.

Article 15

1. This Convention shall be binding only upon those Members of the International Labour Organisation whose ratifications have been registered with the Director-General.

2. It shall come into force twelve months after the date on which the ratifications of two Members have been registered with the Director-General.

3. Thereafter, this Convention shall come into force for any Member twelve months after the date on which its ratification has been registered.

Article 16

1. A Member which has ratified this Convention may denounce it after the expiration of ten years from the date on which the Convention first comes into force, by an act communicated to the Director-General of the International Labour Office for registration. Such denunciation shall not take effect until one year after the date on which it is registered.

2. Each Member which has ratified this Convention and which does not, within the year following the expiration of the period of ten years mentioned in the preceding paragraph, exercise the right of denunciation provided for in this Article, will be bound for another period of ten years and, thereafter, may denounce this Convention at the expiration of each period of ten years under the terms provided for in this Article.

Article 17

1. The Director-General of the International Labour Office shall notify all Members of the International Labour Organisation of the registration of all ratifica-

tions, declarations and denunciations communicated to him by the Members of the Organisation.

2. When notifying the Members of the Organisation of the registration of the second ratification communicated to him, the Director-General shall draw the attention of the Members of the Organisation to the date upon which the Convention will come into force.

Article 18

The Director-General of the International Labour Office shall communicate to the Secretary-General of the United Nations for registration in accordance with Article 102 of the Charter of the United Nations full particulars of all ratifications, declarations and acts of denunciation registered by him in accordance with the provisions of the preceding Articles.

Article 19

At such times as it may consider necessary the Governing Body of the International Labour Office shall present to the General Conference a report on the working of this Convention and shall examine the desirability of placing on the agenda of the Conference the question of its revision in whole or in part.

Article 20

1. Should the Conference adopt a new Convention revising this Convention in whole or in part, then, unless the new Convention otherwise provides,

(a) the ratification by a Member of the new revising Convention shall *ipso jure* involve the immediate denunciation of this Convention, notwithstanding the provisions of Article 16 above, if and when the new revising Convention shall have come into force;

(b) as from the date when the new revising Convention comes into force this Convention shall cease to be open to ratification by the Members.

2. This Convention shall in any case remain in force in its actual form and content for those Members which have ratified it but have not ratified the revising Convention.

Article 21

The English and French versions of the text of this Convention are equally authoritative.

Right to Organise and Collective Bargaining Convention (No. 98)

Adopted: 1 July 1949
Entered into force: 18 July 1951

The General Conference of the International Labour Organisation,

Having been convened at Geneva by the Governing Body of the International Labour Office, and having met in its Thirty-second Session on 8 June 1949, and

Having decided upon the adoption of certain proposals concerning the application of the principles of the right to organise and to bargain collectively, which is the fourth item on the agenda of the session, and

Having determined that these proposals shall take the form of an international Convention,

adopts this first day of July of the year one thousand nine hundred and forty-nine the following Convention, which may be cited as the Right to Organise and Collective Bargaining Convention, 1949:

Article 1

1. Workers shall enjoy adequate protection against acts of anti-union discrimination in respect of their employment.

2. Such protection shall apply more particularly in respect of acts calculated to:

(a) make the employment of a worker subject to the condition that he shall not join a union or shall relinquish trade union membership;

(b) cause the dismissal of or otherwise prejudice a worker by reason of union membership or because of participation in union activities outside working hours or, with the consent of the employer, within working hours.

Article 2

1. Workers' and employers' organisations shall enjoy adequate protection against any acts of interference by each other or each other's agents or members in their establishment, functioning or administration.

2. In particular, acts which are designed to promote the establishment of workers' organisations under the domination of employers or employers' organisations, or to support workers' organisations by financial or other means, with the object of placing such organisations under the control of employers or employers' organisations, shall be deemed to constitute acts of interference within the meaning of this Article.

Article 3

Machinery appropriate to national conditions shall be established, where necessary, for the purpose of ensuring respect for the right to organise as defined in the preceding Articles.

Article 4

Measures appropriate to national conditions shall be taken, where necessary, to encourage and promote the full development and utilisation of machinery for voluntary negotiation between employers or employers' organisations and workers' organisations, with a view to the regulation of terms and conditions of employment by means of collective agreements.

Article 5

1. The extent to which the guarantees provided for in this Convention shall apply to the armed forces and the police shall be determined by national laws or regulations.

2. In accordance with the principle set forth in paragraph 8 of Article 19 of the Constitution of the International Labour Organisation the ratification of this Convention by any Member shall not be deemed to affect any existing law, award, custom or agreement in virtue of which members of the armed forces or the police enjoy any right guaranteed by this Convention.

Article 6

This Convention does not deal with the position of public servants engaged in the administration of the State, nor shall it be construed as prejudicing their rights or status in any way.

Article 7

The formal ratifications of this Convention shall be communicated to the Director-General of the International Labour Office for registration.

Article 8

1. This Convention shall be binding only upon those Members of the International Labour Organisation whose ratifications have been registered with the Director-General.

2. It shall come into force twelve months after the date on which the ratifications of two Members have been registered with the Director-General.

3. Thereafter, this Convention shall come into force for any Member twelve months after the date on which its ratification has been registered.

Article 9

1. Declarations communicated to the Director-General of the International Labour Office in accordance with paragraph 2 of Article 35 of the Constitution of the International Labour Organisation shall indicate:

(a) the territories in respect of which the Member concerned undertakes that the provisions of the Convention shall be applied without modification;

(b) the territories in respect of which it undertakes that the provisions of the Convention shall be applied subject to modifications, together with details of the said modifications;

(c) the territories in respect of which the Convention is inapplicable and in such cases the grounds on which it is inapplicable;

(d) the territories in respect of which it reserves its decision pending further consideration of the position.

2. The undertakings referred to in subparagraphs (a) and (b) of paragraph 1 of this Article shall be deemed to be an integral part of the ratification and shall have the force of ratification.

3. Any Member may at any time by a subsequent declaration cancel in whole or in part any reservation made in its original declaration in virtue of subparagraph (b), (c) or (d) of paragraph 1 of this Article.

4. Any Member may, at any time at which the Convention is subject to denunciation in accordance with the provisions of Article 11, communicate to the Director-General a declaration modifying in any other respect the terms of any former declaration and stating the present position in respect of such territories as it may specify.

Article 10

1. Declarations communicated to the Director-General of the International Labour Office in accordance with paragraph 4 or 5 of Article 35 of the Constitution of the International Labour Organisation shall indicate whether the provisions of the Convention will be applied in the territory concerned without modification or subject to modifications; when the declaration indicates that the provisions of the Convention will be applied subject to modifications, it shall give details of the said modifications.

2. The Member, Members or international authority concerned may at any time by a subsequent declaration renounce in whole or in part the right to have recourse to any modification indicated in any former declaration.

3. The Member, Members or international authority concerned may, at any time at which the Convention is subject to denunciation in accordance with the provisions of Article 11, communicate to the Director-General a declaration modifying in any other respect the terms of any former declaration and stating the present position in respect of the application of the Convention.

Article 11

1. A Member which has ratified this Convention may denounce it after the expiration of ten years from the date on which the Convention first comes into force, by an act communicated to the Director-General of the International Labour Office for registration. Such denunciation shall not take effect until one year after the date on which it is registered.

2. Each Member which has ratified this Convention and which does not, within the year following the expiration of the period of ten years mentioned in the preceding paragraph, exercise the right of denunciation provided for in this Article, will be bound for another period of ten years and, thereafter, may denounce this Convention at the expiration of each period of ten years under the terms provided for in this Article.

Article 12

1. The Director-General of the International Labour Office shall notify all Members of the International Labour Organisation of the registration of all ratifications, declarations and denunciations communicated to him by the Members of the Organisation.

2. When notifying the Members of the Organisation of the registration of the second ratification communicated to him, the Director-General shall draw the attention of the Members of the Organisation to the date upon which the Convention will come into force.

Article 13

The Director-General of the International Labour Office shall communicate to the Secretary-General of the United Nations for registration in accordance with Article 102 of the Charter of the United Nations full particulars of all ratifications, declarations and acts of denunciation registered by him in accordance with the provisions of the preceding Articles.

Article 14

At such times as it may consider necessary the Governing Body of the International Labour Office shall present to the General Conference a report on the working of this Convention and shall examine the desirability of placing on the agenda of the Conference the question of its revision in whole or in part.

Article 15

1. Should the Conference adopt a new Convention revising this Convention in whole or in part, then, unless the new Convention otherwise provides:

(a) the ratification by a Member of the new revising Convention shall *ipso jure* involve the immediate denunciation of this Convention, notwithstanding the provisions of Article 11 above, if and when the new revising Convention shall have come into force;

(b) as from the date when the new revising Convention comes into force, this Convention shall cease to be open to ratification by the Members.

2. This Convention shall in any case remain in force in its actual form and content for those Members which have ratified it but have not ratified the revising Convention.

Article 16

The English and French versions of the text of this Convention are equally authoritative.

ELIMINATION OF ALL FORMS OF FORCED OR COMPULSORY LABOUR

Forced labour occurs where work or service is exacted by the State or by individuals who have the will and power to threaten workers with severe deprivations, such as withholding food or land or wages, physical violence or sexual abuse, restricting people's movements or locking them up.

For example, a domestic worker is in a forced labour situation where the head of a household takes away identity papers, forbids the worker to go outside and threatens him or her with, for instance, beatings or non-payment of salary in case of disobedience. The domestic may also work for an unbearably low wage, but that is another matter. If he or she were free to leave, this would not amount to forced labour but to exploitation.

Another example of forced labour arises where villagers, whether they want to or not, have to provide substantial help in the construction of roads, the digging of irrigation channels, etc., and where government administrators, police officers or traditional chiefs brandish a credible menace if the requisitioned men, women or children do not turn up.

Bonding workers through debts is, in fact, a widespread form of forced labour in a number of developing countries. Sometimes it originates with a poor and illiterate peasant pledging labour services to an intermediary or a landowner to work off a debt over a period of time. Sometimes the obligation is passed on from one family member to another, even down to children, and from one generation to another. The labour service is rarely defined or limited in duration, and it tends to be manipulated in such a way that it does not pay off the debt. The worker becomes dependent on the intermediary or on the landowner and labours in slave-like conditions. The threat and, indeed, the occurrence of violence or other penalties for failing to work turns an economic relationship - one-sided as it is to start with - into a forced labour situation.

Labour trafficking can give rise to forced labour. One way in which traffickers tend to put themselves into a threatening position is to confiscate the identity papers of the person they move for employment purposes. Another is to trap people through indebtedness by cash advances or loans. Traffickers may also resort to kidnapping, notably of children. At any rate, traffickers, the persons linked to them or the employers at the point of destination, give their victims no choice as to what work to perform and under which conditions. Intimidation can range from revealing the victim's illegal status to the police, to physical assault and sexual abuse.

Forced Labour Convention (No. 29)

Adopted: 28 June 1930
Entered into force: 1 May 1932

The General Conference of the International Labour Organisation,

Having been convened at Geneva by the Governing Body of the International Labour Office, and having met in its Fourteenth Session on 10 June 1930, and

Having decided upon the adoption of certain proposals with regard to forced or compulsory labour, which is included in the first item on the agenda of the session, and

Having determined that these proposals shall take the form of an international Convention,

adopts this twenty-eighth day of June of the year one thousand nine hundred and thirty the following Convention, which may be cited as the Forced Labour Convention, 1930, for ratification by the Members of the International Labour Organisation in accordance with the provisions of the Constitution of the International Labour Organisation:

Article 1

1. Each Member of the International Labour Organisation which ratifies this Convention undertakes to suppress the use of forced or compulsory labour in all its forms within the shortest possible period.

2. With a view to this complete suppression, recourse to forced or compulsory labour may be had, during the transitional period, for public purposes only and as an exceptional measure, subject to the conditions and guarantees hereinafter provided.

3. At the expiration of a period of five years after the coming into force of this Convention, and when the Governing Body of the International Labour Office prepares the report provided for in Article 31 below, the said Governing Body shall consider the possibility of the suppression of forced or compulsory labour in all its forms without a further transitional period and the desirability of placing this question on the agenda of the Conference.

Article 2

1. For the purposes of this Convention the term "forced or compulsory labour" shall mean all work or service which is exacted from any person under the menace of any penalty and for which the said person has not offered himself voluntarily.

2. Nevertheless, for the purposes of this Convention, the term "forced or compulsory labour" shall not include:

(a) any work or service exacted in virtue of compulsory military service laws for work of a purely military character;

(b) any work or service which forms part of the normal civic obligations of the citizens of a fully self-governing country;

(c) any work or service exacted from any person as a consequence of a conviction in a court of law, provided that the said work or service is carried out under the supervision and control of a public authority and that the said person is not hired to or placed at the disposal of private individuals, companies or associations;

(d) any work or service exacted in cases of emergency, that is to say, in the event of war or of a calamity or threatened calamity, such as fire, flood, famine, earthquake, violent epidemic or epizootic diseases, invasion by animal, insect or vegetable pests, and in general any circumstance that would endanger the existence or the well-being of the whole or part of the population;

(e) minor communal services of a kind which, being performed by the members of the community in the direct interest of the said community, can therefore be considered as normal civic obligations incumbent upon the members of the community, provided that the members of the community or their direct representatives shall have the right to be consulted in regard to the need for such services.

Article 3

For the purposes of this Convention the term "competent authority" shall mean either an authority of the metropolitan country or the highest central authority in the territory concerned.

Article 4

1. The competent authority shall not impose or permit the imposition of forced or compulsory labour for the benefit of private individuals, companies or associations.

2. Where such forced or compulsory labour for the benefit of private individuals, companies or associations exists at the date on which a Member's ratification of this Convention is registered by the Director-General of the International Labour Office, the Member shall completely suppress such forced or compulsory labour from the date on which this Convention comes into force for that Member.

Article 5

1. No concession granted to private individuals, companies or associations shall involve any form of forced or compulsory labour for the production or the collection of products which such private individuals, companies or associations utilise or in which they trade.

2. Where concessions exist containing provisions involving such forced or compulsory labour, such provisions shall be rescinded as soon as possible, in order to comply with Article 1 of this Convention.

Article 6

Officials of the administration, even when they have the duty of encouraging the populations under their charge to engage in some form of labour, shall not put constraint upon the said populations or upon any individual members thereof to work for private individuals, companies or associations.

Article 7

1. Chiefs who do not exercise administrative functions shall not have recourse to forced or compulsory labour.

2. Chiefs who exercise administrative functions may, with the express permission of the competent authority, have recourse to forced or compulsory labour, subject to the provisions of Article 10 of this Convention.

3. Chiefs who are duly recognised and who do not receive adequate remuneration in other forms may have the enjoyment of personal services, subject to due regulation and provided that all necessary measures are taken to prevent abuses.

Article 8

1. The responsibility for every decision to have recourse to forced or compulsory labour shall rest with the highest civil authority in the territory concerned.

2. Nevertheless, that authority may delegate powers to the highest local authorities to exact forced or compulsory labour which does not involve the removal of the workers from their place of habitual residence. That authority may also delegate, for such periods and subject to such conditions as may be laid down in the regulations provided for in Article 23 of this Convention, powers to the highest local authorities to exact forced or compulsory labour which involves the removal of the workers from their place of habitual residence for the purpose of facilitating the movement of officials of the administration, when on duty, and for the transport of government stores.

Article 9

Except as otherwise provided for in Article 10 of this Convention, any authority competent to exact forced or compulsory labour shall, before deciding to have recourse to such labour, satisfy itself:

(a) that the work to be done or the service to be rendered is of important direct interest for the community called upon to do the work or render the service;

(b) that the work or service is of present or imminent necessity;

(c) that it has been impossible to obtain voluntary labour for carrying out the work or rendering the service by the offer of rates of wages and conditions of labour not less favourable than those prevailing in the area concerned for similar work or service; and

(d) that the work or service will not lay too heavy a burden upon the present population, having regard to the labour available and its capacity to undertake the work.

Article 10

1. Forced or compulsory labour exacted as a tax and forced or compulsory labour to which recourse is had for the execution of public works by chiefs who exercise administrative functions shall be progressively abolished.

2. Meanwhile, where forced or compulsory labour is exacted as a tax, and where recourse is had to forced or compulsory labour for the execution of public

works by chiefs who exercise administrative functions, the authority concerned shall first satisfy itself:

(a) that the work to be done or the service to be rendered is of important direct interest for the community called upon to do the work or render the service;

(b) that the work or the service is of present or imminent necessity;

(c) that the work or service will not lay too heavy a burden upon the present population, having regard to the labour available and its capacity to undertake the work;

(d) that the work or service will not entail the removal of the workers from their place of habitual residence;

(e) that the execution of the work or the rendering of the service will be directed in accordance with the exigencies of religion, social life and agriculture.

Article 11

1. Only adult able-bodied males who are of an apparent age of not less than 18 and not more than 45 years may be called upon for forced or compulsory labour. Except in respect of the kinds of labour provided for in Article 10 of this Convention, the following limitations and conditions shall apply:

(a) whenever possible prior determination by a medical officer appointed by the administration that the persons concerned are not suffering from any infectious or contagious disease and that they are physically fit for the work required and for the conditions under which it is to be carried out;

(b) exemption of school teachers and pupils and of officials of the administration in general;

(c) the maintenance in each community of the number of adult able-bodied men indispensable for family and social life;

(d) respect for conjugal and family ties.

2. For the purposes of subparagraph (c) of the preceding paragraph, the regulations provided for in Article 23 of this Convention shall fix the proportion of the resident adult able-bodied males who may be taken at any one time for forced or compulsory labour, provided always that this proportion shall in no case exceed 25 per cent. In fixing this proportion the competent authority shall take account of the density of the population, of its social and physical development, of the seasons, and of the work which must be done by the persons concerned on their own behalf in their locality, and, generally, shall have regard to the economic and social necessities of the normal life of the community concerned.

Article 12

1. The maximum period for which any person may be taken for forced or compulsory labour of all kinds in any one period of twelve months shall not exceed sixty days, including the time spent in going to and from the place of work.

2. Every person from whom forced or compulsory labour is exacted shall be furnished with a certificate indicating the periods of such labour which he has completed.

Article 13

1. The normal working hours of any person from whom forced or compulsory labour is exacted shall be the same as those prevailing in the case of voluntary labour, and the hours worked in excess of the normal working hours shall be remunerated at the rates prevailing in the case of overtime for voluntary labour.

2. A weekly day of rest shall be granted to all persons from whom forced or compulsory labour of any kind is exacted and this day shall coincide as far as possible with the day fixed by tradition or custom in the territories or regions concerned.

Article 14

1. With the exception of the forced or compulsory labour provided for in Article 10 of this Convention, forced or compulsory labour of all kinds shall be remunerated in cash at rates not less than those prevailing for similar kinds of work either in the district in which the labour is employed or in the district from which the labour is recruited, whichever may be the higher.

2. In the case of labour to which recourse is had by chiefs in the exercise of their administrative functions, payment of wages in accordance with the provisions of the preceding paragraph shall be introduced as soon as possible.

3. The wages shall be paid to each worker individually and not to his tribal chief or to any other authority.

4. For the purpose of payment of wages the days spent in travelling to and from the place of work shall be counted as working days.

5. Nothing in this Article shall prevent ordinary rations being given as a part of wages, such rations to be at least equivalent in value to the money payment they are taken to represent, but deductions from wages shall not be made either for the payment of taxes or for special food, clothing or accommodation supplied to a worker for the purpose of maintaining him in a fit condition to carry on his work under the special conditions of any employment, or for the supply of tools.

Article 15

1. Any laws or regulations relating to workmen's compensation for accidents or sickness arising out of the employment of the worker and any laws or regulations providing compensation for the dependants of deceased or incapacitated workers which are or shall be in force in the territory concerned shall be equally applicable to persons from whom forced or compulsory labour is exacted and to voluntary workers.

2. In any case it shall be an obligation on any authority employing any worker on forced or compulsory labour to ensure the subsistence of any such worker who, by accident or sickness arising out of his employment, is rendered wholly or partially incapable of providing for himself, and to take measures to ensure the maintenance of any persons actually dependent upon such a worker in the event of his incapacity or decease arising out of his employment.

Article 16

1. Except in cases of special necessity, persons from whom forced or compulsory labour is exacted shall not be transferred to districts where the food and

climate differ so considerably from those to which they have been accustomed as to endanger their health.

2. In no case shall the transfer of such workers be permitted unless all measures relating to hygiene and accommodation which are necessary to adapt such workers to the conditions and to safeguard their health can be strictly applied.

3. When such transfer cannot be avoided, measures of gradual habituation to the new conditions of diet and of climate shall be adopted on competent medical advice.

4. In cases where such workers are required to perform regular work to which they are not accustomed, measures shall be taken to ensure their habituation to it, especially as regards progressive training, the hours of work and the provision of rest intervals, and any increase or amelioration of diet which may be necessary.

Article 17

Before permitting recourse to forced or compulsory labour for works of construction or maintenance which entail the workers remaining at the workplaces for considerable periods, the competent authority shall satisfy itself:

(1) that all necessary measures are taken to safeguard the health of the workers and to guarantee the necessary medical care, and, in particular,
  - (a) that the workers are medically examined before commencing the work and at fixed intervals during the period of service,
  - (b) that there is an adequate medical staff, provided with the dispensaries, infirmaries, hospitals and equipment necessary to meet all requirements, and
  - (c) that the sanitary conditions of the workplaces, the supply of drinking water, food, fuel, and cooking utensils, and, where necessary, of housing and clothing, are satisfactory;

(2) that definite arrangements are made to ensure the subsistence of the families of the workers, in particular by facilitating the remittance, by a safe method, of part of the wages to the family, at the request or with the consent of the workers;

(3) that the journeys of the workers to and from the workplaces are made at the expense and under the responsibility of the administration, which shall facilitate such journeys by making the fullest use of all available means of transport;

(4) that, in case of illness or accident causing incapacity to work of a certain duration, the worker is repatriated at the expense of the administration;

(5) that any worker who may wish to remain as a voluntary worker at the end of his period of forced or compulsory labour is permitted to do so without, for a period of two years, losing his right to repatriation free of expense to himself.

Article 18

1. Forced or compulsory labour for the transport of persons or goods, such as the labour of porters or boatmen, shall be abolished within the shortest possible period. Meanwhile the competent authority shall promulgate regulations determining, *inter alia*, (a) that such labour shall only be employed for the purpose of facilitating the movement of officials of the administration, when on duty, or for the

transport of government stores, or, in cases of very urgent necessity, the transport of persons other than officials, (b) that the workers so employed shall be medically certified to be physically fit, where medical examination is possible, and that where such medical examination is not practicable the person employing such workers shall be held responsible for ensuring that they are physically fit and not suffering from any infectious or contagious disease, (c) the maximum load which these workers may carry, (d) the maximum distance from their homes to which they may be taken, (e) the maximum number of days per month or other period for which they may be taken, including the days spent in returning to their homes, and (f) the persons entitled to demand this form of forced or compulsory labour and the extent to which they are entitled to demand it.

2. In fixing the maxima referred to under (c), (d) and (e) in the foregoing paragraph, the competent authority shall have regard to all relevant factors, including the physical development of the population from which the workers are recruited, the nature of the country through which they must travel and the climatic conditions.

3. The competent authority shall further provide that the normal daily journey of such workers shall not exceed a distance corresponding to an average working day of eight hours, it being understood that account shall be taken not only of the weight to be carried and the distance to be covered, but also of the nature of the road, the season and all other relevant factors, and that, where hours of journey in excess of the normal daily journey are exacted, they shall be remunerated at rates higher than the normal rates.

Article 19

1. The competent authority shall only authorise recourse to compulsory cultivation as a method of precaution against famine or a deficiency of food supplies and always under the condition that the food or produce shall remain the property of the individuals or the community producing it.

2. Nothing in this Article shall be construed as abrogating the obligation on members of a community, where production is organised on a communal basis by virtue of law or custom and where the produce or any profit accruing from the sale thereof remain the property of the community, to perform the work demanded by the community by virtue of law or custom.

Article 20

Collective punishment laws under which a community may be punished for crimes committed by any of its members shall not contain provisions for forced or compulsory labour by the community as one of the methods of punishment.

Article 21

Forced or compulsory labour shall not be used for work underground in mines.

Article 22

The annual reports that Members which ratify this Convention agree to make to the International Labour Office, pursuant to the provisions of Article 22 of the

Constitution of the International Labour Organisation, on the measures they have taken to give effect to the provisions of this Convention, shall contain as full information as possible, in respect of each territory concerned, regarding the extent to which recourse has been had to forced or compulsory labour in that territory, the purposes for which it has been employed, the sickness and death rates, hours of work, methods of payment of wages and rates of wages, and any other relevant information.

Article 23

1. To give effect to the provisions of this Convention the competent authority shall issue complete and precise regulations governing the use of forced or compulsory labour.

2. These regulations shall contain, *inter alia*, rules permitting any person from whom forced or compulsory labour is exacted to forward all complaints relative to the conditions of labour to the authorities and ensuring that such complaints will be examined and taken into consideration.

Article 24

Adequate measures shall in all cases be taken to ensure that the regulations governing the employment of forced or compulsory labour are strictly applied, either by extending the duties of any existing labour inspectorate which has been established for the inspection of voluntary labour to cover the inspection of forced or compulsory labour or in some other appropriate manner. Measures shall also be taken to ensure that the regulations are brought to the knowledge of persons from whom such labour is exacted.

Article 25

The illegal exaction of forced or compulsory labour shall be punishable as a penal offence, and it shall be an obligation on any Member ratifying this Convention to ensure that the penalties imposed by law are really adequate and are strictly enforced.

Article 26

1. Each Member of the International Labour Organisation which ratifies this Convention undertakes to apply it to the territories placed under its sovereignty, jurisdiction, protection, suzerainty, tutelage or authority, so far as it has the right to accept obligations affecting matters of internal jurisdiction; provided that, if such Member may desire to take advantage of the provisions of Article 35 of the Constitution of the International Labour Organisation, it shall append to its ratification a declaration stating:

(1) the territories to which it intends to apply the provisions of this Convention without modification;

(2) the territories to which it intends to apply the provisions of this Convention with modifications, together with details of the said modifications;

(3) the territories in respect of which it reserves its decision.

2. The aforesaid declaration shall be deemed to be an integral part of the ratification and shall have the force of ratification. It shall be open to any Member, by a subsequent declaration, to cancel in whole or in part the reservations made, in pursuance of the provisions of subparagraphs (2) and (3) of this Article, in the original declaration.

Article 27

The formal ratifications of this Convention under the conditions set forth in the Constitution of the International Labour Organisation shall be communicated to the Director-General of the International Labour Office for registration.

Article 28

1. This Convention shall be binding only upon those Members whose ratifications have been registered with the International Labour Office.

2. It shall come into force twelve months after the date on which the ratifications of two Members of the International Labour Organisation have been registered with the Director-General.

3. Thereafter, this Convention shall come into force for any Member twelve months after the date on which the ratification has been registered.

Article 29

As soon as the ratifications of two Members of the International Labour Organisation have been registered with the International Labour Office, the Director-General of the International Labour Office shall so notify all the Members of the International Labour Organisation. He shall likewise notify them of the registration of ratifications which may be communicated subsequently by other Members of the Organisation.

Article 30

1. A Member which has ratified this Convention may denounce it after the expiration of ten years from the date on which the Convention first comes into force, by an act communicated to the Director-General of the International Labour Office for registration. Such denunciation shall not take effect until one year after the date on which it is registered with the International Labour Office.

2. Each Member which has ratified this Convention and which does not, within the year following the expiration of the period of ten years mentioned in the preceding paragraph, exercise the right of denunciation provided for in this Article, will be bound for another period of five years and, thereafter, may denounce this Convention at the expiration of each period of five years under the terms provided for in this Article.

Article 31

At such times as it may consider necessary the Governing Body of the International Labour Office shall present to the General Conference a report on the working of this Convention and shall examine the desirability of placing on the agenda of the Conference the question of its revision in whole or in part.

Article 32

1. Should the Conference adopt a new Convention revising this Convention in whole or in part, the ratification by a Member of the new revising Convention shall *ipso jure* involve denunciation of this Convention without any requirement of delay, notwithstanding the provisions of Article 30 above, if and when the new revising Convention shall have come into force.

2. As from the date of the coming into force of the new revising Convention, the present Convention shall cease to be open to ratification by the Members.

3. Nevertheless, this Convention shall remain in force in its actual form and content for those Members which have ratified it but have not ratified the revising Convention.

Article 33

The French and English texts of this Convention shall both be authentic.

Abolition of Forced Labour Convention (No. 105)

Adopted: 25 June 1957
Entered into force: 17 January 1959

The General Conference of the International Labour Organisation,

Having been convened at Geneva by the Governing Body of the International Labour Office, and having met in its Fortieth Session on 5 June 1957, and

Having considered the question of forced labour, which is the fourth item on the agenda of the session, and

Having noted the provisions of the Forced Labour Convention, 1930, and

Having noted that the Slavery Convention, 1926, provides that all necessary measures shall be taken to prevent compulsory or forced labour from developing into conditions analogous to slavery and that the Supplementary Convention on the Abolition of Slavery, the Slave Trade and Institutions and Practices Similar to Slavery, 1956, provides for the complete abolition of debt bondage and serfdom, and

Having noted that the Protection of Wages Convention, 1949, provides that wages shall be paid regularly and prohibits methods of payment which deprive the worker of a genuine possibility of terminating his employment, and

Having decided upon the adoption of further proposals with regard to the abolition of certain forms of forced or compulsory labour constituting a violation of the rights of man referred to in the Charter of the United Nations and enunciated by the Universal Declaration of Human Rights, and

Having determined that these proposals shall take the form of an international Convention,

adopts this twenty-fifth day of June of the year one thousand nine hundred and fifty-seven the following Convention, which may be cited as the Abolition of Forced Labour Convention, 1957:

Article 1

Each Member of the International Labour Organisation which ratifies this Convention undertakes to suppress and not to make use of any form of forced or compulsory labour:

(a) as a means of political coercion or education or as a punishment for holding or expressing political views or views ideologically opposed to the established political, social or economic system;

(b) as a method of mobilising and using labour for purposes of economic development;

(c) as a means of labour discipline;

(d) as a punishment for having participated in strikes;

(e) as a means of racial, social, national or religious discrimination.

Article 2

Each Member of the International Labour Organisation which ratifies this Convention undertakes to take effective measures to secure the immediate and complete abolition of forced or compulsory labour as specified in Article 1 of this Convention.

Article 3

The formal ratifications of this Convention shall be communicated to the Director-General of the International Labour Office for registration.

Article 4

1. This Convention shall be binding only upon those Members of the International Labour Organisation whose ratifications have been registered with the Director-General.

2. It shall come into force twelve months after the date on which the ratifications of two Members have been registered with the Director-General.

3. Thereafter, this Convention shall come into force for any Member twelve months after the date on which its ratification has been registered.

Article 5

1. A Member which has ratified this Convention may denounce it after the expiration of ten years from the date on which the Convention first comes into force, by an act communicated to the Director-General of the International Labour Office for registration. Such denunciation shall not take effect until one year after the date on which it is registered.

2. Each Member which has ratified this Convention and which does not, within the year following the expiration of the period of ten years mentioned in the preceding paragraph, exercise the right of denunciation provided for in this Article, will be bound for another period of ten years and, thereafter, may denounce this Convention at the expiration of each period of ten years under the terms provided for in this Article.

Article 6

1. The Director-General of the International Labour Office shall notify all Members of the International Labour Organisation of the registration of all ratifications and denunciations communicated to him by the Members of the Organisation.

2. When notifying the Members of the Organisation of the registration of the second ratification communicated to him, the Director-General shall draw the attention of the Members of the Organisation to the date upon which the Convention will come into force.

Article 7

The Director-General of the International Labour Office shall communicate to the Secretary-General of the United Nations for registration in accordance with Article 102 of the Charter of the United Nations full particulars of all ratifications and acts of denunciation registered by him in accordance with the provisions of the preceding Articles.

Article 8

At such times as it may consider necessary the Governing Body of the International Labour Office shall present to the General Conference a report on the working of this Convention and shall examine the desirability of placing on the agenda of the Conference the question of its revision in whole or in part.

Article 9

1. Should the Conference adopt a new Convention revising this Convention in whole or in part, then, unless the new Convention otherwise provides:

(a) the ratification by a Member of the new revising Convention shall *ipso jure* involve the immediate denunciation of this Convention, notwithstanding the provisions of Article 5 above, if and when the new revising Convention shall have come into force;

(b) as from the date when the new revising Convention comes into force this Convention shall cease to be open to ratification by the Members.

2. This Convention shall in any case remain in force in its actual form and content for those Members which have ratified it but have not ratified the revising Convention.

Article 10

The English and French versions of the text of this Convention are equally authoritative.

EFFECTIVE ABOLITION OF CHILD LABOUR

Children enjoy the same human rights accorded to all people. But, lacking the knowledge, experience or physical development of adults and the power to defend their own interests in an adult world, children also have distinct rights to protection by virtue of their age. One of these is protection from economic exploitation and from work that is dangerous to the health and morals of children or hampers the child's development.

The principle of the effective abolition of child labour means ensuring that every girl and boy has the opportunity to develop physically and mentally to her or his full potential. Its aim is to stop all work by children that jeopardizes their education and development. This does not mean stopping all work performed by children. International labour standards allow the distinction to be made between what constitutes acceptable and unacceptable forms of work for children at different ages and stages of development.

The principle extends from formal employment to the informal economy where the bulk of the unacceptable forms of child labour are found. It covers family-based enterprises, agricultural activities, domestic service and unpaid work carried out under various customary arrangements such as children working in return for their keep.

To achieve the effective abolition of child labour, governments should fix and enforce a minimum age or ages at which children can enter into different types of work. Within limits, these ages may vary according to national social and economic circumstances. However, the general minimum age for admission to employment should not be less than the age of completion of compulsory schooling and never be less than 15 years. In some instances, developing countries may make exceptions to this, and a minimum age of 14 years may be applied where the economy and educational facilities are insufficiently developed.

Certain types of work categorized as "the worst forms of child labour" are totally unacceptable for all children under the age of 18 years, and their abolition is a matter for urgent and immediate action. These forms include such inhumane practices as slavery, trafficking, debt bondage and other forms of forced labour; prostitution and pornography; forced recruitment of children for military purposes; and the use of children for illicit activities such as the trafficking of drugs. Dangerous work that can harm the health, safety or morals of children are subject to assessment by governments in consultation with workers' and employers' organizations.

A key characteristic of any effective strategy to abolish child labour is the provision of relevant and accessible basic education. However, education must be an integral part of a wide range of measures that combat many factors, such as poverty, lack of awareness of children's rights and inadequate systems of social protection, that give rise to child labour and allow it to persist.

Minimum Age Convention (No. 138)

Adopted: 26 June 1973
Entered into force: 19 June 1976

The General Conference of the International Labour Organisation,

Having been convened at Geneva by the Governing Body of the International Labour Office, and having met in its Fifty-eighth Session on 6 June 1973, and

Having decided upon the adoption of certain proposals with regard to minimum age for admission to employment, which is the fourth item on the agenda of the session, and

Noting the terms of the Minimum Age (Industry) Convention, 1919, the Minimum Age (Sea) Convention, 1920, the Minimum Age (Agriculture) Convention, 1921, the Minimum Age (Trimmers and Stokers) Convention, 1921, the Minimum Age (Non-Industrial Employment) Convention, 1932, the Minimum Age (Sea) Convention (Revised), 1936, the Minimum Age (Industry) Convention (Revised), 1937, the Minimum Age (Non-Industrial Employment) Convention (Revised), 1937, the Minimum Age (Fishermen) Convention, 1959, and the Minimum Age (Underground Work) Convention, 1965, and

Considering that the time has come to establish a general instrument on the subject, which would gradually replace the existing ones applicable to limited economic sectors, with a view to achieving the total abolition of child labour, and

Having determined that these proposals shall take the form of an international Convention,

adopts this twenty-sixth day of June of the year one thousand nine hundred and seventy-three the following Convention, which may be cited as the Minimum Age Convention, 1973:

Article 1

Each Member for which this Convention is in force undertakes to pursue a national policy designed to ensure the effective abolition of child labour and to raise progressively the minimum age for admission to employment or work to a level consistent with the fullest physical and mental development of young persons.

Article 2

1. Each Member which ratifies this Convention shall specify, in a declaration appended to its ratification, a minimum age for admission to employment or work within its territory and on means of transport registered in its territory; subject to Articles 4 to 8 of this Convention, no one under that age shall be admitted to employment or work in any occupation.

2. Each Member which has ratified this Convention may subsequently notify the Director-General of the International Labour Office, by further declarations, that it specifies a minimum age higher than that previously specified.

3. The minimum age specified in pursuance of paragraph 1 of this Article shall not be less than the age of completion of compulsory schooling and, in any case, shall not be less than 15 years.

4. Notwithstanding the provisions of paragraph 3 of this Article, a Member whose economy and educational facilities are insufficiently developed may, after consultation with the organisations of employers and workers concerned, where such exist, initially specify a minimum age of 14 years.

5. Each Member which has specified a minimum age of 14 years in pursuance of the provisions of the preceding paragraph shall include in its reports on the application of this Convention submitted under Article 22 of the Constitution of the International Labour Organisation a statement:

(a) that its reason for doing so subsists; or,

(b) that it renounces its right to avail itself of the provisions in question as from a stated date.

Article 3

1. The minimum age for admission to any type of employment or work which by its nature or the circumstances in which it is carried out is likely to jeopardise the health, safety or morals of young persons shall not be less than 18 years.

2. The types of employment or work to which paragraph 1 of this Article applies shall be determined by national laws or regulations or by the competent authority, after consultation with the organisations of employers and workers concerned, where such exist.

3. Notwithstanding the provisions of paragraph 1 of this Article, national laws or regulations or the competent authority may, after consultation with the organisations of employers and workers concerned, where such exist, authorise employment or work as from the age of 16 years on condition that the health, safety and morals of the young persons concerned are fully protected and that the young persons have received adequate specific instruction or vocational training in the relevant branch of activity.

Article 4

1. In so far as necessary, the competent authority, after consultation with the organisations of employers and workers concerned, where such exist, may exclude from the application of this Convention limited categories of employment or work in respect of which special and substantial problems of application arise.

2. Each Member which ratifies this Convention shall list in its first report on the application of the Convention submitted under Article 22 of the Constitution of the International Labour Organisation any categories which may have been excluded in pursuance of paragraph 1 of this Article, giving the reasons for such exclusion, and shall state in subsequent reports the position of its law and practice in respect of the categories excluded and the extent to which effect has been given or is proposed to be given to the Convention in respect of such categories.

3. Employment or work covered by Article 3 of this Convention shall not be excluded from the application of the Convention in pursuance of this Article.

Article 5

1. A Member whose economy and administrative facilities are insufficiently developed may, after consultation with the organisations of employers and workers concerned, where such exist, initially limit the scope of application of this Convention.

2. Each Member which avails itself of the provisions of paragraph 1 of this Article shall specify, in a declaration appended to its ratification, the branches of economic activity or types of undertakings to which it will apply the provisions of the Convention.

3. The provisions of the Convention shall be applicable as a minimum to the following: mining and quarrying; manufacturing; construction; electricity, gas and water; sanitary services; transport, storage and communication; and plantations and other agricultural undertakings mainly producing for commercial purposes, but excluding family and small-scale holdings producing for local consumption and not regularly employing hired workers.

4. Any Member which has limited the scope of application of this Convention in pursuance of this Article:

(a) shall indicate in its reports under Article 22 of the Constitution of the International Labour Organisation the general position as regards the employment or work of young persons and children in the branches of activity which are excluded from the scope of application of this Convention and any progress which may have been made towards wider application of the provisions of the Convention;

(b) may at any time formally extend the scope of application by a declaration addressed to the Director-General of the International Labour Office.

Article 6

This Convention does not apply to work done by children and young persons in schools for general, vocational or technical education or in other training institutions, or to work done by persons at least 14 years of age in undertakings, where such work is carried out in accordance with conditions prescribed by the competent authority, after consultation with the organisations of employers and workers concerned, where such exist, and is an integral part of:

(a) a course of education or training for which a school or training institution is primarily responsible;

(b) a programme of training mainly or entirely in an undertaking, which programme has been approved by the competent authority; or,

(c) a programme of guidance or orientation designed to facilitate the choice of an occupation or of a line of training.

Article 7

1. National laws or regulations may permit the employment or work of persons 13 to 15 years of age on light work which is:

(a) not likely to be harmful to their health or development; and,

(b) not such as to prejudice their attendance at school, their participation in vocational orientation or training programmes approved by the competent authority or their capacity to benefit from the instruction received.

2. National laws or regulations may also permit the employment or work of persons who are at least 15 years of age but have not yet completed their compulsory schooling on work which meets the requirements set forth in subparagraphs (a) and (b) of paragraph 1 of this Article.

3. The competent authority shall determine the activities in which employment or work may be permitted under paragraphs 1 and 2 of this Article and shall prescribe the number of hours during which and the conditions in which such employment or work may be undertaken.

4. Notwithstanding the provisions of paragraphs 1 and 2 of this Article, a Member which has availed itself of the provisions of paragraph 4 of Article 2 may, for as long as it continues to do so, substitute the ages 12 and 14 for the ages 13 and 15 in paragraph 1 and the age 14 for the age 15 in paragraph 2 of this Article.

Article 8

1. After consultation with the organisations of employers and workers concerned, where such exist, the competent authority may, by permits granted in individual cases, allow exceptions to the prohibition of employment or work provided for in Article 2 of this Convention, for such purposes as participation in artistic performances.

2. Permits so granted shall limit the number of hours during which and prescribe the conditions in which employment or work is allowed.

Article 9

1. All necessary measures, including the provision of appropriate penalties, shall be taken by the competent authority to ensure the effective enforcement of the provisions of this Convention.

2. National laws or regulations or the competent authority shall define the persons responsible for compliance with the provisions giving effect to the Convention.

3. National laws or regulations or the competent authority shall prescribe the registers or other documents which shall be kept and made available by the employer; such registers or documents shall contain the names and ages or dates of birth, duly certified wherever possible, of persons whom he employs or who work for him and who are less than 18 years of age.

Article 10

1. This Convention revises, on the terms set forth in this Article, the Minimum Age (Industry) Convention, 1919, the Minimum Age (Sea) Convention, 1920, the Minimum Age (Agriculture) Convention, 1921, the Minimum Age (Trimmers and Stokers) Convention, 1921, the Minimum Age (Non-Industrial Employment) Convention, 1932, the Minimum Age (Sea) Convention (Revised), 1936, the Minimum Age (Industry) Convention (Revised), 1937, the Minimum Age (Non-Industrial Employment) Convention (Revised), 1937, the Minimum Age (Fishermen) Convention, 1959, and the Minimum Age (Underground Work) Convention, 1965.

2. The coming into force of this Convention shall not close the Minimum Age (Sea) Convention (Revised), 1936, the Minimum Age (Industry) Convention (Revised), 1937, the Minimum Age (Non-Industrial Employment) Convention (Revised), 1937, the Minimum Age (Fishermen) Convention, 1959, or the Minimum Age (Underground Work) Convention, 1965, to further ratification.

3. The Minimum Age (Industry) Convention, 1919, the Minimum Age (Sea) Convention, 1920, the Minimum Age (Agriculture) Convention, 1921, and the Minimum Age (Trimmers and Stokers) Convention, 1921, shall be closed to further ratification when all the parties thereto have consented to such closing by ratification of this Convention or by a declaration communicated to the Director-General of the International Labour Office.

4. When the obligations of this Convention are accepted:

(a) by a Member which is a party to the Minimum Age (Industry) Convention (Revised), 1937, and a minimum age of not less than 15 years is specified in pursuance of Article 2 of this Convention, this shall *ipso jure* involve the immediate denunciation of that Convention;

(b) in respect of non-industrial employment as defined in the Minimum Age (Non-Industrial Employment) Convention, 1932, by a Member which is a party to that Convention, this shall *ipso jure* involve the immediate denunciation of that Convention;

(c) in respect of non-industrial employment as defined in the Minimum Age (Non-Industrial Employment) Convention (Revised), 1937, by a Member which is a party to that Convention, and a minimum age of not less than 15 years is specified in pursuance of Article 2 of this Convention, this shall *ipso jure* involve the immediate denunciation of that Convention;

(d) in respect of maritime employment, by a Member which is a party to the Minimum Age (Sea) Convention (Revised), 1936, and a minimum age of not less than 15 years is specified in pursuance of Article 2 of this Convention or the Member specifies that Article 3 of this Convention applies to maritime employment, this shall *ipso jure* involve the immediate denunciation of that Convention;

(e) in respect of employment in maritime fishing, by a Member which is a party to the Minimum Age (Fishermen) Convention, 1959, and a minimum age of not less than 15 years is specified in pursuance of Article 2 of this Convention or the Member specifies that Article 3 of this Convention applies to employment in maritime fishing, this shall *ipso jure* involve the immediate denunciation of that Convention;

(f) by a Member which is a party to the Minimum Age (Underground Work) Convention, 1965, and a minimum age of not less than the age specified in pursuance of that Convention is specified in pursuance of Article 2 of this Convention or the Member specifies that such an age applies to employment underground in mines in virtue of Article 3 of this Convention, this shall *ipso jure* involve the immediate denunciation of that Convention, if and when this Convention shall have come into force.

5. Acceptance of the obligations of this Convention:

(a) shall involve the denunciation of the Minimum Age (Industry) Convention, 1919, in accordance with Article 12 thereof;

(b) in respect of agriculture shall involve the denunciation of the Minimum Age (Agriculture) Convention, 1921, in accordance with Article 9 thereof;

(c) in respect of maritime employment shall involve the denunciation of the Minimum Age (Sea) Convention, 1920, in accordance with Article 10 thereof, and of the Minimum Age (Trimmers and Stokers) Convention, 1921, in accordance with Article 12 thereof, if and when this Convention shall have come into force.

Article 11

The formal ratifications of this Convention shall be communicated to the Director-General of the International Labour Office for registration.

Article 12

1. This Convention shall be binding only upon those Members of the International Labour Organisation whose ratifications have been registered with the Director-General.

2. It shall come into force twelve months after the date on which the ratifications of two Members have been registered with the Director-General.

3. Thereafter, this Convention shall come into force for any Member twelve months after the date on which its ratification has been registered.

Article 13

1. A Member which has ratified this Convention may denounce it after the expiration of ten years from the date on which the Convention first comes into force, by an act communicated to the Director-General of the International Labour Office for registration. Such denunciation shall not take effect until one year after the date on which it is registered.

2. Each Member which has ratified this Convention and which does not, within the year following the expiration of the period of ten years mentioned in the preceding paragraph, exercise the right of denunciation provided for in this Article, will be bound for another period of ten years and, thereafter, may denounce this Convention at the expiration of each period of ten years under the terms provided for in this Article.

Article 14

1. The Director-General of the International Labour Office shall notify all Members of the International Labour Organisation of the registration of all ratifications and denunciations communicated to him by the Members of the Organisation.

2. When notifying the Members of the Organisation of the registration of the second ratification communicated to him, the Director-General shall draw the attention of the Members of the Organisation to the date upon which the Convention will come into force.

Article 15

The Director-General of the International Labour Office shall communicate to the Secretary-General of the United Nations for registration in accordance with

Article 102 of the Charter of the United Nations full particulars of all ratifications and acts of denunciation registered by him in accordance with the provisions of the preceding Articles.

Article 16

At such times as it may consider necessary the Governing Body of the International Labour Office shall present to the General Conference a report on the working of this Convention and shall examine the desirability of placing on the agenda of the Conference the question of its revision in whole or in part.

Article 17

1. Should the Conference adopt a new Convention revising this Convention in whole or in part, then, unless the new Convention otherwise provides:

(a) the ratification by a Member of the new revising Convention shall *ipso jure* involve the immediate denunciation of this Convention, notwithstanding the provisions of Article 13 above, if and when the new revising Convention shall have come into force;

(b) as from the date when the new revising Convention comes into force this Convention shall cease to be open to ratification by the Members.

2. This Convention shall in any case remain in force in its actual form and content for those Members which have ratified it but have not ratified the revising Convention.

Article 18

The English and French versions of the text of this Convention are equally authoritative.

Worst Forms of Child Labour Convention (No. 182)

Adopted: 17 June 1999
Entered into force: 19 Nov. 2000

The General Conference of the International Labour Organization,

Having been convened at Geneva by the Governing Body of the International Labour Office, and having met in its 87th Session on 1 June 1999, and

Considering the need to adopt new instruments for the prohibition and elimination of the worst forms of child labour, as the main priority for national and international action, including international cooperation and assistance, to complement the Convention and the Recommendation concerning Minimum Age for Admission to Employment, 1973, which remain fundamental instruments on child labour, and

Considering that the effective elimination of the worst forms of child labour requires immediate and comprehensive action, taking into account the importance of free basic education and the need to remove the children concerned from all such work and to provide for their rehabilitation and social integration while addressing the needs of their families, and

Recalling the resolution concerning the elimination of child labour adopted by the International Labour Conference at its 83rd Session in 1996, and

Recognizing that child labour is to a great extent caused by poverty and that the long-term solution lies in sustained economic growth leading to social progress, in particular poverty alleviation and universal education, and

Recalling the Convention on the Rights of the Child adopted by the United Nations General Assembly on 20 November 1989, and

Recalling the ILO Declaration on Fundamental Principles and Rights at Work and its Follow-up, adopted by the International Labour Conference at its 86th Session in 1998, and

Recalling that some of the worst forms of child labour are covered by other international instruments, in particular the Forced Labour Convention, 1930, and the United Nations Supplementary Convention on the Abolition of Slavery, the Slave Trade, and Institutions and Practices Similar to Slavery, 1956, and

Having decided upon the adoption of certain proposals with regard to child labour, which is the fourth item on the agenda of the session, and

Having determined that these proposals shall take the form of an international Convention;

adopts this seventeenth day of June of the year one thousand nine hundred and ninety-nine the following Convention, which may be cited as the Worst Forms of Child Labour Convention, 1999.

Article 1

Each Member which ratifies this Convention shall take immediate and effective measures to secure the prohibition and elimination of the worst forms of child labour as a matter of urgency.

Article 2

For the purposes of this Convention, the term "child" shall apply to all persons under the age of 18.

Article 3

For the purposes of this Convention, the term "the worst forms of child labour" comprises:

(a) all forms of slavery or practices similar to slavery, such as the sale and trafficking of children, debt bondage and serfdom and forced or compulsory labour, including forced or compulsory recruitment of children for use in armed conflict;

(b) the use, procuring or offering of a child for prostitution, for the production of pornography or for pornographic performances;

(c) the use, procuring or offering of a child for illicit activities, in particular for the production and trafficking of drugs as defined in the relevant international treaties;

(d) work which, by its nature or the circumstances in which it is carried out, is likely to harm the health, safety or morals of children.

Article 4

1. The types of work referred to under Article 3(d) shall be determined by national laws or regulations or by the competent authority, after consultation with the organizations of employers and workers concerned, taking into consideration relevant international standards, in particular Paragraphs 3 and 4 of the Worst Forms of Child Labour Recommendation, 1999.

2. The competent authority, after consultation with the organizations of employers and workers concerned, shall identify where the types of work so determined exist.

3. The list of the types of work determined under paragraph 1 of this Article shall be periodically examined and revised as necessary, in consultation with the organizations of employers and workers concerned.

Article 5

Each Member shall, after consultation with employers' and workers' organizations, establish or designate appropriate mechanisms to monitor the implementation of the provisions giving effect to this Convention.

Article 6

1. Each Member shall design and implement programmes of action to eliminate as a priority the worst forms of child labour.

2. Such programmes of action shall be designed and implemented in consultation with relevant government institutions and employers' and workers' organizations, taking into consideration the views of other concerned groups as appropriate.

Article 7

1. Each Member shall take all necessary measures to ensure the effective implementation and enforcement of the provisions giving effect to this Convention including the provision and application of penal sanctions or, as appropriate, other sanctions.

2. Each Member shall, taking into account the importance of education in eliminating child labour, take effective and time-bound measures to:

(a) prevent the engagement of children in the worst forms of child labour;

(b) provide the necessary and appropriate direct assistance for the removal of children from the worst forms of child labour and for their rehabilitation and social integration;

(c) ensure access to free basic education, and, wherever possible and appropriate, vocational training, for all children removed from the worst forms of child labour;

(d) identify and reach out to children at special risk; and,

(e) take account of the special situation of girls.

3. Each Member shall designate the competent authority responsible for the implementation of the provisions giving effect to this Convention.

Article 8

Members shall take appropriate steps to assist one another in giving effect to the provisions of this Convention through enhanced international cooperation and/ or assistance including support for social and economic development, poverty eradication programmes and universal education.

Article 9

The formal ratifications of this Convention shall be communicated to the Director-General of the International Labour Office for registration.

Article 10

1. This Convention shall be binding only upon those Members of the International Labour Organization whose ratifications have been registered with the Director-General of the International Labour Office.

2. It shall come into force 12 months after the date on which the ratifications of two Members have been registered with the Director-General.

3. Thereafter, this Convention shall come into force for any Member 12 months after the date on which its ratification has been registered.

Article 11

1. A Member which has ratified this Convention may denounce it after the expiration of ten years from the date on which the Convention first comes into force, by an act communicated to the Director-General of the International Labour Office for registration. Such denunciation shall not take effect until one year after the date on which it is registered.

2. Each Member which has ratified this Convention and which does not, within the year following the expiration of the period of ten years mentioned in the preceding paragraph, exercise the right of denunciation provided for in this Article, will be bound for another period of ten years and, thereafter, may denounce this Convention at the expiration of each period of ten years under the terms provided for in this Article.

Article 12

1. The Director-General of the International Labour Office shall notify all Members of the International Labour Organization of the registration of all ratifications and acts of denunciation communicated by the Members of the Organization.

2. When notifying the Members of the Organization of the registration of the second ratification, the Director-General shall draw the attention of the Members of the Organization to the date upon which the Convention shall come into force.

Article 13

The Director-General of the International Labour Office shall communicate to the Secretary-General of the United Nations, for registration in accordance with Article 102 of the Charter of the United Nations, full particulars of all ratifications and acts of denunciation registered by the Director-General in accordance with the provisions of the preceding Articles.

Article 14

At such times as it may consider necessary, the Governing Body of the International Labour Office shall present to the General Conference a report on the working of this Convention and shall examine the desirability of placing on the agenda of the Conference the question of its revision in whole or in part.

Article 15

1. Should the Conference adopt a new Convention revising this Convention in whole or in part, then, unless the new Convention otherwise provides:

(a) the ratification by a Member of the new revising Convention shall *ipso jure* involve the immediate denunciation of this Convention, notwithstanding the provisions of Article 11 above, if and when the new revising Convention shall have come into force;

(b) as from the date when the new revising Convention comes into force, this Convention shall cease to be open to ratification by the Members.

2. This Convention shall in any case remain in force in its actual form and content for those Members which have ratified it but have not ratified the revising Convention.

Article 16

The English and French versions of the text of this Convention are equally authoritative.

ELIMINATION OF DISCRIMINATION IN RESPECT OF EMPLOYMENT AND OCCUPATION

Discrimination at work can occur in many different settings, from high-rise office buildings to rural villages, and in a variety of forms. It can affect men or women on the basis of their sex, or because their race or skin colour, national extraction or social origin, religion or political opinions differ from those of others. Often countries decide to ban distinctions or exclusions and forbid discrimination on other grounds as well, such as disability, HIV status or age. Discrimination at work denies opportunities to individuals and deprives society of what those people can and could contribute.

Eliminating discrimination starts with dismantling barriers and ensuring equality in access to training, education as well as the ability to own and use resources such as land and credit. It continues with fixing conditions for setting up and running enterprises of all types and sizes, and the policies and practices related to hiring, assignment of tasks, working conditions, pay, benefits, promotions, lay-offs and termination of employment. Merit and the ability to do a job, not irrelevant characteristics, should be the guide.

Discrimination in employment or occupation may be direct or indirect. Direct discrimination exists when laws, rules or practices explicitly cite a particular ground, such as sex, race, etc. to deny equal opportunities. For instance, if a wife, but not a husband, must obtain the spouse's consent to apply for a loan or a passport to participate in an occupation, this would be direct discrimination on the basis of sex.

Indirect discrimination occurs where rules or practices appear on the surface to be neutral but in practice lead to exclusions. Requiring applicants to be a certain height could disproportionately exclude women and members of some ethnic groups, for example. Unless the specified height is absolutely necessary to perform the particular job, this would illustrate indirect discrimination.

Equality at work means that all individuals should be accorded equal opportunities to develop fully the knowledge, skills and competencies that are relevant to the economic activities they wish to pursue. Measures to promote equality need to bear in mind diversity in culture, language, family circumstances, and the ability to read and to deal with numbers. For peasants and owners of small or family enterprises, especially women and ethnic groups, equal access to land (including by inheritance), training, technology and capital is key.

In the case of both employees and self-employed or (own-account) workers, non-discrimination at work depends on equal access to quality education prior to entering the labour market. This is of chief importance for girls and disadvantaged groups. A more equal division of work and family responsibilities in the household would also permit more women to improve their work opportunities.

Effective mechanisms are needed to address the obstacles of discrimination when they occur. A common example involves claims for the non-discriminatory payment of wages, which should be set using objective criteria that takes into account the value of the work performed. ILO principles fix minimum thresholds while national laws and practices may well take a broader approach and include more comprehensive means in eliminating discrimination at work.

Equal Remuneration Convention (No. 100)

Adopted: 29 June 1951
Entered into force: 23 May 1953

The General Conference of the International Labour Organisation,

Having been convened at Geneva by the Governing Body of the International Labour Office, and having met in its Thirty-fourth Session on 6 June 1951, and

Having decided upon the adoption of certain proposals with regard to the principle of equal remuneration for men and women workers for work of equal value, which is the seventh item on the agenda of the session, and

Having determined that these proposals shall take the form of an international Convention,

adopts this twenty-ninth day of June of the year one thousand nine hundred and fifty-one the following Convention, which may be cited as the Equal Remuneration Convention, 1951:

Article 1

For the purpose of this Convention:

(a) the term "remuneration" includes the ordinary, basic or minimum wage or salary and any additional emoluments whatsoever payable directly or indirectly, whether in cash or in kind, by the employer to the worker and arising out of the worker's employment;

(b) the term "equal remuneration for men and women workers for work of equal value" refers to rates of remuneration established without discrimination based on sex.

Article 2

1. Each Member shall, by means appropriate to the methods in operation for determining rates of remuneration, promote and, in so far as is consistent with such methods, ensure the application to all workers of the principle of equal remuneration for men and women workers for work of equal value.

2. This principle may be applied by means of:

(a) national laws or regulations;

(b) legally established or recognised machinery for wage determination;

(c) collective agreements between employers and workers; or,

(d) a combination of these various means.

Article 3

1. Where such action will assist in giving effect to the provisions of this Convention measures shall be taken to promote objective appraisal of jobs on the basis of the work to be performed.

2. The methods to be followed in this appraisal may be decided upon by the authorities responsible for the determination of rates of remuneration, or, where such rates are determined by collective agreements, by the parties thereto.

3. Differential rates between workers which correspond, without regard to sex, to differences, as determined by such objective appraisal, in the work to be performed shall not be considered as being contrary to the principle of equal remuneration for men and women workers for work of equal value.

Article 4

Each Member shall co-operate as appropriate with the employers' and workers' organisations concerned for the purpose of giving effect to the provisions of this Convention.

Article 5

The formal ratifications of this Convention shall be communicated to the Director-General of the International Labour Office for registration.

Article 6

1. This Convention shall be binding only upon those Members of the International Labour Organisation whose ratifications have been registered with the Director-General.

2. It shall come into force twelve months after the date on which the ratifications of two Members have been registered with the Director-General.

3. Thereafter, this Convention shall come into force for any Member twelve months after the date on which its ratification has been registered.

Article 7

1. Declarations communicated to the Director-General of the International Labour Office in accordance with paragraph 2 of Article 35 of the Constitution of the International Labour Organisation shall indicate:

(a) the territories in respect of which the Member concerned undertakes that the provisions of the Convention shall be applied without modification;

(b) the territories in respect of which it undertakes that the provisions of the Convention shall be applied subject to modifications, together with details of the said modifications;

(c) the territories in respect of which the Convention is inapplicable and in such cases the grounds on which it is inapplicable;

(d) the territories in respect of which it reserves its decisions pending further consideration of the position.

2. The undertakings referred to in subparagraphs (a) and (b) of paragraph 1 of this Article shall be deemed to be an integral part of the ratification and shall have the force of ratification.

3. Any Member may at any time by a subsequent declaration cancel in whole or in part any reservation made in its original declaration in virtue of subparagraph (b), (c) or (d) of paragraph 1 of this Article.

4. Any Member may, at any time at which the Convention is subject to denunciation in accordance with the provisions of Article 9, communicate to the Director-General a declaration modifying in any other respect the terms of any former declaration and stating the present position in respect of such territories as it may specify.

Article 8

1. Declarations communicated to the Director-General of the International Labour Office in accordance with paragraph 4 or 5 of Article 35 of the Constitution of the International Labour Organisation shall indicate whether the provisions of the Convention will be applied in the territory concerned without modification or subject to modifications; when the declaration indicates that the provisions of the Convention will be applied subject to modifications, it shall give details of the said modifications.

2. The Member, Members or international authority concerned may at any time by a subsequent declaration renounce in whole or in part the right to have recourse to any modification indicated in any former declaration.

3. The Member, Members or international authority concerned may, at any time at which this Convention is subject to denunciation in accordance with the provisions of Article 9, communicate to the Director-General a declaration modifying in any other respect the terms of any former declaration and stating the present position in respect of the application of the Convention.

Article 9

1. A Member which has ratified this Convention may denounce it after the expiration of ten years from the date on which the Convention first comes into force, by an act communicated to the Director-General of the International Labour Office for registration. Such denunciation shall not take effect until one year after the date on which it is registered.

2. Each Member which has ratified this Convention and which does not, within the year following the expiration of the period of ten years mentioned in the preceding paragraph, exercise the right of denunciation provided for in this Article, will be bound for another period of ten years and, thereafter, may denounce this Convention at the expiration of each period of ten years under the terms provided for in this Article.

Article 10

1. The Director-General of the International Labour Office shall notify all Members of the International Labour Organisation of the registration of all ratifications, declarations and denunciations communicated to him by the Members of the Organisation.

2. When notifying the Members of the Organisation of the registration of the second ratification communicated to him, the Director-General shall draw the attention of the Members of the Organisation to the date upon which the Convention will come into force.

Article 11

The Director-General of the International Labour Office shall communicate to the Secretary-General of the United Nations for registration in accordance with Article 102 of the Charter of the United Nations full particulars of all ratifications, declarations and acts of denunciation registered by him in accordance with the provisions of the preceding Articles.

Article 12

At such times as it may consider necessary the Governing Body of the International Labour Office shall present to the General Conference a report on the working of this Convention and shall examine the desirability of placing on the agenda of the Conference the question of its revision in whole or in part.

Article 13

1. Should the Conference adopt a new Convention revising this Convention in whole or in part, then, unless the new Convention otherwise provides:

(a) the ratification by a Member of the new revising Convention shall *ipso jure* involve the immediate denunciation of this Convention, notwithstanding the provisions of Article 9 above, if and when the new revising Convention shall have come into force;

(b) as from the date when the new revising Convention comes into force this Convention shall cease to be open to ratification by the Members.

2. This Convention shall in any case remain in force in its actual form and content for those Members which have ratified it but have not ratified the revising Convention.

Article 14

The English and French versions of the text of this Convention are equally authoritative.

Discrimination (Employment and Occupation) Convention (No. 111)

Adopted: 25 June 1958
Entered into force: 15 June 1960

The General Conference of the International Labour Organisation,

Having been convened at Geneva by the Governing Body of the International Labour Office, and having met in its Forty-second Session on 4 June 1958, and

Having decided upon the adoption of certain proposals with regard to discrimination in the field of employment and occupation, which is the fourth item on the agenda of the session, and

Having determined that these proposals shall take the form of an international Convention, and

Considering that the Declaration of Philadelphia affirms that all human beings, irrespective of race, creed or sex, have the right to pursue both their material well-being and their spiritual development in conditions of freedom and dignity, of economic security and equal opportunity, and

Considering further that discrimination constitutes a violation of rights enunciated by the Universal Declaration of Human Rights,

adopts this twenty-fifth day of June of the year one thousand nine hundred and fifty-eight the following Convention, which may be cited as the Discrimination (Employment and Occupation) Convention, 1958:

Article 1

1. For the purpose of this Convention the term "discrimination" includes:

(a) any distinction, exclusion or preference made on the basis of race, colour, sex, religion, political opinion, national extraction or social origin, which has the effect of nullifying or impairing equality of opportunity or treatment in employment or occupation;

(b) such other distinction, exclusion or preference which has the effect of nullifying or impairing equality of opportunity or treatment in employment or occupation as may be determined by the Member concerned after consultation with representative employers' and workers' organisations, where such exist, and with other appropriate bodies.

2. Any distinction, exclusion or preference in respect of a particular job based on the inherent requirements thereof shall not be deemed to be discrimination.

3. For the purpose of this Convention the terms "employment" and "occupation" include access to vocational training, access to employment and to particular occupations, and terms and conditions of employment.

Article 2

Each Member for which this Convention is in force undertakes to declare and pursue a national policy designed to promote, by methods appropriate to national conditions and practice, equality of opportunity and treatment in respect of employment and occupation, with a view to eliminating any discrimination in respect thereof.

Article 3

Each Member for which this Convention is in force undertakes, by methods appropriate to national conditions and practice:

(a) to seek the co-operation of employers' and workers' organisations and other appropriate bodies in promoting the acceptance and observance of this policy;

(b) to enact such legislation and to promote such educational programmes as may be calculated to secure the acceptance and observance of the policy;

(c) to repeal any statutory provisions and modify any administrative instructions or practices which are inconsistent with the policy;

(d) to pursue the policy in respect of employment under the direct control of a national authority;

(e) to ensure observance of the policy in the activities of vocational guidance, vocational training and placement services under the direction of a national authority;

(f) to indicate in its annual reports on the application of the Convention the action taken in pursuance of the policy and the results secured by such action.

Article 4

Any measures affecting an individual who is justifiably suspected of, or engaged in, activities prejudicial to the security of the State shall not be deemed to be discrimination, provided that the individual concerned shall have the right to appeal to a competent body established in accordance with national practice.

Article 5

1. Special measures of protection or assistance provided for in other Conventions or Recommendations adopted by the International Labour Conference shall not be deemed to be discrimination.

2. Any Member may, after consultation with representative employers' and workers' organisations, where such exist, determine that other special measures designed to meet the particular requirements of persons who, for reasons such as sex, age, disablement, family responsibilities or social or cultural status, are generally recognised to require special protection or assistance, shall not be deemed to be discrimination.

Article 6

Each Member which ratifies this Convention undertakes to apply it to non-metropolitan territories in accordance with the provisions of the Constitution of the International Labour Organisation.

Article 7

The formal ratifications of this Convention shall be communicated to the Director-General of the International Labour Office for registration.

Article 8

1. This Convention shall be binding only upon those Members of the International Labour Organisation whose ratifications have been registered with the Director-General.

2. It shall come into force twelve months after the date on which the ratifications of two Members have been registered with the Director-General.

3. Thereafter, this Convention shall come into force for any Member twelve months after the date on which its ratification has been registered.

Article 9

1. A Member which has ratified this Convention may denounce it after the expiration of ten years from the date on which the Convention first comes into force, by an act communicated to the Director-General of the International Labour Office for registration. Such denunciation shall not take effect until one year after the date on which it is registered.

2. Each Member which has ratified this Convention and which does not, within the year following the expiration of the period of ten years mentioned in the preceding paragraph, exercise the right of denunciation provided for in this Article, will be bound for another period of ten years and, thereafter, may denounce this Convention at the expiration of each period of ten years under the terms provided for in this Article.

Article 10

1. The Director-General of the International Labour Office shall notify all Members of the International Labour Organisation of the registration of all ratifications and denunciations communicated to him by the Members of the Organisation.

2. When notifying the Members of the Organisation of the registration of the second ratification communicated to him, the Director-General shall draw the attention of the Members of the Organisation to the date upon which the Convention will come into force.

Article 11

The Director-General of the International Labour Office shall communicate to the Secretary-General of the United Nations for registration in accordance with Article 102 of the Charter of the United Nations full particulars of all ratifications and acts of denunciation registered by him in accordance with the provisions of the preceding Articles.

Article 12

At such times as it may consider necessary the Governing Body of the International Labour Office shall present to the General Conference a report on the working of this Convention and shall examine the desirability of placing on the agenda of the Conference the question of its revision in whole or in part.

Article 13

1. Should the Conference adopt a new Convention revising this Convention in whole or in part, then, unless the new Convention otherwise provides:

(a) the ratification by a Member of the new revising Convention shall *ipso jure* involve the immediate denunciation of this Convention, notwithstanding the provisions of Article 9 above, if and when the new revising Convention shall have come into force;

(b) as from the date when the new revising Convention comes into force this Convention shall cease to be open to ratification by the Members.

2. This Convention shall in any case remain in force in its actual form and content for those Members which have ratified it but have not ratified the revising Convention.

Article 14

The English and French versions of the text of this Convention are equally authoritative.

ILO DECLARATION ON FUNDAMENTAL PRINCIPLES AND RIGHTS AT WORK AND ITS FOLLOW-UP (Adopted: 18 June 1998)

Whereas the ILO was founded in the conviction that social justice is essential to universal and lasting peace;

Whereas economic growth is essential but not sufficient to ensure equity, social progress and the eradication of poverty, confirming the need for the ILO to promote strong social policies, justice and democratic institutions;

Whereas the ILO should, now more than ever, draw upon all its standard-setting, technical cooperation and research resources in all its areas of competence, in particular employment, vocational training and working conditions, to ensure that, in the context of a global strategy for economic and social development, economic and social policies are mutually reinforcing components in order to create broad-based sustainable development;

Whereas the ILO should give special attention to the problems of persons with special social needs, particularly the unemployed and migrant workers, and mobilize and encourage international, regional and national efforts aimed at resolving their problems, and promote effective policies aimed at job creation;

Whereas, in seeking to maintain the link between social progress and economic growth, the guarantee of fundamental principles and rights at work is of particular significance in that it enables the persons concerned to claim freely and on the basis of equality of opportunity their fair share of the wealth which they have helped to generate, and to achieve fully their human potential;

Whereas the ILO is the constitutionally mandated international organization and the competent body to set and deal with international labour standards, and enjoys universal support and acknowledgement in promoting fundamental rights at work as the expression of its constitutional principles;

Whereas it is urgent, in a situation of growing economic interdependence, to reaffirm the immutable nature of the fundamental principles and rights embodied in the Constitution of the Organization and to promote their universal application;

The International Labour Conference,

1. Recalls:

(a) that in freely joining the ILO, all Members have endorsed the principles and rights set out in its Constitution and in the Declaration of Philadelphia, and have undertaken to work towards attaining the overall objectives of the Organization to the best of their resources and fully in line with their specific circumstances;

(b) that these principles and rights have been expressed and developed in the form of specific rights and obligations in Conventions recognized as fundamental both inside and outside the Organization.

2. Declares that all Members, even if they have not ratified the Conventions in question, have an obligation, arising from the very fact of membership in the Organization, to respect, to promote and to realize, in good faith and in accordance with the Constitution, the principles concerning the fundamental rights which are the subject of those Conventions, namely:

(a) freedom of association and the effective recognition of the right to collective bargaining;

(b) the elimination of all forms of forced or compulsory labour;

(c) the effective abolition of child labour; and

(d) the elimination of discrimination in respect of employment and occupation.

3. Recognizes the obligation on the Organization to assist its Members, in response to their established and expressed needs, in order to attain these objectives by making full use of its constitutional, operational and budgetary resources, including by the mobilization of external resources and support, as well as by encouraging other international organizations with which the ILO has established relations, pursuant to Article 12 of its Constitution, to support these efforts:

(a) by offering technical cooperation and advisory services to promote the ratification and implementation of the fundamental Conventions;

(b) by assisting those Members not yet in a position to ratify some or all of these Conventions in their efforts to respect, to promote and to realize the principles concerning fundamental rights which are the subject of those Conventions; and

(c) by helping the Members in their efforts to create a climate for economic and social development.

4. Decides that, to give full effect to this Declaration, a promotional follow-up, which is meaningful and effective, shall be implemented in accordance with the measures specified in the annex hereto, which shall be considered as an integral part of this Declaration.

5. Stresses that labour standards should not be used for protectionist trade purposes, and that nothing in this Declaration and its follow-up shall be invoked or otherwise used for such purposes; in addition, the comparative advantage of any country should in no way be called into question by this Declaration and its follow-up.

Annex

Follow-up to the Declaration

I. Overall purpose

1. The aim of the follow-up described below is to encourage the efforts made by the Members of the Organization to promote the fundamental principles and rights enshrined in the Constitution of the ILO and the Declaration of Philadelphia and reaffirmed in this Declaration.

2. In line with this objective, which is of a strictly promotional nature, this follow-up will allow the identification of areas in which the assistance of the Organization through its technical cooperation activities may prove useful to its Members to help them implement these fundamental principles and rights. It is not a substitute for the established supervisory mechanisms, nor shall it impede their functioning; consequently, specific situations within the purview of those mechanisms shall not be examined or re-examined within the framework of this follow-up.

3. The two aspects of this follow-up, described below, are based on existing procedures: the annual follow-up concerning non-ratified fundamental Conventions will entail merely some adaptation of the present modalities of application of Article 19, paragraph 5(e), of the Constitution; and the global report will serve to obtain the best results from the procedures carried out pursuant to the Constitution.

II. Annual follow-up concerning non-ratified fundamental conventions

A. Purpose and scope

1. The purpose is to provide an opportunity to review each year, by means of simplified procedures to replace the four-year review introduced by the Governing Body in 1995, the efforts made in accordance with the Declaration by Members which have not yet ratified all the fundamental Conventions.

2. The follow-up will cover each year the four areas of fundamental principles and rights specified in the Declaration.

B. Modalities

1. The follow-up will be based on reports requested from Members under Article 19, paragraph 5(e), of the Constitution. The report forms will be drawn up so as to obtain information from governments which have not ratified one or more of the fundamental Conventions, on any changes which may have taken place in their law and practice, taking due account of Article 23 of the Constitution and established practice.

2. These reports, as compiled by the Office, will be reviewed by the Governing Body.

3. With a view to presenting an introduction to the reports thus compiled, drawing attention to any aspects which might call for a more in-depth discussion, the Office may call upon a group of experts appointed for this purpose by the Governing Body.

4. Adjustments to the Governing Body's existing procedures should be examined to allow Members which are not represented on the Governing Body to provide, in the most appropriate way, clarifications which might prove necessary or useful during Governing Body discussions to supplement the information contained in their reports.

III. GLOBAL REPORT

A. Purpose and scope

1. The purpose of this report is to provide a dynamic global picture relating to each category of fundamental principles and rights noted during the preceding four-year period, and to serve as a basis for assessing the effectiveness of the assistance provided by the Organization, and for determining priorities for the following period, in the form of action plans for technical cooperation designed in particular to mobilize the internal and external resources necessary to carry them out.

2. The report will cover, each year, one of the four categories of fundamental principles and rights in turn.

B. Modalities

1. The report will be drawn up under the responsibility of the Director-General on the basis of official information, or information gathered and assessed in accordance with established procedures. In the case of States which have not ratified the fundamental Conventions, it will be based in particular on the findings of the aforementioned annual follow-up. In the case of Members which have ratified the Conventions concerned, the report will be based in particular on reports as dealt with pursuant to Article 22 of the Constitution.

2. This report will be submitted to the Conference for tripartite discussion as a report of the Director-General. The Conference may deal with this report separately from reports under Article 12 of its Standing Orders, and may discuss it during a sitting devoted entirely to this report, or in any other appropriate way. It will then be for the Governing Body, at an early session, to draw conclusions from this discussion concerning the priorities and plans of action for technical cooperation to be implemented for the following four-year period.

IV. IT IS UNDERSTOOD THAT:

1. Proposals shall be made for amendments to the Standing Orders of the Governing Body and the Conference which are required to implement the preceding provisions.

2. The Conference shall, in due course, review the operation of this follow-up in the light of the experience acquired to assess whether it has adequately fulfilled the overall purpose articulated in Part I.

The foregoing is the ILO Declaration on Fundamental Principles and Rights at Work and its Follow-up duly adopted by the General Conference of the International Labour Organization during its Eighty-sixth Session which was held at Geneva and declared closed the 18 June 1998.

IN FAITH WHEREOF we have appended our signatures this nineteenth day of June 1998.

The President of the Conference,
JEAN-JACQUES OECHSLIN

The Director-General of the International Labour Office,
MICHEL HANSENNE

ANNEXES

ANNEX 1

LIST OF RATIFICATIONS OF MARITIME LABOUR CONVENTIONS (as at 31 December 2007)

	No. of ratifications
Minimum Age (Sea) Convention, 1920 (No. 7)	53
Unemployment Indemnity (Shipwreck) Convention, 1920 (No. 8)	60
Placing of Seamen Convention, 1920 (No. 9)	41
Minimum Age (Trimmers and Stokers) Convention, 1921 (No. 15) *	69
Medical Examination of Young Persons (Sea) Convention, 1921 (No. 16)	82
Seamen's Articles of Agreement Convention, 1926 (No. 22)	60
Repatriation of Seamen Convention, 1926 (No. 23)	47
Officers' Competency Certificates Convention, 1936 (No. 53)	37
Holidays with Pay (Sea) Convention, 1936 (No. 54) +	6
Shipowners' Liability (Sick and Injured Seamen) Convention, 1936 (No. 55)	18
Sickness Insurance (Sea) Convention, 1936 (No. 56)	20
Hours of Work and Manning (Sea) Convention, 1936 (No. 57)	5
Minimum Age (Sea) Convention (Revised), 1936 (No. 58)	51
Food and Catering (Ships' Crews) Convention, 1946 (No. 68)	25
Certification of Ships' Cooks Convention, 1946 (No. 69)	38
Social Security (Seafarers) Convention, 1946 (No. 70) *	7
Seafarers' Pensions Convention, 1946 (No. 71)	13
Paid Vacations (Seafarers) Convention, 1946 (No. 72) +	5
Medical Examination (Seafarers) Convention, 1946 (No. 73)	46
Certification of Able Seamen Convention, 1946 (No. 74)	29
Accommodation of Crews Convention, 1946 (No. 75) +	5
Wages, Hours of Work and Manning (Sea) Convention, 1946 (No. 76)	1
Paid Vacations (Seafarers) Convention (Revised), 1949 (No. 91) +	25
Accommodation of Crews Convention (Revised), 1949 (No. 92)	47
Wages, Hours of Work and Manning (Sea) Convention (Revised), 1949 (No. 93)	6
Seafarers' Identity Documents Convention, 1958 (No. 108) *	64
Wages, Hours of Work and Manning (Sea) Convention (Revised), 1958 (No. 109)	17

(continued overleaf)

	No. of ratifications
Minimum Age (Fishermen) Convention, 1959 (No. 112)	29
Medical Examination (Fishermen) Convention, 1959 (No. 113)	30
Fishermen's Articles of Agreement Convention, 1959 (No. 114)	23
Fishermen's Competency Certificates Convention, 1966 (No. 125)	10
Accommodation of Crews (Fishermen) Convention, 1966 (No. 126)	23
Accommodation of Crews (Supplementary Provisions) Convention, 1970 (No. 133)	32
Prevention of Accidents (Seafarers) Convention, 1970 (No. 134)	29
Continuity of Employment (Seafarers) Convention, 1976 (No. 145)	17
Seafarers' Annual Leave with Pay Convention, 1976 (No. 146)	17
Merchant Shipping (Minimum Standards) Convention, 1976 (No. 147)	55
Protocol of 1996 to the Merchant Shipping (Minimum Standards) Convention, 1976	23
Seafarers' Welfare Convention, 1987 (No. 163)	16
Health Protection and Medical Care (Seafarers) Convention, 1987 (No. 164)	14
Social Security (Seafarers) Convention (Revised), 1987 (No. 165)	3
Repatriation of Seafarers Convention (Revised), 1987 (No. 166)	13
Labour Inspection (Seafarers) Convention, 1996 (No. 178)	14
Recruitment and Placement of Seafarers Convention, 1996 (No. 179)	10
Seafarers' Hours of Work and the Manning of Ships Convention, 1996 (No. 180)	21
Seafarers' Identity Documents Convention (Revised), 2003 (No. 185) *	12
One Provisional Application (Article 9)	
Maritime Labour Convention, 2006	2
TOTAL	**1 270**

* Conventions which are not included in the Maritime Labour Convention, 2006.

+ Conventions which did not receive the requisite number of ratifications.

ANNEX II

LIST OF MARITIME LABOUR RECOMMENDATIONS

Hours of Work (Fishing) Recommendation, 1920 (No. 7)

National Seamen's Codes Recommendation, 1920 (No. 9)

Unemployment Insurance (Seamen) Recommendation, 1920 (No. 10)

Repatriation (Ship Masters and Apprentices) Recommendation, 1926 (No. 27)

Labour Inspection (Seamen) Recommendation, 1926 (No. 28)

Seamen's Welfare in Ports Recommendation, 1936 (No. 48)

Hours of Work and Manning (Sea) Recommendation, 1936 (No. 49)

Seafarers' Social Security (Agreements) Recommendation, 1946 (No. 75)

Seafarers (Medical Care for Dependants) Recommendation, 1946 (No. 76)

Vocational Training (Seafarers) Recommendation, 1946 (No. 77)

Bedding, Mess Utensils and Miscellaneous Provisions (Ships' Crews) Recommendation, 1946 (No. 78)

Ships' Medicine Chests Recommendation, 1958 (No. 105)

Medical Advice at Sea Recommendation, 1958 (No. 106)

Seafarers' Engagement (Foreign Vessels) Recommendation, 1958 (No. 107)

Social Conditions and Safety (Seafarers) Recommendation, 1958 (No. 108)

Wages, Hours of Work and Manning (Sea) Recommendation, 1958 (No. 109)

Vocational Training (Fishermen) Recommendation, 1966 (No. 126)

Vocational Training (Seafarers) Recommendation, 1970 (No. 137)

Seafarers' Welfare Recommendation, 1970 (No. 138)

Employment of Seafarers (Technical Developments) Recommendation, 1970 (No. 139)

Crew Accommodation (Air Conditioning) Recommendation, 1970 (No. 140)

Crew Accommodation (Noise Control) Recommendation, 1970 (No. 141)

Prevention of Accidents (Seafarers) Recommendation, 1970 (No. 142)

Protection of Young Seafarers Recommendation, 1976 (No. 153)

Continuity of Employment (Seafarers) Recommendation, 1976 (No. 154)

Merchant Shipping (Improvement of Standards) Recommendation, 1976 (No. 155)

Seafarers' Welfare Recommendation, 1987 (No. 173)

Repatriation of Seafarers Recommendation, 1987 (No. 174)

Labour Inspection (Seafarers) Recommendation, 1996 (No. 185)

Recruitment and Placement of Seafarers Recommendation, 1996 (No. 186)

Seafarers' Wages, Hours of Work and the Manning of Ships Recommendation, 1996 (No. 187)

Work in Fishing Recommendation, 2007 (No. 199)

ANNEX III

CHART OF RATIFICATIONS OF MARITIME CONVENTIONS AND OTHER INTERNATIONAL LABOUR CONVENTIONS REFERRED TO IN THIS VOLUME
(as at 31 December 2007)

Member States (182)	Total	Ratifications of maritime Conventions (Brackets = not in force for this country.)
Afghanistan	3	100, 105, 111
Albania	18	16, 29, (58), 81, 87, 98, 100, 105, 111, (112), 129, 138, 144, 147, P147, 178, 182, 185
Algeria	24	29, 56, (58), 68, 69, 70, 71, (72), 73, 74, 81, 87, 91, 92, 98, 100, 105, 108, 111, 122, 138, 144, 147, 182
Angola	17	(7), 29, 68, 69, 73, 74, 81, 87, 91, 92, 98, 100, 105, 108, 111, 138, 182
Antigua and Barbuda	12	29, 81, 87, 98, 100, 105, 108, 111, 122, 138, 144, 182
Argentina	23	(7), 8, 9, (15), 16, 22, 23, 29, 53, 58, 68, 71, 73, 81, 87, 98, 100, 105, 111, 129, 138, 144, 182
Armenia	11	29, 81, 87, 98, 100, 105, 111, 122, 138, 144, 182
Australia	27	7, 8, (9), (15), 16, 22, 29, 57, 58, 69, 73, 76, 81, 87, 92, 93, 98, 100, 105, 109, 111, 112, 122, 133, 144, 166, 182
Austria	11	29, 81, 87, 98, 100, 105, 111, 122, 138, 144, 182
Azerbaijan	24	16, 23, 29, 69, 73, 81, 87, 92, 98, 100, 105, (108), 111, 113, 122, 126, 129, 133, 134, 138, 144, 147, 182, 185
Bahamas	14	(7), 22, 29, 81, 87, 98, 100, 105, 111, 138, 144, 147, 182, 185
Bahrain	5	29, 81, 105, 111, 182
Bangladesh	12	15, 16, 22, 29, 81, 87, 98, 100, 105, 111, 144, 182
Barbados	16	(7), 22, 29, 74, 81, 87, 98, 100, 105, 108, 111, 122, 138, 144, 147, 182
Belarus	15	(15), 16, 29, (58), 81, 87, 98, 100, 105, 108, 111, 122, 138, 144, 182
Belgium	39	(7), 8, 9, (15), 16, 22, 23, 29, 53, (54), 55, 56, (57), (58), 68, 69, 73, 74, 81, 87, 91, 92, 98, 100, 105, 111, (112), 113, 114, 122, 125, 126, 129, 138, 144, 147, P147, 180, 182

(continued overleaf)

Member States (182)	Total	Ratifications of maritime Conventions (Brackets = not in force for this country.)
Belize	24	(7), 8, (15), 16, 22, 23, 29, 55, 58, 81, 87, 92, 98, 100, 105, 108, 111, 133, 134, 138, 144, 147, P147, 182
Benin	10	29, 81, 87, 98, 100, 105, 111, 138, 144, 182
Bolivia	11	29, 81, 87, 98, 100, 105, 111, 122, 129, 138, 182
Bosnia and Herzegovina	28	8, 9, 16, 22, 23, 29, 53, 56, 69, 73, 74, 81, 87, 91, 92, 98, 100, 105, 109, 111, 113, 114, 122, 126, 129, 138, 144, 182
Botswana	9	29, 87, 98, 100, 105, 111, 138, 144, 182
Brazil	32	(7), 16, 22, 29, 53, (58), 81, (91), 92, 93, 98, 100, 105, 108, 109, 111, 113, 122, 125, 126, 133, 134, 138, 144, 145, 146, 147, 163, 164, 166, 178, 182
Bulgaria	41	(7), 8, (9), (15), 16, 22, 23, 29, 53, 54, 55, 56, (57), (58), 68, 69, 71, 72, 73, 75, 81, 87, 98, 100, 105, 108, 111, (112), 113, 138, 144, 146, 147, P147, 163, 164, 166, 178, 179, 180, 182
Burkina Faso	11	29, 81, 87, 98, 100, 105, 111, 129, 138, 144, 182
Burundi	10	29, 81, 87, 98, 100, 105, 111, 138, 144, 182
Cambodia	9	29, 87, 98, 100, 105, 111, 122, 138, 182
Cameroon	15	9, 15, 16, 29, 81, 87, 98, 100, 105, 108, 111, 122, 138, 146, 182
Canada	18	7, 8, 15, 16, 22, 58, 68, 69, 73, 74, 87, 100, 105, 108, 111, 122, 147, 182
Cape Verde	8	29, 81, 87, 98, 100, 105, 111, 182
Central African Republic	11	29, 81, 87, 98, 100, 105, 111, 122, 138, 144, 182
Chad	10	29, 81, 87, 98, 100, 105, 111, 138, 144, 182
Chile	16	(7), 8, 9, (15), 16, 22, 29, 87, 98, 100, 105, 111, 122, 138, 144, 182
China	11	(7), (15), 16, 22, 23, 100, 111, 122, 138, 144, 182
Colombia	18	(7), 8, 9, (15), 16, 22, 23, 29, 81, 87, 98, 100, 105, 111, 129, 138, 144, 182
Comoros	10	29, 81, 87, 98, 100, 105, 111, 122, 138, 182
Congo	10	29, 81, 87, 98, 100, 105, 111, 138, 144, 182
Costa Rica	21	8, 16, 29, 81, 87, 92, 98, 100, 105, 111, (112), 113, 114, 122, 129, 134, 138, 144, 145, 147, 182
Côte d'Ivoire	12	29, 81, 87, 98, 100, 105, 111, 129, 133, 138, 144, 182
Croatia	27	8, (9), 16, 22, 23, 29, 53, 56, 69, 73, 74, 81, 87, 91, 92, 98, 100, 105, 109, 111, 113, 122, 129, 138, 147, 179, 182
Cuba	26	(7), 8, 9, (15), 16, 22, 23, 29, 53, (58), (72), 81, 87, 91, 92, 93, 98, 100, 105, 108, 111, (112), 113, 122, 138, 145
Cyprus	19	(15), 16, 23, 29, (58), 81, 87, 92, 98, 100, 105, 111, 114, 122, 138, 144, 147, P147, 182

Member States (182)	Total	Ratifications of maritime Conventions (Brackets = not in force for this country.)
Czech Republic	13	29, 87, 98, 100, 105, 108, 111, 122, 138, 144, 163, 164, 182
Democratic Republic of the Congo	10	29, 81, 87, 98, 100, 105, 111, 138, 144, 182
Denmark	30	(7), 8, 9, (15), 16, 29, 53, (58), 73, 81, 87, 92, 98, 100, 105, 108, 111, (112), 122, 126, 129, 133, 134, 138, 144, 147, P147, 163, 180, 182
Djibouti	27	9, (15), 16, 22, 23, 29, 53, 55, 56, (58), 69, 71, 73, 81, 87, 91, 98, 100, 105, 108, 111, 122, 125, 126, 138, 144, 182
Dominica	15	8, 16, 22, 29, 81, 87, 98, 100, 105, 108, 111, 138, 144, 147, 182
Dominican Republic	12	(7), 29, 81, 87, 98, 100, 105, 111, 122, 138, 144, 182
Ecuador	14	29, 81, 87, 98, 100, 105, 111, 112, 113, 114, 122, 138, 144, 182
Egypt	27	9, 22, 23, 29, 53, 55, 56, 68, 69, 71, 73, 74, 81, 87, 92, 98, 100, 105, 111, 129, 134, 138, 144, 145, 147, 166, 182
El Salvador	12	29, 81, 87, 98, 100, 105, 111, 122,129, 138, 144, 182
Equatorial Guinea	10	29, 68, 87, 92, 98, 100, 105, 111, 138, 182
Eritrea	7	29, 87, 98, 100, 105, 111, 138
Estonia	23	(7), 8, 9, (15), 16, 22, 23, 29, 53, 81, 87, 98, 100, 105, 108, 111, 122, 129, 138, 144, 147, P147, 182
Ethiopia	8	29, 87, 98, 100, 105, 111, 138, 182
Fiji	12	8, 29, (58), 87, 98, 100, 105, 108, 111, 138, 144, 182
Finland	36	(7), 8, (9), (15), 16, 22, 29, 53, (72), 73, (75), 81, 87, (91), 92, 98, 100, 105, 108, 111, 122, 129, 133, 134, 138, 144, 145, 146, 147, P147, 163, 164, 178, 179, 180, 182
France	53	8, (9), (15), 16, 22, 23, 29, 53, (54), 55, 56, (58), 68, 69, 70, 71, (72), 73, 74, (75), 81, 87, (91), 92, 98, 100, 105, (108), (109), 111, (112), 113, 114, 122, 125, 126, 129, 133, 134, 138, 144, 145, 146, 147, P147, 163, 164, 166, 178, 179, 180, 182, 185
Gabon	9	29, 81, 87, 98, 100, 105, 111, 144, 182
Gambia	8	29, 87, 98, 100, 105, 111, 138, 182
Georgia	10	29, 87, 98, 100, 105, 111, 122, 138, 163, 182
Germany	36	(7), 8, 9, (15), 16, 22, 23, 29, 53, 56, 73, 81, 87, 92, 98, 100, 105, 111, (112), 113, 114, 122, 125, 126, 129, 133, 134, 138, 144, 146, 147, P147, 164, 166, 180, 182
Ghana	19	8, 15, 16, 22, 23, 29, 58, 69, 74, 81, 87, 92, 98, 100, 105, 108, 111, 147, 182

(continued overleaf)

Member States (182)	Total	Ratifications of maritime Conventions (Brackets = not in force for this country.)
Greece	31	(7), 8, 9, (15), 16, 23, 29, 55, (58), 68, 69, 71, 73, 81, 87, 92, 98, 100, 105, 108, 111, 122, 126, 133, 134, 138, 144, 147, P147, 180, 182
Grenada	16	(7), 8, (15), 16, 29, (58), 81, 87, 98, 100, 105, 108, 111, 138, 144, 182
Guatemala	20	(15), 16, 29, 58, 81, 87, 98, 100, 105, 108, 109, 111, 112, 113, 114, 122, 129, 138, 144, 182
Guinea	17	16, 29, 81, 87, 98, 100, 105, 111, (112), 113, 114, 122, 133, 134, 138, 144, 182
Guinea-Bissau	14	7, 29, 68, 69, 73, 74, 81, 91, 92, 98, 100, 105, 108, 111
Guyana	15	(7), (15), 29, 81, 87, 98, 100, 105, 108, 111, 129, 138, 144, 166, 182
Haiti	8	29, 81, 87, 98, 100, 105, 111, 182
Honduras	11	29, 81, 87, 98, 100, 105, 108, 111, 122, 138, 182
Hungary	23	(7), (15), 16, 29, 81, 87, 98, 100, 105, 111, 122, 129, 138, 144, 145, 147, P147, 163, 164, 165, 166, 182, 185
Iceland	15	(15), 29, (58), 87, 91, 98, 100, 105, 108, 111, 122, 138, 144, 147, 182
India	12	15, 16, 22, 29, 81, 100, 105, 108, 111, 122, 144, 147
Indonesia	11	29, 69, 81, 87, 98, 100, 105, 111, 138, 144, 182
Iran, Islamic Republic of	7	29, 100, 105, 108, 111, 122, 182
Iraq	23	8, (15), 16, 22, 23, 29, (58), 81, 92, 93, 98, 100, 105, 108, 109, 111, 122, 138, 144, 145, 146, 147, 182
Ireland	29	(7), 8, (15), 16, 22, 23, 29, 53, 68, 69, 73, 74, 81, 87, 92, 98, 100, 105, 108, 111, 122, 138, 144, 147, P147, 178, 179, 180, 182
Israel	18	9, 29, 53, 81, 87, 91, 92, 98, 100, 105, 111, (112), 122, 133, 134, 138, 147, 182
Italy	39	(7), 8, 9, (15), 16, 22, 23, 29, 53, 55, (58), 68, 69, 71, 73, 74, 81, 87, (91), 92, 98, 100, 105, 108, 109 ,111, (112), 114, 122, 129, 133, 134, 138, 144, 145, 146, 147, 164, 182
Jamaica	16	(7), 8, (15), 16, 29, (58), 81, 87, 98, 100, 105, 111, 122, 138, 144, 182
Japan	20	(7), 8, 9, (15), 16, 22, 29, (58), 69, 73, 81, 87, 98, 100, 122, 134, 138, 144, 147, 182
Jordan	12	29, 81, 98, 100, 105, 111, 122, 138, 144, 147, 182, 185
Kazakhstan	12	29, 81, 87, 98, 100, 105, 111, 122, 129, 138, 144, 182
Kenya	16	(15), 16, 29, (58), 81, 98, 100, 105, 111, (112), 129, 134, 138, 144, 146, 182

Member States (182)	Total	Ratifications of maritime Conventions (Brackets = not in force for this country.)
Kiribati	4	29, 87, 98, 105
Korea, Republic of	10	53, 73, 81, 100, 111, 122, 138, 144, 182, 185
Kuwait	9	29, 81, 87, 98, 105, 111, 138, 144, 182
Kyrgyzstan	22	16, 23, 29, 69, 73, 81, 87, 92, 98, 100, 105, 108, 111, 113, 122, 126, 133, 134, 138, 144, 147, 182
Lao People's Democratic Republic	3	29, 138, 182
Latvia	22	(7), 8, 9, (15), 16, 29, 81, 87, 98, 100, 105, 108, 111, 122, 129, 133, 138, 144, 147, P147, 180, 182
Lebanon	19	8, 9, (15), 29, 58, 71, 73, 74, 81, 98, 100, 105, 109, 111, 122, 133, 138, 147, 182
Lesotho	10	29, 81, 87, 98, 100, 105, 111, 138, 144, 182
Liberia	21	22, 23, 29, 53, 55, 58, 81, 87, 92, 98, 105, 108, 111, 112, 113, 114, 133, 144, 147, 182, MLC
Libyan Arab Jamahiriya	11	29, 53, 81, 87, 98, 100, 105, 111, 122, 138, 182
Lithuania	15	29, 73, 81, 87, 98, 100, 105, 108, 111, 122, 138, 144, 147, P147, 182
Luxembourg	32	(7), 8, 9, (15), 16, 22, 23, 29, 53, 55, 56, 68, 69, 73, 74, 81, 87, 92, 98, 100, 105, 108, 111, 133, 138, 146, 147, P147, 166, 178, 180, 182
Madagascar	13	29, 81, 87, 98, 100, 105, 111, 122, 129, 138, 144, 182, 185
Malawi	11	29, 81, 87, 98, 100, 105, 111, 129, 138, 144, 182
Malaysia	8	29, 81, 98, 100, (105), 138, 144, 182
Malaysia - Sabah	2	(15), 16
Malaysia - Sarawak	3	(7), (15), 16
Mali	10	29, 81, 87, 98, 100, 105, 111, 138, 144, 182
Malta	22	(7), 8, (15), 16, 22, 29, 53, 73, 74, 81, 87, 98, 100, 105,108, 111, 129, 138, 147, P147, 180, 182
Marshall Islands	1	MLC
Mauritania	18	15, 22, 23, 29, 53, 58, 81, 87, 91, 98, 100, 105, 111, 112, 114, 122, 138, 182
Mauritius	17	(7), 8, (15), 16, 29, (58), 74, 81, 87, 98, 100, 105, 108, 111, 138, 144, 182
Mexico	25	(7), 8, 9, 16, 22, (23), 29, 53, 54, 55, 56, 58, 87, 100, 105, 108, 109, 111, 112, 134, 144, 163, 164, 166, 182
Moldova, Republic of	16	29, 81, 87, 92, 98, 100, 105, (108), 111, 122, 129, 133, 138, 144, 182, 185
Mongolia	10	29, 87, 98, 100, 105, 111, 122, 138, 144, 182
Montenegro	27	8, 9, 16, 22, 23, 29, 53, 56, 69, 73, 74, 81, 87, 91, 92, 98, 100, 105, 111, 113, 114, 122, 126, 129, 138, 144, 182
Morocco	20	(15), 22, 29, 55, 81, 98, 100, 105, 108, 111, 122, 129, 138, 145, 146, 147, 178, 179, 180, 182

(continued overleaf)

Member States (182)	Total	Ratifications of maritime Conventions (Brackets = not in force for this country.)
Mozambique	11	29, 81, 87, 98, 100, 105, 111, 122, 138, 144, 182
Myanmar	5	15, 16, 22, 29, 87
Namibia	8	29, 87, 98, 105, 111, 138, 144, 182
Nepal	8	29, 98, 100, 105, 111, 138, 144, 182
Netherlands	38	(7), 8, 9, (15), 16, 22, 23, 29, (58), 68, 69, 70, 71, 73, 74, 81, 87, (91), 92, 98, 100, 105, 111, (112), 113, 114, 122, 126, 129, 133, 138, 144, 145, 146, 147, P147, 180, 182
New Zealand	24	8, 9, 15, 16, 22, 23, 29, 53, 58, 68, 69, 74, 81, 92, 98, 100, 105, 111, 122, 133, 134, 144, 145, 182
Nicaragua	18	(7), 8, 9, (15), 16, 22, 23, 29, 87, 98, 100, 105, 111, 122, 138, 144, 146, 182
Niger	9	29, 81, 87, 98, 100, 105, 111, 138, 182
Nigeria	20	8, (9), (15), 16, 29, (58), 81, 87, 98, 100, 105, 111, 133, 134, 138, 144, 178, 179, 182, 185
Norway	43	(7), 8, (9), (15), 16, 22, 29, 53, 56, (58), 68, 69, 71, 73, (75), 81, 87, 91, 92, 98, 100, 105, 108, (109), 111, (112), 113, 122, 126, 129, 133, 134, 138, 144, 145, 147, P147, 163, 164, 178, 179, 180, 182
Oman	4	29, 105, 138, 182
Pakistan	14	(15), 16, 22, 29, 81, 87, 98, 100, 105, 111, 138, 144, 182, 185
Panama	32	8, 9, (15), 16, 22, 23, 29, 53, 55, 56, (58), 68, 69, 71, 73, 74, 81, 87, 92, 98, 100, 105, 108, 111, (112), 113, 114, 122, 125, 126, 138, 182
Papua New Guinea	12	(7), 8, 22, 29, 87, 98, 100, 105, 111, 122, 138, 182
Paraguay	10	29, 81, 87, 98, 100, 105, 111, 122, 138, 182
Peru	29	8, 9, 22, 23, 29, 53, 55, 56, 58, 68, 69, 70, 71, 73, 81, 87, 98, 100, 105, 111, 112, 113, 114, 122, 138, 144, 147, 178, 182
Philippines	15	23, 29, 53, 87, 93, 98, 100, 105, 111, 122, 138, 144, 165, 179, 182
Poland	34	(7), 8, 9, (15), 16, 22, 23, 29, 68, 69, 70, 73, 74, 81, 87, 91, 92, 98, 100, 105, 108, 111, (112), 113, 122, 129, 133, 134, 138, 144, 145, 147, 178, 182
Portugal	27	(7), 8, 22, 23, 29, 68, 69, 73, 74, 81, 87, (91), 92, 98, 100, 105, 108, 109, 111, 122, 129, 138, 144, 145, 146, 147, 182
Qatar	6	29, 81, 105, 111, 138, 182
Romania	28	(7), 8, 9, (15), 16, 22, 29, 68, 81, 87, 92, 98, 100, 105, 108, 111, 122, 129, 133, 134, 138, 144, 147, P147, 163, 166, 180, 182
Russian Federation	26	(15), 16, 23, 29, (58), 69, 73, 81, 87, 92, 98, 100, 105, 108, 111, (112), 113, 122, 126, 133, 134, 138, 147, 163, 179, 182

Member States (182)	Total	Ratifications of maritime Conventions (Brackets = not in force for this country.)
Rwanda	9	29, 81, 87, 98, 100, 105, 111, 138, 182
Saint Kitts and Nevis	9	29, 87, 98, 100, 105, 111, 138, 144, 182
Saint Lucia	12	7, 8, 15, 16, 29, 87, 98, 100, 105, 108, 111, 182
Saint Vincent and the Grenadines	13	(7), 16, 29, 81, 87, 98, 100, 105, 108, 111, 138, 180, 182
San Marino	9	29, 87, 98, 100, 105, 111, 138, 144, 182
Sao Tome and Principe	10	29, 81, 87, 98, 100, 105, 111, 138, 144, 182
Saudi Arabia	6	29, 81, 100, 105, 111, 182
Senegal	12	29, 81, 87, 98, 100, 105, 111, 122, 125, 138, 144, 182
Serbia	28	8, 9, 16, 22, 23, 29, 53, 56, 69, 73, 74, 81, 87, 91, 92, 98, 100, 105, 109, 111, 113, 114, 122, 126, 129, 138, 144, 182
Seychelles	20	(7), 8, (15), 16, 22, 29, (58), 73, 81, 87, 98, 100, 105, 108, 111, 138, 144, 147, 180, 182
Sierra Leone	16	7, 8, 15, 16, 22, 29, 58, 81, 87, 98, 100, 105, 111, 125, 126, 144
Singapore	12	(7), 8, (15), 16, 22, 29, 81, 98, 100, (105),138, 182
Slovakia	12	29, 87, 98, 100, 105, 111, 122, 138, 144, 163, 164, 182
Slovenia	31	8, 9, 16, 22, 23, 29, 53, 56, 69, 73, 74, 81, 87, 91, 92, 98, 100, 105, 108, (109), 111, 113, 114, 122, 126, 129, 138, 147, P147, 180, 182
Solomon Islands	5	8, 16, 29, 81, 108
Somalia	6	16, 22, 23, 29, 105, 111
South Africa	9	29, 87, 98, 100, 105, 111, 138, 144, 182
Spain	45	(7), 8, 9, (15), 16, 22, 23, 29, 53, 55, (56), (58), 68, 69, (70), 73, 74, 81, 87, (91), 92, 98, 100, 105, 108, (109), 111, (112), 113, 114, 122, 126, 129, 134, 138, 144, 145, 146, 147, 163, 164, 165, 166, 180, 182
Sri Lanka	16	(7), 8, (15), 16, 29, 58, 81, 87, 98, 100, 105, 108, 111, 138, 144, 182
Sudan	9	29, 81, 98, 100, 105, 111, 122, 138, 182
Suriname	9	29, 81, 87, 98, 105, 112, 122, 144, 182
Swaziland	10	29, 81, 87, 98, 100, 105, 111, 138, 144, 182
Sweden	34	(7), 8, 9, (15), 16, 29, 57, (58), 73, (75), 81, 87, 92, 98, 100, 105, 108, 109, 111, 122, 129, 133, 134, 138, 144, 145, 146, 147, P147, 163, 164, 178, 180, 182
Switzerland	16	8, (15), 16, 23, 29, (58), 81, 87, 98, 100, 105, 111, 138, 144, 163, 182
Syrian Arab Republic	13	29, 53, 81, 87, 98, 100, 105, 111, 125, 129, 138, 144, 182

(continued overleaf)

Member States (182)	Total	Ratifications of maritime Conventions (Brackets = not in force for this country.)
Tajikistan	20	16, 23, 29, 69, 73, 87, 92, 98, 100, 105, 108, 111, 113, 122, 126, 133, 134, 138, 147, 182
Tanzania, United Republic of	12	(15), 16, 29, 87, 98, 100, 105, 111, 134, 138, 144, 182
Tanzania - Tanganyika	2	81, 108
Tanzania - Zanzibar	2	(7), 58
Thailand	6	29, 100, 105, 122, 138, 182
The former Yugoslav Republic of Macedonia	28	8, 9, 16, 22, 23, 29, 53, 56, 69, 73, 74, 81, 87, 91, 92, 98, 100, 105, 109, 111, 113, 114, 122, 126, 129, 138, 144, 182
Togo	9	29, 87, 98, 100, 105, 111, 138, 144, 182
Trinidad and Tobago	14	(15), 16, 29, 81, 87, 98, 100, 105, 111, 125, 138, 144, 147, 182
Tunisia	22	8, 16, 22, 23, 29, 55, (58), 73, 81, 87, 91, 98, 100, 105, 108, 111, (112), 113, 114, 122, 138, 182
Turkey	25	(15), 29, 53, 55, (58), 68, 69, 73, 81, 87, 92, 98, 100, 105, 108, 111, 122, 133, 134, 138, 144, 146, 164, 166, 182
Turkmenistan	6	29, 87, 98, 100, 105, 111
Uganda	11	29, 81, 87, 98, 100, 105, 111, 122, 138, 144, 182
Ukraine	25	(15), 16, 23, 29, (58), 69, 73, 81, 87, 92, 98, 100, 105, 108, 111, (112), 113, 122, 126, 129, 133, 138, 144, 147, 182
United Arab Emirates	7	29, 81, 100, 105, 111, 138, 182
United Kingdom	31	(7), 8, (15), 16, 22, 23, 29, 56, 68, 69, 70, 74, 81, 87, 92, 98, 100,105, 108, 111, 114, 122, 126, 133, 138, 144, 147, P147, 178, 180, 182
United States	10	53, 54, 55, 57, 58, 74, 105, 144, 147, 182
Uruguay	29	(7), 8, 9, (15), 16, 22, 23, 29, 54, (58), 73, 81, 87, 93, 98, 100, 105, 108, 111, (112), 113, 114, 122, 129, 133, 134, 138, 144, 182
Uzbekistan	6	29, 98, 100, 105, 111, 122
Vanuatu	8	29, 87, 98, 100, 105, 111, 182, 185
Venezuela, Bolivarian Republic of	13	(7), 22, 29, 81, 87, 98, 100, 105, 111, 122, 138, 144, 182
Viet Nam	6	29, 81, 100, 111, 138, 182
Yemen	14	(15), 16, 29, 58, 81, 87, 98, 100, 105, 111, 122, 138, 144, 182
Zambia	10	29, 87, 98, 100, 105, 111, 122, 138, 144, 182
Zimbabwe	11	29, 81, 87, 98, 100, 105, 111, 129, 138, 144, 182

ANNEX IV

DECLARATION OF APPLICATION OF MARITIME AND OTHER INTERNATIONAL LABOUR CONVENTIONS TO NON-METROPOLITAN TERRITORIES (as at 31 December 2007)[1]

Member State	Non-metropolitan territory	Total	Conventions applicable (with or without modifications)
Australia	Norfolk Island	10	(15), (16), 29, (58), 87, 98, 100, 105, 112, 122
Denmark	Faeroe Islands	12	7, 8, 9, 15, 16,29, 53, 87, 92, 98, 105, 126
	Greenland	8	7, 15, 16, 29, 87, 105, 122, 126
France	French Guiana	40	8, 9, 15, 16, 22, 23, 29, 53, (54), 55, 56, 58, 68, 69, 70, 71, (72), 73, 74, 81, 87, (91), 92, 98, 100, 105, 108, 109, 111, 112, 113, 114, 125, 126, 129, 133, 144, 145, 146, 147
	French Polynesia	29	9, 15, 16, 22, 23, 29, 53, 55, 56, 58, 69, 71, 73, 81, 87, (91), 98, 100, 105, 108, 111, 122, 125, 126, 129, 144, 145, 146, 147
	French Southern and Antarctic Territories	21	8, 9, 15, 16, 22, 23, 53, 58, 68, 69, 73, 74, 87, 92, 98, 108, 111, 133, 134, 146, 147
	Guadeloupe	40	8, 9, 15, 16, 22, 23, 29, 53, (54), 55, 56, 58, 68, 69, 70, 71, (72), 73, 74, 81, 87, (91), 92, 98, 100, 105, 108, 109, 111, 112, 113, 114, 125, 126, 129, 133, 144, 145, 146, 147
	Martinique	40	8, 9, 15, 16, 22, 23, 29, 53, (54), 55, 56, 58, 68, 69, 70, 71, (72), 73, 74, 81, 87, (91), 92, 98, 100, 105, 108, 109, 111, 112, 113, 114, 125, 126, 129, 133, 144, 145, 146, 147
	New Caledonia	29	9, 15, 16, 22, 23, 29, 53, 55, 56, 58, 69, 71, 73, 81, 87, (91), 98, 100, 105, 108, 111, 122, 125, 126, 129, 144, 145, 146, 147

(continued overleaf)

Member State	Non-metropolitan territory	Total	Conventions applicable (with or without modifications)
France *(cont.)*	Réunion	40	8, 9, 15, 16, 22, 23, 29, 53, (54), 55, 56, 58, 68, 69, 70, 71, (72), 73, 74, 81, 87, (91), 92, 98, 100, 105, 108, 109, 111, 112, 113, 114, 125, 126, 129, 133, 144, 145, 146, 147
	St. Pierre and Miquelon	29	9, 15, 16, 22, 23, 29, 53, 55, 56, 58, 69, 71, 73, 81, 87, (91), 98, 100, 105, 108, 111, 122, 125, 126, 129, 144, 145, 146, 147
Netherlands	Aruba	21	8, 9, 22, 23, 29, (58), 69, 74, 81, 87, 105, 113, 114, 122, 126, (129), 138, 144, 145, 146, 147
	Netherlands Antilles	12	8, 9, 22, 23, 29, 58, 69, 74, 81, 87, 105, 122
New Zealand	Tokelau	4	29, 100, 105, 111
United Kingdom	Anguilla	10	7, 8, 22, 23, 29, 58, 87, 98, 105, 108
	Bermuda	13	7, 15, 16, 22, 23, 29, 58, 87, 98, 105, 108, 133, 147
	British Virgin Islands	9	7, 8, 23, 29, 58, 87, 98, 105, 108
	Falkland Islands (Malvinas)	10	7, 8, 22, 23, 29, 58, 87, 98, 105, 108
	Gibraltar	16	7, 8, 15, 16, 22, 23, 29, 58, 81, 87, 98, 100, 105, 108, 133, 147
	Guernsey	17	7, 8, 15, 16, 22, 29, 56, 69, 74, 81, 87, 98, 105, 108, 114, 122, 182
	Isle of Man	25	7, 8, 15, 16, 22, 23, 29, 56, 68, 69, 70, 74, 81, 87, 92, 98, 105, 108, 122, 126, 133, 147, P147, 178, 180
	Jersey	14	7, 8, 15, 16, 22, 29, 56, 69, 74, 81, 87, 98, 105, 108
	Montserrat	10	7, 8, 15, 16, 29, 58, 87, 98, 105, 108
	St. Helena	10	7, 8, 15, 16, 29, 58, 87, 98, 105, 108
United States	American Samoa	7	53, 54, 55, 57, 58, 144, 147
	Guam	8	53, 54, 55, 57, 58, 74, 144, 147
	Northern Mariana Islands	2	144, 147
	Puerto Rico	8	53, 54, 55, 57, 58, 74, 144, 147
	United States Virgin Islands	8	53, 54, 55, 57, 58, 74, 144, 147

[1] Numbers in parentheses denote Conventions ratified but not in force for the country concerned.

INDEX